The Making of Victorian England

The Making of
Victorian England

BEING THE FORD LECTURES DELIVERED
BEFORE THE UNIVERSITY OF OXFORD

by

G. KITSON CLARK, Litt.D.

*Reader in Constitutional History in the University of Cambridge
and Fellow of Trinity College, Cambridge*

London
METHUEN & CO LTD
11 *New Fetter Lane EC4*

First published 1962
Reprinted three times
Reprinted 1970
ISBN 0 416 25180 3

First published as a University Paperback 1965
Reprinted twice
Reprinted 1970
Reprinted 1973
Reprinted 1975
ISBN 0 416 69320 2

Dedicated with respect and affection to

G. M. Trevelyan

To whom most of this book was read

before publication

NOSTRI HISTORICORUM

GENERIS AUCTORI

Contents

Preface

This book is founded on the Ford lectures which I delivered at Oxford in 1960 and I would like to begin by thanking those who gave me that opportunity. Professor Richard Pares, whose untimely illness and death was one of the most severe blows historical scholarship in Britain has received for a very long time, once wrote that the invitation to give the Ford lectures was "the highest honour . . . an English historian can receive", meaning it is to be presumed that can be received by an historian working in the field of English history, for it is to English history that the Ford lectures are confined. I feel no disposition to quarrel with this statement, though I find it alarming; that, however, does not diminish my gratitude.

The lectures were delivered from notes not a complete text, and it has therefore been necessary to write them out in full before publication. At certain points I have gone into greater detail than I could have done in the time at my disposal, at some points I have done additional research to confirm or check what I said at the time of delivery and on some points I have changed my mind, particularly towards the end of Chapter VI. I have also, for convenience in reading, redistributed and redivided the matter at certain points. Most of what is covered in Chapters III and IV was originally in one lecture, part of Chapter VIII was originally in a lecture which included most of the material in Chapter VII, and the rest of Chapter VIII was combined with a summary which is now contained in Chapter IX. For this reason I think it is better to call my divisions chapters and not lectures; but I do not think that I have at any point substantially altered the argument. What I give here is to all intents and purposes what I gave in the Ford lectures at Oxford.

I have more than the usual reasons for wishing to thank those who have helped me in preparing this book and also for exonerating them from all responsibility for what appears in it. As is the case with other historians nowadays, I have been anxious to write what might be called "history in depth", that is history which gains a perspective from the use, in combination, of the various technical forms of history, each of which gives a special insight into a particular aspect of history. I feel quite sure that this is the right line of development for historiography at this moment, when so much specialized work has been done and it becomes increasingly important to see whether we can not use it to give a deeper reality to our general picture. But it is a line of development which has its own peculiar perils, for it renders necessary the use of professional techniques and specialized forms of knowledge by those who have never been trained to handle them.   In preparing this volume I have been particularly uneasy about my use of economic history and demography. Though primarily a political historian, I have worked alongside economic historians all my life. Sir John Clapham was the first Cambridge historian I ever knew. I have for many years had the advantage of the friendship and advice of Professor Postan, and for the purposes of this book I have had the ready and constant help of Mr Charles Wilson and Mr David Joslin, to whom I am very grateful indeed. At the same time I know that it is one thing to receive expert advice and something quite different to use specialized material as an expert, and I want to emphasize the fact that any mistakes I have made in the handling of the material that comes within the category of economic history come from me not from them.   I also wish to add that even if it turns out that in some of these matters I have got things egregiously wrong, I hope that other political historians will try to use economic history for their purposes for I am sure that very much can be done by combining such history with the detailed political research which is now in fashion.

I have another special obligation of a different sort to record. Since the last war a number of scholars have worked with me at Cambridge as research students. In the preparation of this book I have gained greatly from the ideas and help of those whose work was relevant to its subject. In some instances work by them has already been published or is going to be published very soon. This is, for instance, the case of Dr H. J. Hanham, whose work on *Elections and Party Management* in the time of Gladstone and Disraeli is already well known. Even so, the assistance I have received from Dr Hanham extends to matters which lie outside the compass of that book and goes back to the time when he was working with me as a research student. The same is true of Dr R. Robson, who only for a brief moment worked with me as a research student, but who has helped me continuously during the preparation of this book, and was also kind enough to read it in proof, and of Dr G. F. A. Best, whose most important work on the history of the Ecclesiastical Commissioners is .indeed on the eve of publication. To all these I owe much, but I am also in the debt of several men none of whose work has reached the stage of publication. In particular there is Dr D. Cresap Moore, from whom I learnt a very great deal about the collapse of the old aristocratic control in the counties, Dr R. J. Lambert, from whom I gained much on Sir John Simon and the history of public health in the middle of the 19th century and Mr James Cornford, who has investigated the economic and social background to Conservative politics between 1870 and 1890. I have also to thank Mr F. B. Smith who has given me much help on the Act of 1867, and throughout. To these I would like to add another scholar, who never worked with me as a research student, but who taught in Cambridge for a time, the Rev. J. H. S. Kent. From him I learnt much about religious revivalism in the 19th century; he also helped me to find documents which illustrated the history of Nonconformity in the middle of the century.

I ought to say that, though in each case I was immensely helped by these men in the approach to their subjects, the views I put forward in this book are my own and have been arrived at after research which may have led me to make assertions for which they might not wish to be responsible. I hope therefore that nothing that I say will be taken as an anticipation of what they will in due course publish and I hope that each of them will soon have an opportunity of putting forward his own ideas for himself.

I wish also to express my great debt to Professor David Spring of Johns Hopkins University, Baltimore, who has done important work on the economy and management of the great landed estates in England in the 19th century. I ought to say that in the last two years my help from him has been necessarily by letter and that he has had no opportunity of checking the statements which I refer to his authority. I also wish to thank Professor W. O. Aydelotte of the State University of Iowa State, U.S.A., for his help. I refer to his work in the course of my first lecture and in reply to a question which I referred to him he sent to me a paper which seemed to me of such value and so relevant to part of my argument that with his leave I print it as an appendix at the end of the volume. Dr J. P. C. Roach gave me help with regard to 19th century Universities, Mr Frank Beckwith of the Leeds Library, Commercial Street, Leeds, gave me repeated assistance from his unrivalled knowledge of Yorkshire in the 19th century, Dr A. J. Rook gave me help on medical matters, Professor H. W. R. Wade upon law, the Rt Rev. Mgr A. N. Gilbey on Roman Catholic history in the 19th century and Mr G. O. Pierce help towards the study of a point in Welsh history. Professors Asa Briggs, W. L. Burn, Sydney Checkland, W. O. Chadwick, and Arnold Lloyd and Drs F. C. Mather, W. H. Chaloner and O. Mac-Donagh have all been very kind in answering questions and suggesting lines of thought and I have been helped by others too numerous to mention individually and who will, I hope, forgive me for not naming them.

My list of obligations is very long, and this is not only evidence of the great generosity with which I have been treated, but also of the very large numbers of scholars working on the subject. Indeed, the volume of the work being produced on British history in the 19th century is beginning to present a very serious problem. I will frankly confess that I have not read all the books, articles and unpublished theses which are relevant to the subjects with which I have dealt. To have attempted to do so would have made it impossible to have delivered the Ford lectures in the time granted to me, or would have interposed an unconscionable delay between delivery and publication. It would also have left no time to refer directly to contemporary 19th century documents on points on which it seemed to be important to do so. For this reason I have not produced a list of books which purports to cover the whole subject, but have contented myself with footnotes which refer to books which are directly relevant to particular topics. My time was by the nature of my case somewhat restricted, but I very much doubt whether any writer wishing to write a general book on 19th century Britain even if he had very much more time available, would be able to take into account all the work, of reasonable importance, which has been done on the subjects which he has been handling; and each year this problem is rather rapidly getting worse. The solution to it, however, is not to give up the attempt to write general history books and so to allow the body of history to be torn in pieces by the specialists, nor is it to write general history by the old impressionistic methods without any relation to specialist studies and techniques; the solution must be to make repeated attempts to write general histories which take account of the depth and exactitude which specialized studies afford. Only so can we get a little nearer to historical truth. I have, in fact, been anxious to do something of this sort, and where I have failed I hope that I shall at least inspire others to do the work more effectively.

G.K.C.

Cambridge, *April 1961*.

Note

Where in the footnotes reference is made to a work which has been cited already, the page reference *within* the square bracket refers to the page in *this* book on which the first citation can be found, the number *outside and following* the bracket to the pages in the work cited to which reference is made.

CHAPTER I

The Task of Revision

In what follows I want to consider some of the factors which might be said to have created Victorian England. This does not mean that I wish to write a complete history of Victorian England, or even to draw a comprehensive composite picture of the Victorian period. Both tasks have been done repeatedly and very well. Recently Professor Asa Briggs in his *Age of Improvement* produced a general history which though it started at an earlier date went well into the Victorian period, in 1936 there was published the full version of that remarkable *tour de force* G. M. Young's *Portrait of an Age*, there are the volumes of Elie Halévy who must always remain the master of those who try to write the history of England in the nineteenth century, and there are many others upon whose excellences it would be impertinent to comment. I have no ambition to rival any of these books. What I want to do is to call attention to some particular factors, or possibly it would be best to call them forces, which called into existence a historic situation with special characteristics in England in the middle of the nineteenth century. To that situation it is best to give the nickname of 'Victorian', but since these creative forces did not cease to operate in 1837 or in 1850 I want to try to show not only how Victorian England was made but also how it developed towards the point when it could be called Victorian England no longer.

I believe that the existence of some of these forces has been at times neglected or the results of their action misapprehended, so that I hope this work may help the next person who turns his hand to the task of writing a new history of Victorian England. For however excellent are the existing books that work will have to be done again. The account of the past which satisfies a particular generation must be regarded as a working hypothesis, no more. We can use what we have received to give form and direction to our thought, but we have no right to regard it as an unquestionably and exhaustively correct view of what actually happened, or of the meaning of what happened. As we see further we ought to realize the defects of what we have written and thought, so that as soon as we have finished writing our histories we ought to start to write them all over again. Each revision we must hope will tell a little more about humanity and its arrangements, but it is not possible that any revision will be final.

'The Priest who slew the slayer and shall himself be slain'; that is, and should be, the condition of the scholar who tries to describe any period of history, and the turn-over is likely to be at its most rapid for those who try their hand on Victorian England which is the subject of so many men's active thought and research. I have no great anxiety to play a leading part at either stage of that transaction; but even though I do not aim at a complete revision of previous work and have no expectation of replacing it by a new comprehensive picture I still think it is necessary to clear the ground a little before I start operations. In doing this I want to do two things. I want to get out of the way certain mistaken conceptions, and I want to suggest methods of work which will I hope challenge those habits of mind which I believe have been the cause of error. I fully realize that those methods may be turned with destructive effect on assumptions that I shall make later, or suggestions that I shall put forward, but that is only as things should be.

II

The tools for any reconstruction of English nineteenth-century history must be forged from the great mass of evidence which is now available for the student—the very large and varied collections of documents, reams of newspapers local and national, ephemeral literature, the results of Government enquiries, etc., etc. It is I believe a larger mass than exists for any country in any previous century, though heaven alone can know what we are depositing now. Upon that mass an almost comparably large swarm of research students has settled, and part of the work of anyone trying to deal with nineteenth-century history must be an attempt, probably an unsuccessful attempt, to cover the relevant work which is being done on his subject; he must also gain for himself some direct experience of the varied evidence which is now so profusely available.

At first sight many of the new details which will emerge from all this may not seem worth all this trouble, for they will often be the details of events in relatively obscure places and often be facts concerning people whose utmost claim to notice might be that they were of secondary importance. The nineteenth century printed its records about its great men and important events very industriously, and, though their habits in editing the private letters which they printed often left a great deal to be desired, a good many of the major facts about important people have in fact been recorded. Certainly there are some strange gaps and no doubt even about the primary characters there is still much to come to light; what however exists in the greatest profusion is unpublished information which the biographers and editors thought to be of no interest, and it is precisely from such information that, or so I believe, the larger changes in our view of nineteenth-century history will come.

For the nineteenth-century historian, and these things are often enough true about historians writing on other centuries, often worked on his central figures and events very carefully, but he filled in their background more easily, accepting generalizations about it without paying much critical attention to them. Those generalizations had sometimes actually been inherited from contemporaries of the events themselves, who might have been strong partisans of one side or other in the conflicts of the period; sometimes, as was inevitable, they had been suggested by the fact that the historian was himself emotionally committed on the issue with which he was treating, but most often they had been accepted casually, simply because scholars had got into the habit of repeating set phrases about certain groups or particular periods without checking their truth in any systematic fashion, or even expending much thought on what they might mean. Now, however, historians have begun to use the vast wealth of evidence which is available for them and to recover a great deal of information about the men and women who were the units covered by these large generalizations, and it would not be too bold to say that wherever this has been done the results have always been surprising and very often revolutionary.

Of course, to assemble this evidence for effective use is a very laborious and sometimes a very dreary task. It is indeed a laborious, and it must be said sometimes a rather dreary task, to try to cover the work of those who have already worked on the evidence, particularly since so much of it is in the form of unpublished Ph.D. theses. But it will I believe become more and more dangerous to write history which has not at least been checked by reference to some of this detail. And it ought to be so. The old bland confident general statements about whole groups of men, or classes, or nations ought to disappear from history; or if something of their sort must remain, and it is difficult to say anything about history or politics or society without making use of general statements, they must remain under suspicion, as expedients which are convenient, possibly necessary, for use at the moment, but are not the best that we shall be able to do in the way of truth.

This matter concerns all historians—the biographer, or the historian of art, or of religion, or of the law and not simply those who are trying to make quantitative generalizations about society as a whole. Indeed, every historical statement even if it is about the most individual of individuals is also a statement about society as a whole, and it is also true that in order to discuss any individual case generalizations about society must be assumed. The subject of a biographer emerges from a particular environment, he lives in a particular environment, if he is a writer he must write for a contemporary public, if he is a politician or a divine he must operate on human raw material provided by the circumstances of his time. To understand him it is necessary to think carefully about these things and not to assume general impressions about them, or to take statements about them ready made from someone else. But this is not always done, indeed even what one might have thought were obviously relevant facts are sometimes neglected because they are at one remove from the central figure. For instance, the lives of statesmen are still too frequently described entirely in terms of the relationships between important individuals at the centre of politics without any thought for the party organizations on which a politician's effectiveness largely depended, still less for the changing social conditions in the constituencies to which they had at some time to appeal. But to leave out these things is to leave out at least half of the factors which determined a man's success or failure. It is history without background, and therefore obviously questionable; but history without background seems to me to be better than history with a false background provided by well-worn general phrases about whose general accuracy no one has ever bothered to think.

May I give, as an example of what goes to create such a false background, the phrases connected with two words, which as I believe have done more to stultify thought about Victorian England than anything else? They are the words 'middle class'. It may be that straight historians, the historians so to speak of the legitimate stage, have by now become a little uneasy about the use of those words, but what one might call para-historians —the writers and broadcasters on the history of art, the literary critics, the politicians and preachers dabbling in history—still use those words with avidity and with them the whole weary range of phrases which have become normal in any description of England at any period of the nineteenth century—'the rising middle class', 'the predominant middle class', 'middle-class taste', and perhaps above all 'middle-class morality'. These conceptions are still offered with a great deal of confidence as a complete explanation for much that was done or produced in the nineteenth century. Nor have the writers of text books, nor I am afraid many of the teachers in schools, abandoned that curious legend that the middle class came to dominate politics and the country immediately after the Reform Bill of 1832 and remained in control till, presumably, the working classes took over—but those who write in this way are normally a little vague on that point.

Now all this needs probing and correcting, indeed it should become the custom, when anyone shews a tendency to talk about the middle class, to make him answer this simple but very difficult question—'Who precisely were the middle class?' Presumably they were all the people who at any given moment came in income, or in social estimation, between the nobility and landed gentry on the one hand and the manual labourers on a weekly or daily wage on the other. If so, the bracket is a wide one. On this calculation a merchant prince in Liverpool would be middle class or a banker in the City and at the same time a linen draper in Exeter would be middle class and so would be those cheeky shabby clerks you so often meet in Dickens. The range of income must have been very great, and the variety in ways of life almost beyond calculation, particularly if you include not only the town but the country-side, the tenant farmers, the corn merchants, the millers, in fact all that society which George Eliot knew so well.

As their environment differed, so did their culture. The middle class included some of the most refined and cultivated people in the kingdom; it provided the society which produced men like William Roscoe of Liverpool, the historian of Lorenzo the Magnificent, Shorthouse of Birmingham, the author of *John Inglesant*, or Thomas Hodgkin, the author of *Italy and her Invaders*; and it also produced, in large numbers, the Philistines of the sort that Matthew Arnold met and disliked in his business as a school inspector. The middle class filled every kind of religious denomination. The nonconformists were held to be distinctively middle class, but the relatively large congregations which the enumerators of the census of 1851 found in Anglican churches cannot all have been gentry or working class, parti-cularly in the towns. The middle class were the backbone at least of the constituency organization of all political parties. In fact, the people who at any given moment might be called middle class vary so widely in so many different ways that there seems to be a high probability that any general statement that purports to include them all must be fallacious, any common attribute credited to them all must be a delusion.

Of course, the general expression 'middle class' remains useful, as a name for a large section of society. Moreover, it is necessary to remember that a belief in the importance and significance of the middle class in the nineteenth century derives from contemporary opinion. From fairly early on in the century men were fond of discussing the part which they thought the middle class was likely to play in the life of the nation. They do not always say clearly whom they have in mind, and since the possible varieties are so great a modern writer should follow them with great caution coupling any reference to the middle class with as precise an analysis as possible of what groups are under discussion.

Above all things it is most important not to attribute too readily to middle-class characteristics, whatever they may have been, matters in which people who were palpably not middle class took part, possibly a leading part. For instance the decay of taste after the elegancies of the regency period has been attributed to the pervasive influence of the 'rising middle class'; this however seems to be very doubtful when it is considered how readily and how widely the aristocracy was infected. Middle-class morality presents a more difficult question, since that is connected with the conception of 'respectability' which was considered to be almost the determining characteristic of the middle class. But it must be remembered that many members of the working classes and even of the aristocracy were 'respectable', while many in the middle income groups palpably were not.

Nor did the middle class, however defined, dominate the country after 1832. Certainly they were deemed to be politically important at the time of that Reform Bill, and that Bill was proposed and passed largely as a recognition of their importance; but after the Bill the final control in politics still lay without question in the hands of the old governing classes, the nobility and gentry. It is sometimes suggested that the repeal of the Corn Laws in 1846 is a sign that by then the decisive political power had passed to the middle classes. Again it is unquestionable that the case for repeal had been vehemently pressed by what was on any calculation a middle-class body, the Anti-Corn Law League; but the actual repeal was carried through by the head of one aristocratic party because he believed it to be desirable with the assent of the other because, at least, he believed it to be expedient. It seems to be very doubtful that Cobden and Bright and the Anti-Corn Law League could have forced the repeal of the Corn Law if neither Sir Robert Peel nor Lord John Russell had agreed with the policy, and what is not doubtful at all is that after the repeal of the Corn Laws as before the final control of politics still remained in the hands of the old governing classes. It was a control which Bright devoted all his powers to fight, yet in spite of all his efforts any further reform of Parliament was postponed another twenty years.

III

The history of the repeal of the Corn Laws has however another lesson for those who would revise history. In most of the older

histories the account of the behaviour and the case of each side
to this controversy came directly from the political statements
of the leaders of the Anti-Corn Law League, unmodified and
unquestioned. In the official life of Disraeli and in the writings
of Mr Charles Whibley a differently balanced account was
given, but it did not convince many and was not much attended
to. The other side's point of view held the field and nobody
bothered to go directly to the contemporary documents to see
whether all the statements made by the champions of the
League in the heat of the battle were consistent with ascertain-
able fact, or whether the accusations which the League rather
profusely made against their opponents could be answered or
balanced by anything that was said on the other side.

To take one question of fact. The spokesmen of the League
always asserted that the main opponents of the repeal of the
Corn Laws were the aristocracy and the squires, but that the
farmers could be persuaded that the repeal was in their interest,
when it was possible to make contact with them. At that date
this was a natural claim to make for the purposes of propaganda,
but a review of the evidence does not confirm it. The strongest
and most passionate objections to repeal seem to have been
entertained by the tenant farmers, whose economic margin was
small and who were terrified at what might be the result if
repeal were passed. This feeling comes out in the various
agitations among the farmers between 1830 and 1846 about
which the older historians were silent. It is also very marked in
the behaviour of farmers at the general elections of 1837 and
1841, and particularly in the elections for county seats which
took place in 1846 itself, about which also the older historians
said nothing. In contrast to this, many of the country gentry
seemed to have been divided in mind, or at least in allegiance,
on the matter of the Corn Laws, for they were pushed in one
direction by their leader Sir Robert Peel but pulled in the other
by their farming constituents, and it seems that the attitude of
members of the House of Lords was even more equivocal. None
of this required very much research to uncover, but the older
historians did not feel the need to do research, since they
accepted the League's account of the crisis as obvious truth.

Or to take another point. As was natural in the circumstances
the League asserted that the tenants of the aristocracy were

forced by the threat of eviction to vote for protectionist candidates, a statement which has been repeated by most historians without the rider that exactly the same electoral influence or pressure was at that time being exerted on their dependants by landlords and employers on the other side in politics, and, further, that there is every reason to believe that agricultural tenants wished to vote for protectionist candidates and that trouble did occur on several occasions even between landlord and tenant when the tenants suspected that the proposed candidate was not sufficiently sound upon protection. In fact, at the time of the Anti-Corn Law controversy accusations of undue influence were being violently made by each side against the other, but it has only been the accusations of the Anti-Corn Law League that have managed to lodge themselves in the history books. Nor till recently was there any reconsideration of the very interesting question of the relation of the behaviour of the League to the disturbances of 1842, though it caused much interest at the time.[1]

It would probably be unreasonable to blame the older historians for accepting a one-sided account of this particular transaction. What happened here has happened so often that it must be considered one of the ordinary hazards of historiography. The case for one side to a controversy has seemed so coherent and cogent that historians have accepted it as evident truth; it has not seemed to be necessary to waste time checking it, or troubling about what the other side had to say. After all, in the ordinary business of life *audi alteram partem* is one of the least frequently observed of all important maxims; considerations of urgency and lack of time seem normally to forbid attention to it. But without any desire to attack his predecessors a revising historian must pay attention to this habit particularly because it is the normal habit of partisans to make, and believe, dogmatic statements of fact for which they have little or no evidence, and it is of some importance that these should be recognized, tested and if necessary removed from the historical canon.

Indeed, another example of party statements taking their place unblushingly as the solemn results of research can be

[1] G. Kitson Clark *Transactions of the Royal Historical Society*, 'The Electorate and the Repeal of the Corn Laws', 5th Series, Vol I (1951). G. Kitson Clark *Journal of Modern History*, 'Hunger and Politics in 1842' (Chicago), Vol XXV, No. 4. N. McCord *The Anti-Corn Law League* (London 1958)

found in a matter of recurrent importance in Victorian history, the statements which are made from time to time as to why a particular party won or lost a general election. These are sometimes the guess of an historian long after the event, but very often they derive from a phrase made by a party orator who wished to point the moral of the election as soon as it was over, particularly if his side had lost. Such statements were usually made in good faith, but there is seldom much reason to believe that they were made after any close study of the facts. Now elections are won or lost in the constituencies, and in order to learn what happened in any given general election it has proved to be necessary to make a rather close local study of particular constituencies. A statement based upon a general impression and not upon this research is worth very little, and one made by an active politician on the morrow of a hard-fought election which has occupied all his energies must be of this nature, even if it were not also inevitably highly coloured by strong party feelings. It is not therefore fair to perpetuate such a statement as if it were a serious contribution to history. As a matter of fact there has been of recent years a good deal of very close work on electoral matters, material has been found in local newspapers, in solicitors' offices, in collections of private papers, and the results have been both complicated and interesting. These results do not seem to bear any very close relationship to the naïve dogmatic statements which still do duty for history in too many books when the results of a particular general election are to be explained.

When historians accept the statement of a partisan as a truth of history they often put themselves at the mercy of a bias which is not their own, the word of a controversialist is received without criticism because it is convenient to do so and not because the historian shares the controversialist's passions; indeed he may never have given much thought about the direction in which those passions might have pulled the statements he accepts. But of course there are many instances when the historian's own emotions are committed. This is liable to happen in all sorts of ways to the student of any history at any period; but as far as English history in the nineteenth century is concerned the student is nowadays less likely to feel himself to be emotionally involved in the quarrels between Liberal and

Conservative or Free Trader and Protectionist than in the issues raised by the whole question of poverty and wealth in the England of the Industrial Revolution.

Emotional commitment on this issue may lead the student to accept consciously, or unconsciously, a pattern of history suggested by a belief in economic conflict and the class struggle as the overriding factor in history, to assume the truth of statements which conform to this pattern and to allow this pattern to give a particular meaning to facts and statements which a normal interpretation would by no means naturally attribute to them. It would of course be idle to deny that economic conflict and the class struggle gives its shape to much of English nineteenth-century history; the danger is that they should be called on to explain too much and to explain it too easily, particularly when political motives are in question. In fact, it is often very difficult to detect the link between political action and economic interest and no historian has a right to believe that he knows, by *a priori* methods and without direct evidence, what it was in any individual case. He has no right to assume that in any action a man has been activated by a regard for his economic interest and by nothing else, he has no right to assume that he knows without enquiry all of a man's economic interests, nor, without direct evidence on the point, that he knows what political action a man might have thought was best suited to further his economic interests.

For instance, a wealthy man in an important position is very likely to have a good many different economic interests and consideration for one of them might easily seem to work for the destruction of another. It is not possible to begin to calculate which affected his politics until they are all known, and also till it is known in what order he valued them. In addition to this a politician, particularly a politician before 1870, is often partially swayed by the hope of Government employment or other favours for himself and his relatives. This may rank as a motive inspired by economic interest, but it will not be discovered by disinterring his sources of income. A poorer man, a wage earner, may have to face a simpler economic problem, but an historian has no right to be sure that he will interpret his economic interest according to the terms of the class war as conceived by someone writing a long time afterwards, or in the confirmed belief that there must be a necessary clash of interest between capital and labour; in fact, it is clear that many of the working men who followed and believed in John Bright did not think in this fashion.

It is necessary to say this because some very crude work has sometimes been published on the relation between economic interest and political action and it will be impossible to think about the problems of Victorian England unless this problem is brought into more accurate focus. But, in fact, most historians are unlikely to adopt these oversimplified economic categories, they are more likely to distribute their sympathies according to rather loosely conceived divisions of the rich and poor, the established and the dispossessed, the comfortable and the miserable. This distribution is likely to be suggested by very natural feelings. Nineteenth-century Britain, especially early nineteenth-century Britain, was a very harsh place, and it has probably been made to seem harsher to us than the Britain of earlier centuries because we know more about it. In the circumstances it is natural for a generous-minded man to feel for the sufferers, and to be angry with those who may have been callous about their sufferings, who may even have inflicted them and who certainly did not redress them. These feelings may be the stronger because many feel that the conditions and the classes which caused them are not yet extinct. Nor has history always been the loser by these tendencies to honest indignation. They have lent enthusiasm to research and imaginative force to the work that has resulted.

But indignation, however honest, is a dangerous passion for historians. Dislike tends to simplify the men and women disliked and to make it impossible for them to be seen for what they were, complex human beings, creatures of a moment necessarily purblind with the prejudices of the time and ignorant of much that it would have been better for them to know. Historians with strong feelings often tend to forget that the people they dislike were possibly victims of incapacity and ignorance and ascribe their actions too consistently to simple inhumanity and greed. Accusations on such counts are of course not easy to answer when little direct evidence survives about a man's thoughts, which therefore must be supplied by supposition. But they may not be just.

An example of the loss and gain in this matter can be found in the work of J. L. and Barbara Hammond. No one interested in nineteenth-century studies should refuse to be grateful to them. They uncovered much, and the strong emotions which inspired their work were in many ways appropriate, for there is material which ought not to be considered in cold blood. But those emotions were not always good servants. Their use of evidence in some instances has been severely questioned, but what is more relevant here, their very strong feelings have too often led them to see the classes they disliked as odious stereotypes with few individual and no mitigating characteristics, about whom merciless generalization was relatively easy. It may indeed be worth while to re-read the two, relatively short, chapters 'On the mind of the Rich' and 'The Conscience of the Rich' in *The Town Labourer* and to note the facility with which the authors slip into talking generally about what the 'Upper Classes' in general thought and felt, and the ease with which they disregard the very difficult problem of what a man of a different era could be reasonably expected to understand or to do. It is also well worth while to compare the very disagreeable picture which the authors draw of Hannah More and Wilberforce with the longer accounts of those two in the books on them by Miss Gwladys Jones and Sir Reginald Coupland, books which possibly show how much more complex are the problems of men and women when they are studied in greater detail than the Hammonds afforded, and with less indignation.

The work of the Hammonds was written some time ago, and in many ways they deserved well of history. It would be harsh to criticize them now, if it were not for the fact that the tendencies which they exemplify still sometimes affect history as written today, and particularly as taught in the schools. Such tendencies are not of course peculiar to any particular type of history. They are common to all history written with strong feelings in which men have to generalize about people they dislike. They are common in religious history and very common in nationalist history. Indeed, the most important task of historical revision is to rescue real men and women who have been shrunk by historians into the bloodless units of a generalization, or have become the ugly depersonalized caricatures of partisan legend or modern prejudice. It is a task well worth doing, since from the contemplation of the stereotypes which have been drawn by historians and by politicians is engendered much of the hatred of the world. The appeal must always be to contemporary documents, and since the number of those which have survived from the England of the nineteenth century is almost overwhelming, we ought, if we have courage and industry, to find it easier to break the existing patterns and to creep a little nearer reality when describing Victorian England than when dealing with most communities in most earlier centuries.

IV

This work needs courage and industry and organizing power and it is necessary to think a little how to do it. Possibly the most effective way to organize the mass of evidence available is to appeal to arithmetic where this is possible. It might perhaps be a good thing to say to anyone who has to make a large quantitative statement about a group or class, 'do not guess, try to count, and if you can not count admit that you are guessing'. The appropriate reply to such a challenge might, however, well be to admit at once that most historical generalizations are necessarily founded on guesses, guesses informed by much general reading and relevant knowledge, guesses shaped by much brooding on the matter in hand, but on guesses none the less. This is, however, not a matter of which there is any reason to be ashamed; it is rather a matter for pride. If it were not for guesses the historical imagination could never build up a complete picture of any period, event or man, and much of the most valuable, and all of the most attractive, work of the historian would remain undone. Nevertheless, the result of that work should be seen for what it is, an hypothesis about the past and no more. As an hypothesis it must always wait to be tested, and one of the most salutory tests to which it can be subjected might be called the discipline of arithmetic. It is particularly healthy to ask of any generalization the questions how many? how often? how much and in what proportion?

The appeal to figures is, however, neither easy, nor certain in its action. Figures can be treacherous. If a mistake is made in the premises of the calculation or in the identification of the units to be counted, the resulting figures can be simply a source of error. Nor are figures always easy to use and it is probable that more historians should learn about the technique of handling them than now do. Yet with all this they may introduce an element of relative certainty into a generalization which no speculation, however intelligent, can ever provide.

One of the most interesting attempts to use figures in research in political history which is going forward at the moment is being practised on British material on the very threshold of what I have called Victorian England. Professor W. O. Aydelotte of the State University of Iowa has investigated the members of the British Parliament which was elected in 1841 and sat till 1847. He has endeavoured to find out all about each one of them, their sources of wealth, their family connections, their personal histories and to correlate these by the technique of the punched card and the calculating machine with their political behaviour in debates and divisions. Perhaps it is as yet too early to express an opinion on the results of this method, but three things I think it has demonstrated already: first, how diverse were the economic interests of individual members of Parliament, second, how complicated is the problem of establishing a relationship between these interests and the way in which they voted, and third, how crude and unsatisfactory are some of the general statements which in the past have been made on that topic.

In many cases, however, arithmetic can not be easily used because a complete count can not be made. Even so, it is better to multiply instances as far as is possible, so that the cases produced are in some way examples of a group of analogous facts large enough to be significant, and not simply illustrations produced to support an intuition or enforce a prejudice. For instance, it is a matter of considerable importance, when trying to estimate what was the condition of agricultural labourers at any point in nineteenth-century England, to find out how many of them controlled a vegetable garden or a potato patch which they could cultivate as an addition to their wages. Sir John Clapham, in his *Early Railway Age*, tackles the question as best he can. He accumulates evidence on this point from various counties for the first thirty years of the century. There is a good deal of it, but not enough, or so one would have said, to make a complete count. It would be difficult to be sure from what he collects exactly what proportion of agricultural labourers of that period possessed gardens, or at least gardens of any appreciable size. This is no doubt unsatisfactory, but it is more satisfying than the conclusion of Mr and Mrs Hammond. When summarizing the events of the period 1760-1832 they said without qualification that the English labourers 'had lost their gardens', giving as their sole evidence, according to Sir John Clapham, 'one extract from a Kentish newspaper'. Sir John called attention to Mr and Mrs Hammond's statement in a footnote, and in the next edition of *The Village Labourer* the statement about the English labourers having lost their gardens disappeared. But in the version which is published today a new sentence has been added that 'They had lost their pigs and fowls'. It is a little difficult to reconcile this statement with the contemporary evidence that a good many agricultural labourers did in fact possess pigs in 1830 and the years that immediately preceded 1830, which appear on the pages which immediately succeed in Sir John Clapham's book his stricture on the Hammonds' original statement. Since Mr and Mrs Hammond presumably dropped their original statement as a result of Sir John Clapham's work they had presumably read these pages, unless they were so clear that they knew what they were talking about that they had not the curiosity to turn over.[1]

Now I suppose that it would not be asserted that there were no labourers in 1830 who were unable to keep pigs where their predecessors had kept them; there may have been a good many. But Mr and Mrs Hammond's statement purports to be 'the whole truth'. This it palpably is not. Therefore it can not be said to be 'nothing but the truth'. It is indeed a very notable example of how much better it is to collect a series of separate instances from the contemporary evidence even though the tale is never going to be complete enough to build up into a generalization than to be so sure of your generalization that you feel justified

[1] Sir John Clapham *An Economic History of Great Britain. The Early Railway Age* (Cambridge 1926) pp. 119-21 (see note 3, p. 119). Mr and Mrs Hammond *The Village Labourer*, ed. 1911, pp. 241-2. In the 1920 edition (pp. 217-18) the remark about gardens is repeated. In the 1927 edition it is dropped out and is replaced by the general statement: 'The general conditions of their daily lives had changed for the worse' (p. 218). In the Guild Books edition first published 1948, the statement about 'pigs and fowls' is made (Vol II, p. 42)

in ignoring any number of separate instances, even when they are brought under your nose.

The effect of such detailed work may very well be disheartening, its result may be to break up an existing picture and replace it with nothing that can be seen as a whole, to lead to a kind of historical nominalism with innumerable accidentals and no universals. Indeed, much of Sir John Clapham's work has seemed to students to produce just this effect. But even if this must be its result, if it is accepted that history should have anything to do with truth the work of accepting this detail into history must be done and the vast accumulation of evidence which is available for Britain in the nineteenth century must be used to do it. Perhaps when the work has been done new patterns, a new general story, may be produced to replace the old to serve their turn and then be discarded when the time comes. But the revision of history cannot wait until the new generalizations appear. Before they appear the results of detailed research must be used even if their only result is to destroy.

V

Certainly there is much that they will destroy. As far as nineteenth-century Britain is concerned this detailed research based on the close study of local evidence will necessarily check and may alter much that men have been accustomed to say about social conditions. It will necessarily check and will certainly alter much that they used to say about politics and elections, and it will probably modify the way men have handled the history of how men and women thought and felt, for on this too there is a good deal of detailed contemporary evidence.

Anyone who has engaged in the kind of research, in old newspapers or in very dead ephemeral literature, to which the study of elections and local politics inevitably leads will have been struck by the number of controversial points of view which clearly excited great feeling at the time, either in support of them or in antagonism to them, which have now sunk without trace into the dust of history, as if no one ever had bothered to think about them. Sometimes the whole controversy which

produced them has been forgotten or nearly forgotten, or
sometimes it has seemed afterwards that one side was so decisively right that historians have not bothered to find out what
the other side had to say for itself, or how much it appealed to
contemporaries. A case in point is the controversy over monetary
matters which raged in the 'twenties and 'thirties after Peel's
Act of 1819. Until recently historians have by no means
realized how cogent were the arguments against the return to
a currency based on gold and how bitterly many people, particularly farmers, attributed all the ills they suffered in the next
two decades to this return.[1] Even now I do not think that sufficient account is taken of the great potential political importance
of this opinion. But it was an opinion that was held in opposition
to the views of the great orthodox economists, who were by
assumption right on these matters and so it has been thought to
be eccentric, not worthy of the attention of history, and has
been left out.

This fate it has shared with a good many other opinions
which in their day gained approval, often enthusiastic approval,
from considerable sections of the community. In some ways
what may be called intellectual history or the history of opinion
suffers from much the same tendencies as those which have
distorted political history. In political history historians concentrated too much on the principal characters—the kings, the
generals, the ambassadors and the leaders of the people—and
did not bother about what seemed to be the secondary characters or the communities in the background. In the history of
opinion there has been a tendency to concentrate attention on
those men whose intellectual standing is still recognized today.
Their influence has therefore been exaggerated, or at least there
has been some neglect to look for others who might have been
influential as well. It is a very natural tendency. The great
figures obviously present themselves for consideration, they
have not to be sought out; their thought has normally come to
be accepted as being within the canon of those opinions which
rational men could possibly entertain: it seems to be intelligible,
if not necessarily acceptable. There is little doubt that their

[1] Asa Briggs *Age of Improvement* (London 1959) pp. 204-5. See also A. Briggs *Cambridge Historical Journal*, 'Thomas Attwood and the Economic background of the
Birmingham Political Union', Vol IX, No. 2 (1948) (IV) pp. 190-216

influence was often considerable. Why then seek further? Why seek for other influences among the obscure, the probably confused, the deservedly forgotten? Like other men, historians find it difficult to believe that human beings in the mass can be powerfully affected by men into whose minds they cannot enter, or by ideas which seem to them to be rubbish, expressed in language which sounds to them very like gibberish.

There is a probable example of the exaggeration of the influence of one very important thinker in the usual estimate of the influence of Jeremy Bentham in the first half of the nineteenth century, a matter on which Dr Oliver MacDonagh has written a very revealing article.[1] Of course, no one would be foolish enough to deny the very great importance of Bentham and his disciples in the history of the political thought and philosophy of that period. The trouble is that far too much of the legislative and administrative development which helped to create Victorian England has been simply labelled 'applied Benthamism', as if it were simply the unfolding of Bentham's political philosophy, and as if Bentham's followers were the only systematic thinkers of their day. This, palpably, they were not, and when the framers of policy were Benthamites the needs of action might often lead them away from the dogmas of the master. In fact, as Dr MacDonagh has pointed out, a great deal of administrative and legislative development was the result of the empirical actions and hard-bought experience of a number of officials, many of whom had probably never heard of Bentham, but on whom public demands had imposed novel and very difficult tasks.

There may be special reasons for an exaggeration of Bentham's influence. Most thought about English legislation in the nineteenth century naturally starts with Dicey's *Law and Opinion*, and Dicey was perhaps a great jurist rather than a great historian looking instinctively more to the philosophical principle behind legislation which Bentham's thought summarized, or might have been held to summarize, rather than to the agencies which actually developed policy, in which he might have had less share. The greatest of the historians who have worked on the history of England in the nineteenth century,

[1] Oliver MacDonagh *The Historical Journal*, 'The Nineteenth Century Revolution in Government: a Reappraisal', Vol I (1958) pp. 52-67

Elie Halévy, was first attracted into English nineteenth century by his interest in Bentham and did important work upon him, and was therefore likely to put emphasis on his thought. Moreover, the great Fabian historians probably found Bentham congenial, since he was in so many ways their ancestor. But no special arguments are needed to explain the tendency to simplify and rationalize history by grouping a large diverse historical movement under the name of one obviously outstanding man whose arguments the ordinary scholar can appreciate since he knows about them from what the great man himself wrote or, what is more likely, from what others have written about him.

To check the estimate of Bentham's importance it is necessary to turn to practice, to the acts of government and to the motives and thought of the men who were behind the acts of government or had to serve as government agents. In other cases when it is necessary to bring into due perspective the importance of an orthodox opinion, the significance of an accepted thinker's philosophy, it is necessary to revitalize dead controversialists and also to ask of contemporary documents what actually moved the people in these matters. There are enough and more than enough of those documents for nineteenth-century Britain for the answer to that question to be a comprehensive one and I think it is probable that the most accurate answer may well be that the people were as often as not moved by men appealing to the sanctions of the Christian religion, particularly if they spoke the language of those brands of Christianity which were not acceptable to educated opinion, or propagated by the leading intelligences of Oxford and Cambridge.

In fact, it might not be too extravagant to say of the nineteenth century that probably in no other century, except the seventeenth and perhaps the twelfth, did the claims of religion occupy so large a part in the nation's life, or did men speaking in the name of religion contrive to exercise so much power. The century opens with a great agitation against slavery, nationwide, highly emotional, magnificently organized, which was largely responsible for one of the most drastic changes in the world's polity there has ever been, the abolition of the age-old institution of chattel slavery. This was the model of many agitations which gave direction and effectiveness to moral indignation; indeed, so attractive and effective did this model become that the agitation against the Corn Laws though launched by secular politicians was consciously given this form by those who organized it.

Behind all this, fermenting in the country from before the beginning of the century, was the Evangelical revival. It helped to renew the life of the Church of England. It created a large Wesleyan Church highly disciplined and inclined to be Tory in politics, it developed other smaller Methodist sects, it gave new life to the Congregationalists and Baptists. It enormously increased the number of Nonconformists in the first quarter of the century, and then returned to revivify them with the second Evangelical revival after 1858. It led Britain to share in the great nineteenth-century movement for overseas missions which despatched representatives of Christianity and white civilization to every quarter of the globe, and, what in Britain at least could be of considerable political importance, provided excitable audiences to listen to the missionaries on the subject of the wrongs of the aborigines when they came back.

Unfortunately this new ferment put new force into old quarrels and did not remove old prejudices. The growing strength of Protestant Nonconformity renewed the battle between Church and Dissent to such an effect that it became at times, for instance in the early 'thirties and the late 'sixties, one of the most important in English politics. Or, to take account of a more primitive feeling, possibly the most deep seated and dangerous prejudice in the English and Scottish mind had at least a religious form, it was the old passionate belief in Protestantism and the wickedness of the Church of Rome which formed so important an element in the political philosophy of many old-fashioned people and was the natural vehicle for the emotions of humbler men and women who in English and Scottish towns found themselves too near neighbours of the unhappy immigrant Irish.

Yet no one would have guessed the importance of this factor from the way the older historians have handled the period. In his book on *Christian Apologetics* Mr Alan Richardson prints a complaint that the only reference to missionaries in the general index of the old *Cambridge Modern History* is to 'missionary ridge', the scene of some fighting in the American Civil War.[1] The

[1] Alan Richardson, B.D., *Christian Apologetics* (London 1947) pp. 97-8, Note i

implications of this are not quite fair. Missionaries are at times mentioned in the text of that history, as for instance in the chapter on early nineteenth-century South Africa, which indeed it would have been impossible to write without referring to them.[1] But the references might be said to be meagre, and it would be very hard to gain from the old *Cambridge Modern History* any idea of the forces behind them in Britain, or of the leaven working generally in the country. The history of Great Britain from 1799 to 1841 is dealt with very competently in three chapters by Messrs Gooch and Temperley.[2] In these chapters the Dissenters are mentioned, but only in the most general and the vaguest terms, nor do the authors allow the word Evangelical to sully their pages. A careless reader of Gooch's Chapter XX might conceive that the only force behind the emancipation of the slaves was the 'growth of the humanitarian spirit'.[3] Wilberforce, Zachary Macaulay and Lord Shaftesbury are indeed mentioned, but it has not seemed necessary to name, much less to discuss, their beliefs. This may have been for considerations of space; Temperley had after all written about Methodism in the eighteenth-century volume and that may have seemed enough for that kind of thing. In these chapters he did however devote about five of the large pages of this volume to Jeremy Bentham.[4]

Such was the conception of British nineteenth century in 1907. The picture was afterwards rectified in the great history of Elie Halévy, a Frenchman who saw England with a fresh eye. He made his mistakes it is true; he tended to confuse, for instance, the various bodies who claimed the common name of Methodist, whose differences socially and politically are of considerable importance. But his are the venial mistakes of a pioneer, and his contribution was great. He recognized the importance of this factor, and how necessary it is to separate in history the various strands in Nonconformity. Even so, it may be questioned whether in fact the lesson has yet been fully learnt. In recent books there is still very little about the second Evangelical revival, little about the movement in Wales, little about Sankey and Moody, not very much about Spurgeon.

[1] *C.M.H.* Vol XI (1908) cap. XXVII (3)
[2] *C.M.H.* Vol IX (1906) cap. XXII, Vol X (1907) caps. XVIII and XX
[3] *C.M.H.* Vol X, p. 658
[4] Ibid., pp. 594-9

The missionaries are still neglected, no one has written that history of nineteenth-century Nonconformity which is so badly needed.

Now, why should there be a reluctance to discuss things which were not only obviously important to a great many people in their own right but as obviously very important in their influence on the history of the country? It may be partly the result of one very curious habit which historians are apt to develop. They are inclined to assume that certain things are important in certain centuries, and when they occur in the wrong centuries they are at liberty to leave them out or play them down because they want to talk about other things. Thus by the tradition of the writing of history religion is important in the seventeenth century, but in the nineteenth century interest should concentrate on democracy, nationalism, industrial development and the social question.

There is, however, probably something more profound at work here; what it is, is possibly demonstrated by the selection from English nineteenth-century religious topics which people have in fact studied fully. The Evangelical Movement is studied till the death of Wilberforce in 1833 or possibly that of Simeon in 1836, after that no one knows what happened to the Evangelicals or much cares. There is great interest in the Oxford Movement till 1845, when Newman left Oxford; after that the interest dies away. Surely these selections are significant. Wilberforce and the Clapham sect were obviously at the centre of the stage, Simeon was at least at Cambridge, which is near the centre though not as near as Oxford. But after 1836 the social and political distinction of the Evangelicals seems to fade with Lord Shaftesbury as a notable exception. They became people on the periphery working in the dim streets of provincial towns, while for many people their ideas remained, what they always had been, intellectually beyond the pale. From 1833 to 1845 Oxford is the scene of an intellectual and spiritual drama which has always fascinated most men of intelligence, whatever their creed, partly because it had at its centre one of the most subtle and attractive minds of the century. After 1845 the Oxford Movement becomes distressingly parochial, and historians, other than ecclesiastical, have not been much interested in what happens in parishes. The Protestant Dissenters have never had their moment at the centre and in consequence their great men, their domestic crises, their varying beliefs have little troubled the ordinary historian. Indeed, one might almost say that historians have cared to know little more about Dissenters than that they normally voted Liberal and that they could on occasion when appropriately stimulated evince strong moral indignation which might have political results.

This is in effect another example of the tendency of historians to concentrate on the figures in the limelight at the centre of the stage to the neglect of those in the shadows in the wings. Yet there is even more to it than that. As I have said, in the history of opinion one of the attractions of the figures at the centre of the stage is that they are not only easy to find but they are also easy to understand, or at least they appear to be easy to understand, since ready made explanations of their ideas are normally available. As intelligible, and therefore attractive, are those people who are moved by the ordinary common-sense motives which most people share. History can easily be written in the terms of such people, in so far as it concerns them it makes a story that can be understood and believed. When others whose experience and values are of a different nature interfere the story becomes incomprehensible, and it is difficult to believe that what is incomprehensible can have been important or decisive; therefore there is a strong temptation to play such people down or leave them out. For this reason there has been a tendency to concentrate on those men and women whose ideas were drawn from the commonly understood world of political expediency rather than from the less generally frequented world of spiritual experience, that is on the Liberal politician rather than on the revivalist preacher, except in so far as he was an ally of the Liberal politician.

The result of this concentration on the readily intelligible has been to suggest that the ideas which have controlled history are those which appear to be rational, or at least intelligible, to the writers of it. Nothing of course could be further from the truth. At best the ideas which have controlled humanity have been only partly rational, if by rational is meant an idea based on an argument which might appeal to an ordinary educated man who is contemporary with ourselves, which is the meaning normally attached to that word. Even where a recognizable argument has apparently controlled action it has normally received its strength from some already prevailing emotion or from some deep-seated belief or prejudice which has supplied the premises. In many cases, however, there has been little argument, and what there has been mainly served to explain or justify what was already accepted; indeed often there has been nothing that can be called argument, or an attempt to reason, at all, only the direct reference to an emotion or a creed. Therefore, in order to understand the springs of action it is important to try to understand the emotions, the irrational feelings, the prejudices, the experiences which form men's minds, and this is precisely what rationally minded historians are likely to fail to do.

For this reason it is very important to put back religion, particularly popular religion, into the picture of nineteenth-century England. But these underlying emotional factors were by no means only religious. It would be hard, for instance, to call the popular Protestantism that could exert so strong a pull religious, at least it seems when it appears in the back streets to be rooted in feelings more analogous to anti-Semitism in a continental town than any true spiritual emotion, and there are other emotional factors which are not religious to be investigated if investigation is possible. Investigation will admittedly not be easy, partly because it is not clear what evidence should be used; but there is one very large mass of evidence available throughout the nineteenth century which may help. It is the popular literature of the period the drama, the songs, and above all the novels and magazine stories. This will not appeal through its good sense or its truth to life, on the contrary the wildness and absurdity and tastelessness of a great deal of it can hardly be exaggerated. These are certainly wildly distorting mirrors, but they reflect something, they reflect the mind of the people who liked to look into them. The generalizations men accept about life, the morality which commends itself to them, are in some way reflected in the plays they see, in the songs they sing, in the stories they enjoy; and it is our duty as historians to try to understand that reflection.

In that task we have no right to reject anything because it seems to us extravagant, or silly, or because it offends our taste. What by our standards could seem to be so extravagant as the literature produced by the group known as Young Ireland between 1842 and 1848? How absurd to us seems much of Meagher's much admired speech on the 'sword', how inflated seem many of the phrases even of Davis, how utterly second rate much of Mangan's poetry! Yet all this was produced in deadly earnest by able men who were prepared to die for their beliefs, and, what is more important, this literature played an important part in the renewal of Irish nationalism. Indeed, if one set about the task of looking at what was being written, sung and declaimed in a variety of European countries, it seems not impossible that at and about this time one would find the same kind of literature playing the same kind of rôle for nationalism elsewhere.

This is not to say that this ephemeral literature is easy to use as historical evidence. A good deal of work has, in fact, been done of late in the popular nineteenth-century novel, the popular nineteenth-century song and the Victorian melodrama, the results of which have not been altogether satisfactory for the general historian. This is partly, perhaps, because of some of those researching have not always been very clear what they were looking for. It is of course always easy to exhibit curiosities and raise a laugh; the problem is what the researcher is to do after that. It is obviously of historic significance that people in one period were prepared to accept and enjoy literature which in another period they reject as absurd, the types and actions that they are ready to admire or detest are obviously significant —but in what way are these things significant? The danger is that at that point in the argument the generalizations which are supposed to be established, the connections which are suggested between those generalizations and ordinary history, tend to become uncomfortably subjective and very often rather unconvincing.

VI

But if this line of thought is worth exploring it is only one of the ways in which history must add to it its perceptions, as it must also continuously check and correct its methods. The task is endless, and the result will never be satisfactory. Nevertheless, it is probably worth while to attempt it, for it may enable us to get a little nearer to the truth about matters which are of importance to mankind. However, the work of revision cannot be of much value if it is all destructive and none of it is constructive, and in my next chapter it will be necessary to turn from criticism to what it is hoped will be the constructive consideration of that Victorian England which is the subject-matter of this book.

CHAPTER II

Progress and Survival in Victorian England

In my first chapter I tried to suggest certain ways in which I believe the revision of nineteenth-century history ought to be attempted, and one of them was the re-examination of certain words and phrases. The example I gave was the phrase 'middle class'. Now, one difficulty about those words is that they have been in currency so long and men have used them so often when they have talked and written about the nineteenth century that they are sure that they know what they mean, although in fact they have no precise and accurate meaning. But the way in which they have been used presents another difficulty. They have been used often enough to describe men and women who were profoundly respected, or very actively disliked, and as a result their meaning has been darkened by the veneer deposited by past controversy and the emotional needs of those who have used them. And in my very title there is another word which has suffered in the same way—the word 'Victorian'. I used it because it is convenient, but it is clearly unsatisfactory. It too is ambiguous, and, much more strongly than the words 'middle class', it has been coloured by the uses to which it has been put. It was used, so Professor Asa Briggs has told us, fairly early in the reign itself,[1] but the colours in which we now know it were received from those who used it at the very end of the reign, or immediately after it, when young men and young women were against all those things for which, so they felt, the Queen and her reign had stood.

In Act III of Bernard Shaw's play *Pygmalion* Clara Eynsford Hill says brightly: 'Such nonsense all this early Victorian prudery'. She is being rather daring: in fact she is just about to be tempted by the insufferable Professor Higgins to repeat the

[1] Professor Asa Briggs *Age of Improvement* [op. cit. p. 18] 446

word 'bloody'. But she is not being particularly original. If you look into the dictionary you will find from about the date of the play not a few examples of the use of the words 'Early Victorian' to describe furniture, dress or habits; they are usually derogatory, for Miss Eynsford Hill's use was symptomatic. It was the defiance of a past generation, in this case, it is true, rather a safe defiance for her mother was merely bewildered and wondered whether she would have to use that horrid word 'bloody' herself; still it was no doubt the kind of thing which many young people were saying at that time with their eyes on their parents' reactions.

Even when the Queen's reign receded into the past they went on saying the same kind of things. No doubt the battle was most often fought out on the domestic hearth-rug, but it also produced a literature of which Lytton Strachey's elegant libels were probably the most distinguished examples. With him, however, the word 'Early' had been dropped out, and the word Victorian had come to be used by itself so that the whole reign began to shrink in people's eyes into one coherent whole to be included in one comprehensive denigration. Men criticized and sneered at what they called 'Victorianism', or they hotly defended it, or, in due course, they expressed nostalgic regret for it, and it must be presumed that they all thought that they knew what they were talking about.

But did they? Certainly the word 'Victorian' as it came to be used raises one or two difficult questions. For instance, does it refer only to what could be found in the Queen's dominions during her life, or alternatively does it refer to what was contemporaneous with her but to be found not only in Great Britain but in foreign countries at the same stage of development? The question is not unimportant because much of what is written on this subject is surprisingly insular. Conditions in Great Britain are described as if they were unique, and causes are ascribed to them which could only have been effective in this country; indeed, many writers are ready to derive much more than seems to be probable from the character of the occupant of the throne herself, or from her husband. But as a matter of fact much that we consider to be typically Victorian was shared by the United States, where, at least till after the Civil War, the ways of life and thought resembled those of this country much more closely than many people on either side of the Atlantic would have desired to believe. More than this, much that we know as Victorian is to be found on the continent of Europe; there it is known often enough by a different name, but it is unmistakably the same. Indeed, it seems probable that much of what we call Victorian came to us from across the Channel, some from France, even more from Germany, though not I think in the luggage of the Prince Consort.

However, even if we disregard this consideration another question immediately proposes itself. If we confine our view to Britain, or even to England, what region or what section of society have we in mind? I have sometimes tried to apply characteristics which are said to be typically Victorian—this famous 'prudery' for instance, or the painstaking earnestness in serious endeavour of which we hear so much—to what one learns from time to time of the racing set at any period of the Queen's reign, but they do not seem to fit. They are less generally appropriate for those who gathered for the spring meetings at Newmarket than for, say, those who flocked to the May meetings of the philanthropic societies at Exeter Hall. This, however, is only one of the many contrasts presented by a society in which at any given moment there were more sharply differentiated habits and ideals of life, varieties of fortune, styles of dress or language than exist now.

And to the questions 'who?' and 'where?' must be added the question 'when?'. The Queen's reign is a very long one in a period of swiftly moving change. It starts with bishops in cauliflower wigs and the great ones of the world driving in coaches with footmen behind, it ends with expensive people driving in motor cars and a leader of the House of Commons who rode a bicycle; it starts with gentlemen fighting duels, it ends with gentlemen playing golf, and all the time essential change in much more important matters than these is rapidly going forward. Yet all this varied, violently contrasted, rapidly changing life can be included in the one word Victorian.

However, the word is convenient, and I think can be used satisfactorily if we take appropriate precautions. It is desirable, for instance, to remember from time to time that much that seems in England to be essentially Victorian is the product of a cosmopolitan culture that England shared with most of what was not aboriginal in North America and all that was not peasant or hopelessly reactionary in Europe; and, also, that the things which we call Victorian did not in fact prevail in every part of England in any year of the Queen's reign. Above all things it is necessary to define the period that is to be discussed, so that there will be no danger of straggling on to include in an imaginary unity the events and conditions of the whole of an artificial period like a reign which because it has an obvious name may seem to have a greater coherence than in fact it possesses. If, however, we remember these things and define what we are discussing there is probably something we can talk about.

In order, therefore, to limit and define my subject I propose to choose for my period the third quarter of the nineteenth century between 1850 and 1875, and to call that the 'High Noon of Victorianism' for those who like such phrases. In choosing that period I am choosing a period which I intend to seem arbitrary and artificial, for my subject is in fact an historic situation which I believe came piecemeal into existence in the first half of the century, prevailed for a period and then began to disappear before the century ended, if many characteristic elements survived into the twentieth century. Clearly to ascribe to anything with such uncertain beginnings and indefinite endings any dates that claim to mean anything would be misleading.

If, however, it were desirable to choose a more significant date it would be easier to do so for the beginning than for the end. For the beginning of the period it might be possible to choose 1848, in Europe the year of revolutions, in Britain the last effective year of Chartism; for this would seem to be the end that is of that era of hope, pain, suffering and fear which had lasted intermittently from the outbreak of the French Revolution up to the beginning of what may be called the Victorian interlude, an era of peace, relative contentment and well-being. To select, however, any significant date for the end of this interlude would be difficult and probably a mistake. For a variety of reasons there might be a case for cutting the matter very short and choosing the date of the second Reform Act of 1867 or the general election which followed it, that of 1868; or following the same line of thought it might be better to choose the date of that much more efficient instrument of change, the third Reform Act, that of 1884, or, in this case, the election that preceded it, that of 1880, when rather important changes in the political structure of the country began to be effective; or to take account of other matters than politics it might be better to choose the whole decade between 1860 and 1870 as being not only the decade in which there were important constitutional and political changes but also that in which Darwinism was being accepted by the learned world and when there were other significant intellectual developments; or 1873 and 1874 might be chosen because of their economic significance, 1873 being the date normally given for the beginning of the 'great depression' and 1874 as the beginning of the nineteenth-century disaster to British agriculture.

Since, however, the Queen herself survived into the next century, and much else that must be considered as being typically Victorian went on after that, a twentieth-century date might seem to be suitable. If so, an obvious one might seem to be the general election of 1906, or, most significant moment of all, the evening of August 4th 1914 when so many of the lights of Europe were put out never to be lighted again. There is in fact some case for each of these dates, but there can be no conclusive case for deciding on any one of them, and it is probably better to choose for the end what is obviously an arbitrary date of convenience, that is 1875. Certainly there are things which seem to be dying at about that time, or turning towards death.

II

If, however, either 1850 or 1848 is chosen for the beginning of the period, it stands to reason that what preceded those dates had an important part to play in the making of Victorian England. For instance, as has been suggested, the years before 1850 supplied a contrast to the secure opulence and peace of what came after. Before 1848 and 1850 there had been intermittently a great deal of suffering and a great deal of bitterness. Within living memory there was the dread precedent of the French Revolution, to many a source of fear, to others a symbol of the terrible but probable punishment which must come if hearts remained hard and the unjustly privileged recalcitrant, and to some the inspiration to wild and dangerous hopes. After 1850 that shadow faded, the tensions went out of society and some of the hardships disappeared. There was still much endemic poverty and some very bad years, yet there was greater and more secure prosperity even for sections of the working class and there seems to have been more general content. After 1850 popular disturbances seem to have been for a season fewer and not so menacing, and it has been suggested that after that point working-class activities seem more often to be inspired by a hope of bettering conditions and less often by the prick of immediate disaster or the fear of things getting worse.[1] In fact, it might be said that to a dangerous night and a stormy morning had succeeded an afternoon which was sunlit and serene, even if it was only the interval before the hours of darkness came again.

The significance of the years before 1850 for what came afterwards was, however, not only that of contrast. In many ways what continued through that date into the Victorian period was more important than what came to an end before it started. The strain and stress of an unstable social and economic situation inflamed by the hope and terror inspired by what had happened in Paris in the last ten years of the eighteenth century were not the sole moving forces in politics in Britain in the first half of the nineteenth century. To a considerable extent those politics formed part, and the French Revolution itself formed part, of a larger movement in history which started much earlier and which went on throughout the nineteenth century, a movement which it might be held has not yet come to an end. This was the tide which swept through human affairs and carried away the *ancien régime* with its aristocracies, its hereditary monarchies, its prescriptive rights and left in its stead a world whose values, on the whole, we still accept.

This movement is too complicated and too extensive to be given any single descriptive name, or to be ascribed to any particular cause. The agents of change were numerous. A philosophy was developed by which the old régime was comprehensively condemned, new classes emerged to challenge the

---

[1] On this see E. J. Hobsbawm *Economic History Review*, 'Economic Fluctuations and some Social Movements since 1800', 2nd Series, Vol V, No. 1 (1952) pp. 1-25.

position claimed by those who had enjoyed a monopoly of privilege and power, changes in politics took place after which it was impossible to turn back. What happened in politics was connected undeniably if mysteriously with the romantic movement in literature and that in its turn was connected, possibly even more mysteriously, with a reawakening in religion. Without doubt the connections between all these movements are often tenuous and always obscure; they moved very different people in very different directions and often enough brought them into conflict with one another. But they all tended to one result. The old régime—oligarchic, superficial, self-satisfied, cruel and corrupt—had been weighed in the balance and found wanting, though amongst whom its kingdom was to be divided was not yet revealed.

These forces had gathered head in Britain before the French Revolution. The crisis in domestic politics in the first twenty years of George III's reign, the American Revolution and the American war, all together produced in Ireland the volunteer movement and the momentary and modified independence of Grattan's Parliament, and in England the movement for the reform of Parliament. At about the same time men like Joseph Priestley were developing theories in political thought which led in due course towards the ideas of Jeremy Bentham. There was in eighteenth-century Britain a renewal of religion and the development of a higher standard of morality. This is too often narrowed down to what is called the Evangelical revival, and traced too exclusively to Wesley and his friends. But that is a mistake. Even when men were moved by what can be strictly defined as Evangelical doctrine it was not necessarily Methodist in its inspiration or origin, and in any case something was happening which was much broader in its sweep than the word evangelical can cover. There were many who were not technically Evangelical at all but who were nevertheless anxious to take their religion more seriously or to do their duties more conscientiously than men had normally done in the immediate past, and it was such men, conscientious but not necessarily converted, who as much as anyone else were going to effect a moral revolution in the working of British institutions and in the tone of English life.

The French Revolution cut across all this. To some it was an inspiration, but to many more of those who had any chance to influence politics it was a challenge and a threat, and it led the Government to strike blindly at men whom it feared were revolutionaries, while even moderate men felt inhibited from pressing reforms. Revolution was followed by war and by devastating rebellion in Ireland. It was a serious set-back, and yet during all that winter of war and fear and reaction the seed that had been sown before 1789 lay in the ground ready to germinate when the time came. The ideas that had challenged the England of Lord North remained to condemn the Government of the Prince Regent and George IV, with whatever of inspiration or of warning the first French Revolution had left behind to give them new force. It is indeed a matter of great importance that what might be called the basic democratic principle, the claim that political power should be under the control of all ordinary men without distinction of person, should have been present throughout the century in most men's minds as a point, at the least, to be considered. In a country like early nineteenth-century England, so near in time and thought to the old pre-revolutionary régime, loaded with hereditary rights, in which men were accustomed to very great inequalities of wealth, this claim might not be considered very seriously, or it might only excite anger and fear; but from the beginning the challenge was always present, and the hope, or for some people the threat, of democracy must have played some part in the thoughts of any man or woman not unusually stupid, or preoccupied, or torpid. It was one of the points by which, throughout the century, political thought and debate was orientated.

Moreover, throughout the war, and particularly in the last ten years of it, there had been incubating those modes of thought which were not compatible with the values and practices of the old régime. It is probable that Jeremy Bentham did not in fact provide a blueprint which was faithfully followed by all nineteenth-century administrators, but he did supply a radical philosophy, sober but drastic, to be the cogent working creed for the enemies of prescription and of the stupidities of the law. The great men like Ricardo who were developing the new science of economics may have produced what seemed to be but grim doctrine to those who were troubled by human suffering, but they applied the methods of rational and systematic

thought to a field in which public policy was to a large
extent the combined result of thoughtless opportunism, meaningless survivals and the selfish shortsighted pressure of interested groups. Romilly and those who supported him called
attention to the ugly barbarities of the criminal law, and the
land was full of political reformers ranging from extreme
radicals to moderate Whigs, all of whom desired some change,
revolutionary or moderate, in the institutions of the country.

Even before Waterloo these voices were getting louder, and
at the same time what could be called the Evangelical Movement proper, the movement inspired by a conviction of sin and
a belief in the possibility of salvation by grace, was continually
growing in strength and volume. Its greatest apostle John
Wesley had left for his immediate followers a very tightly
disciplined society, with a very awkward constitution, and
because of this, and also in part because the political Toryism
which was part of the Wesley tradition was uncongenial to
many of the people drawn into Wesleyanism, the history of
Wesleyan Methodism in the first half of the nineteenth century
is one of many secessions; indeed, they had started in Wesley's
lifetime with the differences between Wesley and Whitefield.
These secessions are important because often enough the
seceding bodies were able to adapt themselves in different ways
to different classes in various parts of the country, but their
effect on the general spread of Methodism should not be
exaggerated. The old connection, the parent body of Methodism continued to grow in spite of secessions, and with the
members of the various secession bodies the Methodists in
general came to control a very considerable section of the
nation's life, the largest after the Church of England. Nor was
the development of this body the only result of the Evangelical
revival. From about the year 1800 the older Dissenting bodies
seem to have caught fire from the revival, particularly the
Congregationalists, or Independents, and the Baptists, and the
numbers of their chapels, and, where these can be ascertained,
of their Church members increased continually from the
beginning of the century. The Evangelical Movement had,
however, started in the Church of England, and although John
Wesley's followers had formed a separate body which gradually
diverged, the leaven continued to spread in the Church. It

infected a certain number of the parochial clergy and it inspired the very remarkable group of the Clapham saints of whom Wilberforce was the leading figure.

These religious bodies and movements were going to play an important part in the making of Victorian England and they will have to be considered later on in that constructive capacity. Here their destructive effect is most relevant, the extent to which they helped to unmake the England of the old régime, to make it clear even in the first twenty years of the nineteenth century that the methods and morals of the eighteenth could not continue indefinitely to satisfy. It is true that the Evangelical revival had its conservative side. Many of those who came under its influence shrank from the godless Jacobin revolution; there were Tories among the Clapham sect, though not all were Tories, and it is possible also that the revival diverted from revolution those of the working classes whom it converted to religion. This fact, however, would be perhaps more important if the danger of a successful violent revolution in the first twenty years of the nineteenth century had been greater than it seems likely that it was; for considering the nature of English society at that time and the numbers of people who, however discontented, still preferred order to revolution, it is difficult to believe that the danger of effective revolution can at any time have been very great. On the other hand, both by enforcing moral standards which were at variance with eighteenth-century practice and also by enabling classes which till now had not counted for much to express themselves, and by providing vehicles for their activity, the Evangelical revival did a very great deal to change the order of society in England.

Its earliest and in many ways its most spectacular exploit was the attack on negro slavery. This was largely directed by the Clapham saints, but it was carried into every corner of the kingdom by one of the most remarkable general agitations that had yet taken place. It was successful, the slave trade as far as Britain was concerned was abolished in 1807 and slavery in British dominions in 1833. The abolition of the slave trade and slavery was in itself a sufficiently significant event. Chattel slavery was an institution which went back to the dawn of history, it had often been deplored, but it had always survived and now it was to be eliminated, in due course from the whole world with trifling exceptions. But the anti-slavery crusade had another significance in British domestic history. In order to bring it to success a new political weapon of great power had been forged, the weapon of organized moral indignation. All sorts of expedients were used to excite opinion against slavery and to bring it to bear on Parliament, and these expedients appealed in particular to relatively humble people who would not otherwise have had much influence in politics. It gave importance in the nation's affairs to a new section of the population, and it provided a precedent. Other moral agitations followed, to protect the aborigines in areas into which European settlers or traders were penetrating, to put down heavy drinking and to abolish the Corn Laws. It might perhaps have been thought that the question of agricultural protection would have been taken as a problem of economic expediency rather than as a moral issue; but in fact the attack on the Corn Laws was consciously planned on the model of the anti-slavery agitation, the Corn Laws were attacked not only as an inconvenience but as a sin, and a chorus of ministers of religion was invoked to pronounce the anathema.

This incident of the Anti-Corn Law agitation, however, demonstrates how difficult it was in nineteenth-century Britain to separate what was religious and what was secular. The conflicts between classes or parties took on a religious form and colour, and religious growth served to emphasize the struggles between classes and parties. If the passing and retention of the Corn Laws was a sin, it was a sin in a very special category. It derived, so its opponents believed, from the very nature of aristocratic society, it exposed the moral evil of aristocratic privilege, and therefore the attack upon it was a natural rallying point for those who wished to attack the aristocracy. But there were other points at which the increasing strength of religious feeling brought new power to the attack on the aristocracy. The Evangelical revival had increased and was increasing the number and liveliness of the Nonconformists, particularly of the Congregationalists and the Baptists, and the Nonconformists had political issues to face which had their seat nearer home than negro slavery, and were more continuously resented than the Corn Laws. At the beginning of the nineteenth century they still suffered under serious civil disabilities. By the Test and

Corporation Acts they were prevented from holding office in the Corporate towns. If the Churchwardens so decreed they might have to pay a rate for the upkeep of the parish church and the provision of what was necessary for the services there, in most cases it was necessary for them to be married in the parish church and often impossible for them to be buried in the parish churchyard. They could not matriculate at Oxford, or take a degree at Cambridge.

These were disabilities imposed on men for ostensibly religious reasons because of their religious scruples, yet in truth they were even more pronouncedly a symbol of social and political divisions. It seems probable that there were many members of the Church of England who were middle class, but there were singularly few members of the aristocracy who were Protestant Nonconformists. The disabilities imposed on Dissenters were probably at least in part maintained because of the low esteem in which classes lower than their own were held by those who governed the country, and the privileges of the Church of England were certainly attacked as being the most notorious part of the whole iniquitous mass of privilege by which the aristocracy maintained itself. In the towns it may be that the difference between Church and Dissent was probably not so much social as political. Those associated with the parish church were the group who by tradition governed the towns and those associated with the leading Chapels were in opposition to them; but in this case, as in most other cases, it would be quite impossible to say whether a man joined a particular denomination because he accepted its claims to present Christianity in a particular way, or whether he did so because it suited his position in society. Nor does it seem to matter, for in whatever way you look at it the growth of nonconformity and the increasing anger at the disabilities of the Nonconformists point to the same important historical conclusion, the increase in numbers in power and in consciousness of those who could not accept the old régime.

In the first quarter of the nineteenth century it was becoming increasingly clear that what was politically, socially, intellectually and spiritually a new society was growing up in England for which neither the institutions, nor the ideas, that had been inherited from the eighteenth century would suffice.

New classes were developing in wealth and self-consciousness and were beginning to demand a place in society which its old traditional order based on hereditary privilege would not grant to them. Men were learning to require greater humanity, greater justice and greater common sense in the methods of government and the law. Some men were inspired by the revival of religion to accept for themselves a higher standard of morality and to condemn practices which the earlier eighteenth century and all preceding centuries had accepted without question, and it was inevitable that men, and in due course even women, would demand with increasing insistence, as a matter of right, a share in the control of the state under which they lived.

If before 1815 these stirrings had in some sort been kept down by the pressure and danger of war, when the French at last broke at Waterloo that excuse was forfeit. As to all wars there succeeded to this one a confused, unhappy, disappointing time with serious social disorders; but even the menace of those disorders grew less in 1819 and men began to concentrate not so much on the possible threat to society of the radicals as on the certainly repressive actions of the Government. In 1820 when George IV became King he immediately involved himself in an unseemly quarrel with his Queen and the whole growing unpopularity and discontent discharged itself at him and at his ministers and their works. The feeling found its immediate expression in support of the cause of the wretched Queen Caroline, but this was only the symbol of a deeper malaise, as was realized by an unusually sensitive young Tory politician at that moment resting after an exhausting tour of duty in Ireland. In a letter written that March, Robert Peel asked his friend Croker whether he did not think that the tone of England was 'more liberal—to use an odious but intelligible phrase—than the policy of the government', and whether there was not 'a feeling, becoming daily more general and more confirmed', in favour of some undefined change in the mode of governing the country.[1]

He was of course right, probably more profoundly right than

---

[1] *The Correspondence and Diaries of the Late Rt. Hon. John Wilson Croker* edited by Louis Jennings (London 1884) Vol I, p. 170. R. Peel to J. W. Croker, 23rd March 1820

he knew. He could not at that moment know how drastic were the changes which were to be demanded by that Liberalism which he referred to with so much distaste, and it was as well for his peace of mind that he should not at that moment know how critical and controversial was the part which he was to play himself. He was soon going to be called into the game. The first cautious adjustments to Liberalism were effected between 1822 and 1827 by Tory ministers in Lord Liverpool's Government, one of whom was by that time Peel himself who as Home Secretary started to mitigate the brutalities of the Criminal Law. Then between 1828 and 1832 came the first notable breach with the past starting with the repeal of the Corporation and Test Acts in 1828, going on to the Emancipation of the Roman Catholics in 1829 and then on, after the resignation of the Tories, to the first bill for the reform of Parliament. This was finally passed in 1832 and there followed a period of active reform by the Whigs, who had been responsible for it. Their impetus began to slacken off in 1837 at the time of the accession of the young Queen and it had almost entirely died away by the time that they were succeeded by the Conservatives in 1841. However, there then ensued the last great ministry of Robert Peel, the culmination of which was the repeal of the Corn Laws in 1846.

Much in fact had been done in the quarter of a century which followed Peel's remark in 1820, and yet there was every sign that there was much more to be done. Many English institutions were still unreformed. England was still a traditional oligarchy and the classes outside the charmed circle of those who enjoyed the hereditary privilege of governing the country were in many cases bitterly discontented with their condition. All through these troubled years there had been signs that men wanted much more than had yet been given to them. From the disturbances at the time of the Reform Bill till Chartism, in the late 'thirties and 'forties, there was continual popular discontent sometimes showing itself in the earnest discussion and promotion of advanced radical schemes and sometimes breaking out into violence, more often perhaps in this a symptom evincing a blind reaction to hardship and injustice than any coherent intention to force a particular practicable political change on the country. At the same time there was continual evidence of what was probably at that time potentially more dangerous, the profound dissatisfaction of large sections of the middle class. This can be seen in the extraordinary bitterness of many of the leaders of the Nonconformists in the years that immediately followed the Reform Bill; it found its expression in much contemporary Radicalism, above all in the agitation against the Corn Laws in the same years as Chartism. It was not as yet powerful enough to alter the fundamental disposition of power in Britain, but those movements are a sign that in Britain, and still more in Ireland, there was still a large and important body of opinion which rejected the old régime. Passions at least in Britain, if not in Ireland, were milder than on the Continent, since British institutions were already more liberal and the Government more flexible; nevertheless, it would seem that there existed in Britain the conditions and emotions which led to the liberal revolutions in Europe and drove men in many lands on to the barricades, or into the field of battle, in 1848 and 1849.

III

1848 is on the eve of my chosen period, and the situation in that year makes it evident that at least part of the legacy of the past to Victorian England is deeply seated social discontent and the thrust of an unsatisfied demand for change. Two years before there had been the great Liberal victory of the repeal of the Corn Laws. It is true that during 1848 it became clear that the Chartist agitation was in obvious dissolution, but to a reasonable reformer that was an advantage for it meant that the claim to change could be pressed without being compromised by futile appeals to violence and the distractions of social disorders. Therefore a man standing on the threshold of the new age might well have been pardoned for thinking that the work of fundamental change must now go swiftly forward, that the citadel of privilege would soon fall and the disinherited classes enter to take their rightful places in the community.

This was what John Bright expected in 1848. But in the sequel he was mistaken. The new bill for Parliamentary reform, the real Reform Bill, for which Bright passionately hoped in 1848, did not come till 1867, and even then it was a very imperfect instrument for reform. After 1848 the classes which had flourished and monopolized power under the old régime showed no intention to retreat from a world in which they should have been anachronisms. In fact, after 1848 their position was stronger than it had been before, for they had abandoned what was indefensible in their position and retained what was material for their power. It would have been impossible to have defended for much longer the palpable absurdities of the electoral system that had existed before 1830; what had taken its place was more tolerable and yet left the controlling power where it had ever been. The hatred of the Corn Laws had proved an effective rallying point for the enemies of the aristocracy, but the Corn Laws had been repealed, the forces that had mustered on that point were dissipated, and yet the aristocracy had in general retained, indeed they were increasing, their wealth.

So in the middle of the nineteenth century, instead of a period of rapidly accelerating reform there seems to be a lull, a centre of indifference, an interlude of relative quiescence and indecision between the political activities of the first half of the century and the even more drastic changes that marked its close. Reforms for which men had clamoured were left incomplete or not passed at all, though some of them were debated often enough. The Dissenters had got rid of the Test and Corporation Acts in 1828, and in 1836 had been relieved of their need to be married in the parish church, but they still remained till after 1867 subject to Church Rates, they still could not secure burial with their own rites in the parish churchyard and though in the 'fifties they gained the right to take degrees at Oxford and Cambridge it was not till 1871 that all posts and prizes at the older universities were opened to them. Other reforms which had been pressed in the 'thirties were not conceded till after 1867. Vote by ballot at Parliamentary elections was not imposed by law till 1872. Flogging remained a peacetime punishment in the Army till 1868. The sale of commissions in the Army had been a standing abuse the dreadful results of which were evident in the Crimea, but it was not abolished till 1871. Violent attacks had for long been made on the recruitment of the Civil Service by aristocratic or political nomination, and the cure, entry by competitive examination, was proposed by the Trevelyan-Northcote report in 1854, but this expedient was not generally used for the Home Civil Service till after 1870.

This period of indecision and delay in the middle of this century of progress and growth had serious results. Probably the most serious loss of opportunity was as ever in Ireland. In his last ministry Peel had tried to get to the root of the Irish troubles, he had appointed the Devon Commission to deal with the basic problem of Irish land tenure and he had attacked the problem of Irish Education; then there had come the tragedy of the potato famine, and Peel's energies were diverted. The sequel was disastrous. In the period after the famine years of 1845-47, when Ireland at least enjoyed the peace of exhaustion and in due course some prosperity, nothing was done, no other states-man turned to the problems of Ireland with the resolution which Peel had shown until his pupil Gladstone took up the matter in 1868, and then nemesis was very near at hand. Only a little less disastrous was the neglect of public education. As sometimes seems to be forgotten, there was a system of public education in England in the middle of the nineteenth century, through the agency of the religious societies, and the general standard of literacy was far higher than it sometimes seems to be believed. But taking England for what she was, the richest and in some ways the most liberal country in Europe, compared to what was provided in Prussia, in Switzerland or in France, what educational facilities were provided for the mass of the people in England were disastrously meagre and poor. It is true that development was impeded by the difficult problem of religious education and the quarrels of the Church, but that problem existed in most countries and it seems to be unquestionable that a determined attack on the problem could have achieved something better for public secondary education and an elementary school for every child before 1870.

There is something of the same pattern in the development of the problem of public health. This was of the greatest impor-tance, for the sanitary condition of the great towns could only be made tolerable by strenuous efforts on the part of the public authorities, otherwise they would remain places where reason-able human lives could not be lived. The great pioneer in this matter was Edwin Chadwick, the secretary of the Poor Law

Commission, whose reports awakened the public mind on the subject. In 1848 the first general public health Act was passed under which a Board of Health was set up upon which Chadwick and Lord Shaftesbury served. They did good work, but they excited opposition, and in 1854 both Shaftesbury and Chadwick were driven from their position. The Board of Health itself was abolished in 1858. As a matter of fact, the effects of these actions were less serious than they might appear to be, for in these middle years, as will be shown, the initiative in matters of public health was largely taken up by enlightened local authorities. Indeed, in judging this middle period it is important to remember how far in such matters as social reform the effective action was still, and by prevailing theory ought to have been, in private hands, or, if public action were needed, localized in scope, the result of the initiative not of a ministry nor of the legislature but of those directly concerned. Nevertheless, the ineffectiveness of Parliament in this middle period is very remarkable, as is also the failure of the concerted forces of Liberalism to dispossess the old rulers of the land. This had two results. In the Victorian mixture, in which progress and liberalism are such important elements, conservatism and the survival of habits, types of human being and institution from earlier, and one might have thought irrelevant, centuries remain important also. The other result was that when the change did come what developed in the end was very different from what the idealists of the first half of the century had shaped in their dreams.

Obviously such frustrations, such delays and such hesitations on the part of Parliament require explanation; and for the hesitations of Parliament at least there is a comparatively simple explanation. Unfortunately for itself this period in the middle of the nineteenth century was the golden age of the private member of the House of Commons. The House of Commons now controlled the legislation of the country, the working of government and the lives of ministries, but there was at the moment no power which could adequately control the members of the House of Commons. In the eighteenth century the members of the House of Commons had been controlled by the power of patronage and the authority of the Crown, in the late nineteenth century and in the twentieth century the Commons were to be kept under discipline by party. Immediately after the Reform Bill there had been a two-party system which closely resembled what was to come, but when Peel repealed the Corn Laws he broke the Conservative party into two. The larger section of it came to be led by Lord Derby and Disraeli, and remained the best organized party in the country; but it was only a fragment and never large enough in these middle years to obtain a majority in the House of Commons and maintain a government. The other section, the immediate followers of Peel, simply added to the number of independent groups that served to confuse politics. On the other side there could not be said to be a coherent Whig or Liberal party. There was usually a Whig Government supported by the traditional apparatus of Whips probably attached to the person of the Prime Minister, but beyond their influence was a shifting mass of individuals or of independent groups like the Peelites or the Manchester men, who might or might not support the Government and its measures.

The result was politics without effective discipline and therefore politics without effective purpose. The House could debate a matter, re-debate it and debate it again and never get anywhere; so it debated Parliamentary reform, so it debated public education. The policy of the ministry, and too often its life, were at the mercy of the whim of the House of Commons. Between 1850 and 1860 there were no less than six different administrations, called into existence to meet Parliamentary necessities and ending their lives because dismissed by the House of Commons sometimes for reasons which would appear to us today to be trivial enough.

If politics were in this condition, small wonder that action was hampered and that reform fell into arrear. That however only throws the question back one stage: why were politics in this condition? An explanation of a situation such as this, which refers solely to the behaviour of politicians or the nature of the organizations which they operate, is likely to be a superficial, or at least a partial, explanation. What politicians do at a particular period is likely to be in part the result of the action of forces operating beyond the control, and normally beyond the knowledge, of the politically conscious, but which provide the conditions under which they act. In many periods a rather difficult and rather complicated social analysis is necessary to discover what these forces may be, though when they are discovered they seem to shew how superficial and unreal is the historical work which explains the course of events entirely in the terms of the day-to-day events which are thrown up in the ordinary commerce of politics. But in this case an explanation of the situation has already suggested itself which is neither abstruse or remote. This interlude was the result of the anodyne of prosperity. Chartism had been the politics of suffering and despair, but now large sections of the working classes were enjoying an improvement of their conditions and a modicum of hope. The Anti-Corn Law League had been to a large extent the product of the depression of the late 'thirties and early 'forties, but that depression was slipping back into history. Even in Ireland after the tremendous clearance of the famine there was probably for a fleeting moment less distress than there had been for years. Most important of all, the prosperity of these middle years was shared by industry and agriculture, so that politics were not disturbed by the discontent of the landed interest as they had been before 1836, or by the warfare between agriculture and industry as they had been between 1838 and 1846. In fact, there was a relaxation of tension, and the passions and the insistent needs that had given shape and direction to politics had for a season lost their strength.

This did not mean that the nature of the country was fundamentally altered or that any of the forces which had made for change had been eliminated. This is a period of hesitations and confusions but not of reaction; men still believed in progress and reform, they had no desire to go back to the old régime, though they sometimes tolerated strange survivals from the eighteenth century as a matter of custom or because they did not see how to remove them. The tone of the country seems to have been liberal, probably more definitely and generally liberal than when Peel wrote to Croker thirty years before. The Governments of the period normally reflected this condition; they were normally Whig, with a strong liberal tincture, the Conservatives never gained a majority in the House of Commons till 1874. There was no going back on protection, the foreign policy of the country was in its way liberal, and in the House of Commons members were prepared to debate liberal reforms, if, too often, there was not enough political discipline, or common resolution, available to secure that they were passed into law.

But even outside the House of Commons the acceptance of liberal principles did not in the third quarter of the century always carry with it an urgent desire for drastic change. Probably at that time most intelligent and educated men held beliefs which may be called liberal, beliefs in the right to freedom, the virtue of mutual toleration and in the effective powers of reason and common sense. For some men the natural corollaries of those beliefs were the promotion of an effective programme of Radical reform, the abolition of the special privileges of the established Church, or of any other way in which the State gave preference to any particular opinion, and the extension of the franchise to anyone who could use it. Such indeed was the creed which John Stuart Mill expounded with great lucidity and all the force of a deeply sincere man with unusually intense emotions. But in the middle of the century there were a good many educated men with generally liberal principles who did not follow him. In particular there were what may be called liberal realists, men like Anthony Trollope, Walter Bagehot or James FitzJames Stephen and the other contributors to the *Saturday Review*, who accepted many basic liberal principles but were not always altogether convinced of the value or safety of popular democratic government. Such men would often be naturally on the liberal side in politics for they would feel no temptation to share the Conservative benches with the well-fed cohorts of the country gentry. They would wish to further administrative reform, fiscal reform or legal reform; but they would feel no reason to welcome the probable results of the next extension of the franchise, if that was to mean the submergence of the educated few beneath the confused and ill-considered rule of the uneducated many.

In the circumstances of the middle of the nineteenth century such an attitude was not unnatural. Except for the American system, which seemed to possess some very unattractive characteristics, and for France during brief and dangerous periods of revolution, there was little experience of the working of democratic government, and the prospect at home was not encouraging. What was most popular in the British form of government, the electoral system in urban constituencies, was often the most unpleasant and corrupt part of it, as Thackeray, Trollope and Bagehot all found to their cost when they tried unsuccessfully to get into Parliament. Indeed, it was to electoral facts and to popular habits of which many of his fellow-members in the House of Commons must have been acutely conscious that Robert Lowe appealed when opposing the Reform Bill of 1866. No doubt there was much to be said against the system of government that existed in Britain in the middle of the nineteenth century; it gave too much power to the landed gentry, it gave too much power to the aristocracy; but it was reasonably liberal, it was government by debate in which educated opinion played its part, and an intelligent man might well consider matters very seriously before he became anxious to change all this for the clumsy tyranny which seemed very likely to result from the direct rule of the people.

Such an attitude of mind did not promise any but the most minor changes in the political system, it certainly held out no expectation that some force would be introduced which would be strong enough to break the spell of indecision and set matters moving again, and the men who inclined to it were men of such intellectual force that they are apt to conceal from us the sources from which an impulse to change might come; for it is difficult not to see mid-nineteenth-century England through their eyes— through the eyes of Trollope in his political novels, and particularly through the eyes of Walter Bagehot in the terms of what is still the best book on the English Constitution that has yet been written. Nothing could be better than the humane and brilliant realism of Bagehot's ringside account of Parliamentary life, and the temptation is to believe that nothing more is to be learnt about the political system of Britain in the middle of the nineteenth century; so clear is the view that it is easy to forget how close is the horizon he has accepted. Yet, in fact, beyond Bagehot's field of vision, in the constituencies and among the unenfranchised, forces were there gathering head while he was yet writing which would make very drastic differences to the game that was being played so prettily at Westminster.

They were possibly not forces which he and those like him found it easy to understand or even to detect. It may not have been easy for those whose eyes were used to the brightly lit professional and Parliamentary world of London to see the growth of new classes in the provinces or to understand the social and economic needs which those classes were likely to propose to the body politic, and even where the eye could see it is possible that the mind could not assess the importance of what was seen because of a complete incapacity to sympathize. To Bagehot, very reasonably, the most satisfactory result of political evolution was government by discussion.[1] Government by discussion seems to imply the civilized exchange of reasonable views in language which one educated man might use to another. But many of the contributions to public discussion in the middle of the nineteenth century did not seem to be couched in such language, many particularly of the contributions of the leaders of nonconformity. They seemed to be inflated and rhetorical, heavy with clichés, often grossly sentimental with an irresistible tendency towards bathos. Against this the clear masculine intelligence of the educated mid-Victorian reacted strongly; what they thought about it can still be read in the trenchant pages of the *Saturday Review*, or in the contemptuous language with which Matthew Arnold describes the modes of thought of the Philistines. Whether these attacks were altogether fair could only be decided after a careful study of the words of the men they scarified, which few but the most devoted students are ever likely to undertake. Nor is it necessary to do this in order to understand the mistake of which those who made them were likely to have been guilty, for it is one that is very often made by intelligent and highly educated men. They underestimate the force and significance of opinions, which are habitually framed in terms which seem to them to be absurd, and by so doing they neglect what are going to be the springs of power.

But in the years immediately after 1850 the possibility of any considerable force gathering head in the constituencies or among the disenfranchised was remote; indeed for most of the period between 1846 and 1866 the description of the English Constitution in Bagehot's book suffices. The people he does not describe had not enough unity of purpose or sense of urgency to intrude often into the game at Westminster. The one point which he does notice about the electorate remains for most of

[1] See W. Bagehot *Physics and Politics* (thirteenth impression) (London 1906) pp. 156-204

the period probably the most important point. He noticed that it was to a curious extent a 'deferential' electorate, and this was true; the most important single political fact in Britain in the middle of the century was the power of the old proprietary classes entrenched in the traditional structure of the countryside, protected by the habit of deference on the part of many sections of the community and using for their own purposes many of the institutions of the State. Britain was Liberal because many of the nobility were Liberal, or knew that they ought to work with Liberals, but it was not a Liberalism that promised an early change in the kind of people who controlled the sinews of power. The pre-revolutionary rulers of the country were still stronger than any force that might try to dispossess them.

There is something of a parallel in the history of Europe. In 1848 the forces of Liberalism, nationalism, romanticism and democracy boiled over, but after a sharp struggle the forces of order and tradition proved to be strong enough to contain the revolutions. As the result during these middle years many political movements were frustrated and dissipated, many emergent nations remained in chains. Italy was neither liberated nor united, Poland, Bohemia and Hungary could not win their freedom, and further east Christian nations still remained under the Turk. On the other hand the Austrian Empire was reprieved, German liberalism failed and German nationalism began to make its dangerous alliance with the power of Prussia. Even in France, the country which was the natural leader of the Liberal forces of Europe the revolution which started in 1848 ended in the Second Empire—that strange compromise between what claimed to be liberal and democratic and what was certainly authoritarian supported uneasily by what was tradiional. Though there were striking differences, the situation in France in the third quarter probably resembled that in Britain more closely than did that of any other great European power. Many Englishmen felt a stronger affinity for the Germans, but German forms of government and society were often more remote from ours than was generally realized, and there was much in German nationalism that was misunderstood, indeed unknown, in England. Britain and France were the two great liberal powers on this side of the Atlantic, and in 1854 as such they fought Russia, which appeared at that time to be the strongest reactionary power in Europe. After that Britain wisely contented herself with making a good deal of noise from the safer side of the touch-line, but the Emperor thought it to be necessary to fight Austria in Italy in 1859, and thereby he destroyed the European balance and opened the way for the Prussian victories of 1866 and 1870. These victories not only destroyed his own régime but they led towards that witches' sabbath in the twentieth century during which so much that was bad, and so much that was good, in Victorian Europe was for ever consumed.

IV

This however raises this difficult question: when did this interlude come to an end and what brought it to an end? Obviously part of the answer has been given. As far as the old Europe is concerned, it was largely brought to an end by war followed by revolution, war largely engineered by the old diplomacy trying to use, or trying to thwart, the power of nationalism. In 1870 the Second Empire went down into irremediable defeat, though the forces that had combined to support it continued to be powerful in the republic of Thiers and MacMahon and were strong enough to be in large part responsible for the Dreyfus case. The rest of Victorian Europe in large part ground itself to pieces between 1914 and 1918. Yet it may be doubted whether, even in the case of Europe, diplomacy and war were the only agents of destruction; certainly they cannot have been so in Britain, where the pattern of change starts sometime before Britain became again fatally involved in the tragedy of Europe.

In fact, as far as politics are concerned in Britain, the beginning of change can perhaps be seen in the same year as it was in France, in 1859, and by a curious coincidence it was a beginning in which the Italian question played a part. In 1859 Gladstone, partly apparently to enable himself to do what he could for Italy, definitely went over to the Whig-Liberal side in politics and joined Lord Palmerston's administration. The period of Peelite hesitation was over, politics could become simpler and more effective, and what was most important from this time onwards the Cabinet contained in Gladstone one who possessed, uniquely, certain characteristics which gave to him the key to the situation. Gladstone could work with the old ruling classes, with whom he had always passed his life, he was not a Whig but he was connected with them by marriage; he had been trained in what had been the best school for statesmen in nineteenth-century English history, Peel's Conservative administration of 1841-46, and yet by 1859 his opinions were definitely liberal, indeed, for that period, radical. Most important of all, however, for the task which history had set him, he was developing a way of speaking that could move the hearts of men who were entirely beyond what might be deemed at that time to be educated circles, a power which possibly evinced itself in him for the first time in his visit to Newcastle in 1862.[1] At first after 1859 there straddled right across the path of Gladstone the Prime Minister Lord Palmerston, who maintained the old Whig compromise with surprising vigour into what seemed likely to be an indefinitely prolonged old age. In 1865, however, it was proved against all expectation that Lord Palmerston was in fact mortal, Lord John Russell succeeded him as Prime Minister with Gladstone as his chief lieutenant and they produced the Reform Bill of 1866. This did not pass, but was followed by the Conservative Bill of 1867 which did, and that in turn was followed by the election of 1868 which brought Gladstone back into power as Prime Minister himself, this time at the head of what has been reasonably called the first truly Liberal administration.[2]

A sense of purpose had returned and with it effective party politics. Gladstone passed his long list of overdue reforms and then the Conservatives won the next general election in 1874, thereby producing the first Conservative majority in the House of Commons since the majority returned in 1841 to support Robert Peel. A new epoch had begun. In 1872 Walter Bagehot, in the introduction to the second edition of his *English Constitution* compared the state of affairs in what year with what it had been in the year 1865 and 1866, which was what he had originally described, and he found the difference very striking indeed.

---

[1] For the significance of the Newcastle visit see Stuart J. Reid *Memoirs of Sir Wemys Reid 1842-1885* (London 1905) pp. 54-7

[2] See *1859. Entering an Age of Crisis*, edited by Philip Appleman, William A. Madden, Michael Wolff (Bloomington U.S.A. 1959) particularly pp. 115-96 for Gladstone. W. E. Williams *The Rise of Gladstone (1859-68)* (Cambridge 1934). Sir Philip Magnus *Gladstone. A Biography* (London 1954) pp. 141-95

'A new world', said he, 'has arisen which is not as the old world; and', he added, 'we naturally ascribe the change to the Reform Act. But this is a complete mistake. If there had been no Reform Act at all there would, nevertheless, have been a great change in English politics.'[1] He did not, as a matter of fact, mean by that that the Reform Act of 1867 had made no difference at all to the kind of House of Commons elected in 1868, on the contrary he believed that the names of the members returned to the new House suggested that the Act of 1867 was completing the work of 1832 and was turning an aristocracy into a plutocracy. There is little means of knowing how exact or how casual his calculations were; later analyses seem to suggest they cannot have been conclusive. What was remarkable about that election was the number of members returned who were prepared to disestablish the Church, a fact which he does not mention. But he was probably completely justified when he said that the change which had taken place in politics was not to be ascribed to the Act of 1867.

The Reform Act of 1867 is an important Act; it enfranchised a good many new voters in the boroughs, and more in the counties than are usually credited to it. In many of the boroughs the new voters were working men, though in some boroughs they seem to have been mainly shopkeepers, clerks, and the like —classes already well represented in the electorate. These large additions to the size of urban constituencies were to have important results for the development of party organization and, in certain cases, on the type of Liberal returned to the House. This, however, was not likely to make an immediate change in the course of politics. To secure an immediate political result it is not enough to increase the number of voters, it is necessary so to distribute them that they can control an increased number of seats. Nothing is effected if the numbers voting in a radical majority in an already radical constituency is increased by many thousands, if the members so returned can still be outvoted by the representatives of a much smaller constituency. The amount of redistribution and disenfranchisement effected at the time of the Act of 1867 was not decisive. In 1867 and 1868, 17 boroughs lost their members entirely, 4 of them for gross

---

[1] W. Bagehot *English Constitution* (London 1872), Introduction to the Second Edition, p. viii

corruption. Thirty-five members were taken from other English boroughs, but 87 boroughs with approximately less than 2,000 electors apiece still returned 105 members, 35 of these had in fact less than approximately 1,000 electors.[1] Some of the surviving boroughs were certainly collectors' pieces for connoisseurs in the more picturesque phases of electoral history, but they had little else to commend them. For instance, Bridgewater and Beverley were notorious for their corruption even in mid-nineteenth-century England. In 1866 Bagehot had been the inevitably unsuccessful Liberal candidate for Bridgewater, in 1868 Anthony Trollope was foolish enough to stand for Beverley. He did not of course get in, it was his money not his person they wanted, but he described the matter afterwards in his novel *Ralph the Heir*, so the effort was not entirely wasted. Both Bridgewater and Beverley were spared by the Act of 1867, as also were certain very small proprietary boroughs like Calne and Woodstock, the preserves of Lord Lansdowne and the Duke of Marlborough respectively. If, therefore, some very large boroughs had been called into being by the Act, there were plenty of others of another sort to balance them when it came to a division in the House of Commons. Meanwhile the countryside was still carefully sealed off from the town and the county franchise carefully limited so that there should be no dangerous infiltration of new voters to disturb the country gentleman's control of his shire.[2]

An Act so devised was not likely to work an immediate political revolution. If as Bagehot asserted a new world had come into existence by 1872, if, as he declared, by that time laws were being passed which would have been unthinkable five years before, then the Reform Act of 1867 can only have been in very small part the cause. Indeed, for the passage of one important Act the Reform Act of 1867 can have been in no way responsible and that was the Reform Act itself, passed after sixteen years' hesitation in apparently such a hurry that the minister in charge, Disraeli, seems not to have understood all its clauses.

---

[1] I owe these figures to Mr F. B. Smith of Trinity College, Cambridge. It should be pointed out that it is not always easy to find out how many electors had been enfranchised in a particular borough.

[2] For the results of the Act of 1867 see H. J. Hanham *Elections and Party Management. Politics in the time of Disraeli and Gladstone* (London 1959) *passim*. I have also gained much knowledge from Mr Hanham's unpublished thesis.

If, therefore, there had been a change, and it seems there had been a change, it is necessary to look beyond the Act of 1867 to find the explanation. Bagehot characteristically looked inwards to the game at Westminster. He said that there had been a change of generation, that certain key personalities had died or retired and so the face of politics had changed. There is probably something in this; there is no doubt that the death of Palmerston made a considerable difference, but there is as little doubt that as an explanation it is incomplete. It is not to be conceived that the death of one old man or of several old men was the sole motive cause in the profound change in politics which Bagehot himself had noticed. In fact, the purely political explanation is again unsatisfactory. The behaviour and fortunes of politicians have no doubt very important results on the course of events, but the situations they have to handle, the forces they must strive to direct must to a very large extent be not of their making, but rather the result of broader movements in the community—social, economic, spiritual—which lie outside the game of politics. Indeed, the nature of these movements does not only affect the fortunes of the statesmen involved: it may mould the statesman himself. Much has been written about the various men and events that influenced Gladstone's mind in the critical ten years between 1858 and 1868, but there is one influence that is not often mentioned though in all probability it was as potent with him as anything else, it was the influence of the popular audiences which were responsive to him. Indeed, a study of his opinions from now onwards suggests that these people had an increasing effect on the ways he thought. It was this characteristic that made him seem to be a renegade from the educated classes.

If this be so, an explanation of what Gladstone said and thought must be sought not only in the history of Gladstone's mind but also in the social history which explains the nature of the crowds who came to hear him and were prepared to applaud certain particular statements in a speech and to enjoy the way in which he said them. But there are other things which require explanation in the political history of this period. There is the Liberal victory of 1868. It cannot, as has been seen, be wholly put down to the changes made by the Reform Act of 1867, the old naïve statement that the 'new electors were grateful to Mr

Gladstone' does not seem to survive a detailed analysis of what happened in particular constituencies. There are indeed signs of a change in earlier elections but 1868 is obviously a critical election, significant not only for the size of the Liberal victory but also for the type of Liberals returned, and even more significant for the phase of politics it seems to have initiated.

What in fact requires an explanation is twenty years of political revolution starting in 1866, and since this is the sequel of the twenty years between 1846 and 1866 it is tempting to give an explanation which is the sequel of the explanation given of the lull in politics in that earlier period. In the middle of the nineteenth century it has been suggested that tensions relaxed because of the development of general prosperity in this period, possibly tension reappeared because that prosperity got less. Probably, again, there is something in this suggestion. In about 1873 what is called the great depression may be said to have started; there is controversy about its nature, but certainly about this time the old confident industrial predominance was challenged and the old unbounded optimism began to disappear. More serious still, after 1874 a series of devastating blows struck British agriculture, starting with those sections of it which were primarily dependent on the price of corn. There is little doubt that the disasters to agriculture affected the structure of politics. The stability of the mid-Victorian period had in part rested upon the balance of prosperity between industry and agriculture. After 1874 that balance was permanently upset, for what happened to agriculture was more serious and more lasting in its results than any set-back which commerce or industry suffered and the disastrous conditions in the countryside helped to shake the aristocratic control of the county constituencies with results that were evident in the general elections of 1880 and 1885.

But any study of conditions in the counties makes it clear that the disasters to agriculture were not the only cause of the crumbling away of the political power of many of the landowners, and it is hard to see in what ways the great depression affected the political history of towns. It may have left some members of the middle class with inflated demands on life and diminished incomes to meet them, but it is difficult to see clearly what effect that would have upon their politics, it was not likely to make them more radical; and the general effect of the depression on working-class prosperity as a whole is much more doubtful. There seems indeed to be evidence that considerable sections of the people were enjoying a rising standard of life. But in any case the political change in the towns seems to start too early to be attributed to a breakdown of prosperity. There are notable signs of change in the general election of 1868 in years when things on the whole were going well.

Moreover, if what happened in and after 1868 is to be attributed to some important change having taken place over large enough areas of the country to affect the course of politics, it cannot be a change that happened overnight; it must be something the origins of which can be traced back to some point much earlier in the century. But if that is possible it is obviously necessary to look more carefully at the period between 1850 and 1866. It may be a period of social peace, and apparently of political stagnation, but is it possible that all the time powerful spiritual and social forces were at work under the surface which were changing the structure of society and preparing the way for the more obvious changes of the last thirty years or so of the nineteenth century? Perhaps one may be too ready to believe that social disturbances are the best evidence of radical social developments, that broken water is the only sign that the current is moving fast. However, to detect such changes it must obviously be necessary to consider the community in England in that period much more closely than I have yet done and perhaps to try to disregard a little that self-conscious, self-confident minority who seem to have made history and certainly have normally written it, whose voices, unless we are careful, are the only ones we are likely to hear from the past.

V

If, however, the picture of the English community in 1850, and of what happened in the years that followed, is to come into focus there is one important point to be realized. It has been said that one very important fact of the history of the middle of the century was the survival of the power of the gentry and nobility to control so much of the political system of the country. But this is not the only survival to be reckoned with. Survivals are in fact to be found round every Victorian corner. Habits, patterns of behaviour, attitudes of mind, conditions of living which had come down from the eighteenth century persisted not only in the life and practices of the aristocracy but also in the ways of life and thought, and where there was not much conscious thought in the instincts and customs, of people much lower down the social scale, particularly of people at the very base of society. It is important to realize this, partly because it is necessary to do so if we are to realize what kind of country Victorian England was, but also because I think we are apt to see the history of England since 1850 foreshortened, to believe that the England of 1850 was much more like the England that we know than in fact it can have been, and so not to understand how great were the social and spiritual changes between 1850 and, say, 1880 or 1900.

It is indeed healthy to reflect how near a neighbour to the eighteenth century was the England of 1850. I believe that most people feel, possibly unconsciously, that somewhere an invisible line crosses history separating our relatively orderly, relatively humane, relatively well-policed society from the wilder, more savage, if more colourful society of the past. On the other side of that line life, however dangerous and uncomfortable for those who had to live it, was picturesque and violent, and I suppose that instinct lurks even in the hearts of sober adult historians, potentially romantic. On our side of the line we think of it as being as commonplace as it may appear to be today. There is of course no question on which side of that line life in the eighteenth century was to be found. Much of life before 1800 was certainly colourful and violent, if on closer acquaintance it appears to have been more ugly and brutal than romance would suggest. It was likely to be violent because the forces available to keep order were normally meagre and futile, and as a result smugglers infested the coasts and the counties adjoining the coasts, and highwaymen the roads, while in the towns and in the countryside there was much violent crime and not infrequent rioting. What the law lacked in force, however, it tried to supply in horror by prescribing the death penalty for a long list of offences, some of them trivial, some of them hardly offences at all. The resultant spectacles at Tyburn were much enjoyed by the crowd. For if the habits of many Englishmen were violent, the tastes of still more of them were coarse and their pleasures callous. They delighted in the fighting or the torturing of animals and in the fighting of human beings— violent and damaging forms of wrestling, cudgel play or prize fighting with the bare fist. Bestial drunkenness was to be found in all classes, and to judge by the accounts in novels and else- where the manners shown towards the unprotected women in the street or in a place like Ranelagh were often free and menacing, or worse. Meanwhile, as the account of any eighteenth-century town will show, the amount of human misery and degradation that filled the background and showed itself in the streets would surprise anyone who was only familiar with the decent conditions of Modern Western Europe.

None of this was new. These things had been part of the ordinary conditions of life in harsh century after harsh century; probably there is less to be surprised at in the fact that they existed than in the fact that a sense of morality coupled with human ingenuity and good fortune has transformed these con- ditions into those of our kinder, much more generally pros- perous, world. But the important point to remember is this. In 1850 that change, in so far that it had taken place, was recent. Any man who was over thirty in 1850 had lived in a world in which there were not only no railways, but also no police to speak of. When he was born, the old terrible criminal code would still be in force, the pillory still used and the cruel sports still legal.

Certainly he would have seen in his lifetime remarkable changes in these matters. In the 'twenties and 'thirties the list of capital offences was severely restricted. The pillory was finally abolished in 1837, and ox driving, cock fighting, the baiting of bulls, badgers and bears were made illegal in 1833 and 1835. Most important, he would have seen the beginning of a campaign to bring the whole country under the peaceful control of an effective civil force. It was a piecemeal campaign. It started in different reigns and at different times. In 1817 the coastal blockade was established in Kent and Sussex to deal with the smugglers, this was followed in 1831 by the organiza- tion of the coastguards, and after a series of pitched battles, the last of which was the battle of Pevensey Sluice in November 1833, the smugglers were beaten. It was probably the first time that any English Government had gained undisputed control of that stretch of coast and of the land behind it.[1] In 1829 the Metropolitan Police were founded and it seems probable that the London mob was finally beaten at the battle of Cold Bath Fields in 1833. However, the Metropolitan Police only covered part of the London area. It was not till after the municipalities had been reformed in 1835, and the rural police Act had been passed in 1839, that police forces were developed in other parts of the country; indeed, the work was not completed till the Act of 1856 had been passed, and in the early years of the police some of the rural police forces seem to be extraordinarily small for the area they were supposed to cover.

By 1850 the forces of order were able, when concentrated, to deal with ease, and so with humanity, with any major disorder, as the history of Chartism demonstrates. But at least in the 'forties they could not as yet maintain secure control of the whole country for the whole time. For instance, in 1843 the Government seems to have found it very difficult to put down the spirited guerrilla campaign which the farmers in South and Central Wales fought against the turnpike companies, in which armed bands dressed as women broke down the gates and drove off the gatekeepers.[2] The Home Office papers for the same years suggest that rural incendiarism in England was peculiarly persistent and difficult to prevent or punish; while to judge by reports in the newspapers and elsewhere there was still a great deal of habitual violence on the open roads, in the wilder streets of the towns, particularly of the ports, in markets and on fairgrounds and anywhere where people might assemble who were the worse for strong drink. No statistical calculation of the incidence of all this has I believe been made, probably no satisfactory calculation would be possible. But the cumulative effect of the evidence is great. It is of course possible to give examples. They can be found for instance in the memoirs of 'Lord' George Sanger, the circus proprietor, who as a showman was on the roads, first with his father and then on his own

---

[1] Neville Williams *Contraband Cargoes: Seven centuries of Smuggling* (London 1959) p. 180 ff.

[2] On this see D. Williams *The Rebecca Riots* (Cardiff 1955), on the effectiveness of the police at the time of the Chartist troubles see F. C. Mather *Public Order in the Age of the Chartists* (Manchester 1959), and on the history of the police see J. M. Hart *The British Police* (London 1951) Chapter II, and Charles Reith, *A New Study of Police History* (London 1956)

account, for a great deal of the century. He has not a few stories of the violence which he witnessed. The last one as it happens actually took place in 1850, when he saw the keeper of a gingerbread stall kicked to death by miners wearing iron-tipped clogs at Stalybridge Wakes. He says that two policemen did in fact come up to investigate the matter, but it was his impression that they were not much surprised at what had happened nor perhaps likely to do very much about it.[1]

When, then, the Victorian interlude began the old harsh wild world of the eighteenth century was only just disappearing; in fact, considerable survivals from it had not disappeared and took some time to go. A middle-aged man in 1850 would not only have seen great changes he would also be used as a matter of everyday fact to much that we would consider very brutal and primitive. For instance, a characteristic entertainment had been the old style Prize Fight before large crowds in some such place as Six Mile Bottom. These assemblies had always been illegal, but it had been impossible to stop them and they went on till 1860, when Sayers fought Heenan. Race-courses were traditionally rough places and continued to be so, as it continued for some time to be the custom to hire boxers to protect jockeys or horses, or to get rid of touts.[2] Elections continued to be the scenes of habitual disturbance, in which mobs were hired to intimidate electors or to fight each other. There was a notorious case in Nottingham in 1865, and as late as 1880 there were election riots in sixteen places apparently for the significant reason that they did not yet possess adequate police forces to stop them.[3] And if the populace was brutal, the law itself was not yet wholly civilized. It is as well to remember when the restriction of the death penalty is considered that transportation might consign a felon to an existence to which a quick death in front of Newgate would have been preferable. Moreover, public executions continued till 1868 and could be watched by old and young sometimes with relish.[4]

[1] 'Lord' George Sanger *Seventy Years a Showman* (London 1926) pp. 190-1
[2] For conditions on the turf in the middle of the century see *The Life and Times of George Hodgman 1840-1900*, edited by Charles R. Warren (London 1901), and H. Custance *Riding Recollections and Turf Stories* (London 1894)
[3] Hanham [op. cit. p. 55] 264 note 1
[4] For the description of a public hanging in the middle of the century see that of the hanging of William Palmer in 1856 in Robert Graves *They hanged my Saintly Billy* (London 1957) pp. 263-269. Others can, however, be found in the newspapers

VI

In fact, in the social life of the country as in its politics the same conflict can be seen, the conflict between what perhaps may be called the forces of 'progress' and the will to survive of institutions, habits and ideas that had come down from the past, sometimes from the remote past. This had started before 1850, but for long after 1850 it was still going on. This conflict was very often between what was to make for a more humane, more civilized and more equitable society in place of indefensible survivals or the product of mere primitive savagery. From that conflict Victorian England derived.

Yet it would be unfortunate to fall into the mistake which was constantly made by the liberals and to believe that this conflict was always in any simple sense between what was new, progressive and enlightened and unselfish on the one hand and what was old, stupid and obscurantist and greedy on the other. What was happening in England was a very complex process in which there were a great many agents involved. There were the forces of the political revolution and the propagators of the march of mind, there were the humanitarians, the romantic writers and the apostles of the religious revival and there were those who affected the result by simply holding on to what they possessed. The relations of these agents are complicated, not always easy to predict and by no means settled or uniform. Nor is it easy to say at any given moment whose ideas are going to prevail, nor whose ideas ought to prevail if human happiness is to be furthered. But there is one point to remember. What is at issue is not the unrolling of a simple political narrative, or the logical account of successive changes in the machinery of government; it is the development of a whole community and therefore the economic growth and cultural development of large classes of men, often of obscure men, are likely to be more important for it than the behaviour of individuals, even of distinguished individuals.

It is clear that such development is going on in Victorian society; indeed, much that is considered to be essentially Victorian seems to be a symptom of it. The concentrated industry of Victorians was the natural habit of men confronted by new and exciting opportunities. The uneasy Victorian snobbery was probably the result of the impact of new classes who wanted to secure their position in a traditional hierarchy, Victorian hypocrisy the result of the attempt to lay claim to new standards of conduct which proved to be too hard to maintain consistently, Victorian prudery the result of a struggle for order and decency on the part of people just emerging from the animalism and brutality of primitive society. These are probably signs of the pressures and strains in a community undergoing the process of growth and change. It was growth partly caused by the play and development of conscious ideas that were gradually penetrating it, but again it is important to remember that not all the forces at work were directed by the conscious purposes of man.

The struggle for political progress was conscious, its advocates were struggling for an object the nature of which they fully understood, and the advocates for conservatism often knew what they were doing and what it was they feared; the apostles of religion knew what they desired, so did the humanitarians. But there were also at work in the country blind forces of great power, the agents for which were not directed or controlled by any conception of the results of their actions for humanity in general. These forces are very significant, in fact two of them must be of primary consideration in any assessment of the Victorian situation for they are of basic importance in every part of it; they are the nineteenth-century increase in the population and the nineteenth-century increase in the powers of production, and to these I will devote my next two chapters.

CHAPTER III

The Increase in Population

When I spoke in my last chapter of the increase in population and the increase in productive capacity in nineteenth-century England as *primary* and *basic* factors in the making of Victorian England I used words which might easily be misunderstood. I meant that these factors are so generally important that there are few problems relating to Victorian England which can be considered without taking them into account, I did not mean those two words to be retranslated into *overriding*. The fact that in almost all contexts those two factors have to be considered does not mean that nothing else must be considered, or that everything else is secondary and derivative, or that they have 'caused' everything else. On the contrary, in many contexts other factors may seem more important and more decisive, if in any case any hierarchy of importance or decisiveness can be properly established, which is much to be doubted. Since, however, their influence is probably universally important, it seems to be convenient to consider them before turning to other things.

Of the two it is best to start with the increase in population. Logically it seems to come first, for it is improbable that the increase of productive capacity such as occurred in nineteenth-century Britain could have occurred without an increase in the size of population; but unfortunately, as will be seen, history makes it quite clear that an increase in population could take place, on the scale of these nineteenth-century increases, without any increase in production except in the capacity to produce the most elementary food crops. In any case the increase of the population of nineteenth-century Britain is one of the most startling facts in history, and if Britain means England, Wales and Scotland it is as well to remember that it did not take place in Britain alone but was in the first half of the century both marked and significant in Ireland also. However, in order to avoid complications at the outset it is better to start with the figures for England and Wales.

When the census was taken in 1801 the population of England and Wales was recorded as being 8,872,980,[1] in 1851 at the beginning of what I have called Victorian England the figure was 17,927,609, in 1871 it was 22,712,266, in 1881 it was 25,974,439. This increase had probably been going on for some time in the eighteenth century, but since even after the most careful use of available material any figures before 1801 remain extremely speculative it is not easy to say by what stages the increase had taken place, or when it started.[2] Indeed, the accuracy of the census of 1801 apparently leaves much to be desired and since its faults are likely to have been rather those of omission than of commission—the leaving out of people that have escaped from the record than the putting in of people who never existed—it may well be that the climb from the actual numbers of the population in 1801 to those of 1851, when the actual numbers are almost certainly more accurately recorded in the census, is a little less steep than the figures given in the census seem to suggest. The necessary correction is, however, likely to be small, and the fact remains that the increase of the population of England and Wales had by 1851 created a community of a completely different order from what had existed in England and Wales before 1800. If nothing else had happened in the first half of the nineteenth century, this alone would have secured that Victorian England was decisively different in a hundred and one ways from the Georgian England of 1800.

II

So much is reasonably clear, the difficulty is to account for the increase. This is an historical problem on which a great deal has been written without so far attaining any very satisfactory result. Much of the discussion is highly technical and upon it

[1] This figure excludes the men in the Army and Navy and the seamen in registered shipping which is given for Britain as 469,188 and the convicts in the hulks who were 1,410.

[2] J. T. Krause *Economic History Review*, 'Changes in English Fertility and Mortality 1781-1850', 2nd Series, Vol XI, No. 1 (August 1958) pp. 52-70

I have no right to any conclusion, though by sheer chance I was present as a mute observer at the opening of an important phase of it. As a young man I knew well another young man of the name of G. T. Griffith who was working under Sir John Clapham on the question of the growth of population in England in the late eighteenth and early nineteenth centuries. As he worked them out he explained his ideas to me, though I was a mere sounding-board incapable of relevant comment or criticism. In due course he published his ideas in his book *Population Problems of the Age of Malthus*.[1] It is important to remember it was a young man's book published when its author was only twenty-seven and that when he published it he had already left the work of research and become a schoolmaster, so that he had no opportunity to revise his ideas or to develop them. Nevertheless, though it was criticized, his work held the centre of the stage in population studies for a quarter of a century, and even those who were not expert in these matters have been inclined to rely pretty heavily on two of the ideas that he had used: the first was that the increase of population in the late eighteenth and early nineteenth centuries derived rather from a decrease in the death rate than an increase in the birth rate, and the second that this decrease came largely from the improvement of the medical facilities and skills available to the population in general.

Unfortunately, of late years these two conclusions have been effectively criticized. The figures have been reviewed and scholars have come to the conclusion that an increase in the birth rate has played a much more important part in the increase of the population than Griffith credited to it. It seems probable that this increase is likely to have been caused in part at least by a lowering of the age at which women got married, which would give them a longer period of fertile marriage, or an increase in the proportion of marriageable women who did in fact get married. Something in fact must have happened to encourage people to form unions who would otherwise have not done so, and probably to loosen the precautions against early or improvident marriages or connections, which often exist in a rural community, imposed by the force of custom or parental control, and which have as their object the restriction

[1] G. T. Griffith *Population Problems of the Age of Malthus* (Cambridge 1926)

of the families to the number of holdings available. A number of possible changes might have these results. The development of some form of industrialism might offer opportunities of non-agricultural employment, whole or part-time, which had not existed before and so loosen the discipline which membership of a community exclusively based on traditional farming might impose. New methods of cultivation or of marketing might bring an end to subsistence farming and possibly also the enclosure of individual holdings. The end of the system by which farm workers lived in the house of the farmer might lead them to set up households of their own at an earlier age than they would have done in past conditions, or the possibility of raising a family on potatoes may have led to the development of more households in a community than older methods of cultivation could have supported, or allowed to come into existence. There seems to be evidence that most of these things happened in the appropriate period, but unfortunately research does not seem to have revealed which, if any, of them was decisive, or which was decisive in what districts.[1] Moreover, the problem as it stands presents this difficulty. The same conditions do not seem to prevail in both England and Ireland, and it is not altogether satisfactory that the same increase in population should take place at the same time in two neighbouring countries and yet in either country be attributed to entirely different causes.[2] Probably the only satisfactory way of reconciling this divergence would be to suggest that there was some common factor operating at the same time in both countries which permitted different local causes to take effect.

The other line of criticism of Griffith's work has been to suggest that he exaggerated the possible effects on the death rate of improved medical facilities in the late eighteenth and early nineteenth centuries. Certainly the increase in the eighteenth century in the number of hospitals, dispensaries and clinics and in the number of physicians and surgeons is very impressive, and certainly by the end of the eighteenth century one very important prophylactic discovery had been made, the

[1] On some of the factors which may have affected the age of marriage, etc., see J. T. Krause *The Journal of Economic History*, 'Some Neglected Factors in the English Industrial Revolution', Vol XIX, No. 4 (New York Dec. 1959) pp. 528-40

[2] K. H. Connell *Irish Historical Studies*, 'Some Unsettled Problems in English and Irish Population History' Vol VII, No. 28 (Sept. 1951) pp. 225-34

effectiveness of vaccination as a precaution against smallpox, which had been a major killing disease. But though the use of infection from cow-pox as a preventative against smallpox had probably been known traditionally in various parts of England and Ireland, Jenner's invention of vaccination was not available till after 1800, by which time, as far as can be seen, the increase in population had already started. Nor is it easy to believe that immediately after 1800 it was used on so large a scale as to affect decisively the death rate of the whole country. Vaccination only became free in England in 1840 and was not compulsory for infants till 1853. There had certainly been attempts before that to popularize vaccination, but they seem to have been frustrated by the fact that many poor people suspected it while others seem to have known nothing about it and if they did anything at all practised the much more dangerous method of inoculation.[1]

This, however, raises an important general question. Supposing that these new medical facilities were likely to save and prolong life, to how large a proportion of the population in those areas of the country where it is known that an increase in the population took place had these improved facilities been available? Certainly in Connaught in Ireland the medical facilities seem to have been negligible, but the increase in population in Connaught was marked.[2] In other parts of Ireland, and still more in England and Scotland, medical facilities were no doubt more often to hand, particularly in the towns, and their effect may have been greater. But there is this fact to remember. Before 1851 it has been calculated that the majority of the population, even of England, lived in what could be called rural conditions, and the census of 1851 shows that even then one of the largest single sections of the working population was the agricultural labourers, while there is evidence that the great towns were constantly being filled by immigrants who had not been born in them. It would seem, therefore, that increase in population, even in England, must have been largely a rural phenomenon deriving from causes to be found in the countryside where access to doctors, hospitals

---

[1] J. A. Delmege *Towards National Health* (London 1931) p. 179, and for an example, 'Lord' George Sanger *Seventy Years a Showman* (London 1926) pp. 61-5
[2] K. H. Connell *The Population of Ireland 1750-1845* (Oxford 1950) pp. 184-220

and clinics would be least easy. This endorses the lesson, not only of Connaught but of other parts of Ireland as well, that there could be large increases of population in areas in which the improvement of medical facilities in the late eighteenth and early nineteenth centuries were unlikely to have had much effect.

However, even where there were improved medical facilities it is not clear how effective they were likely to have been in actually saving life. The removal of a patient to hospital in the eighteenth century might perhaps improve his personal hygiene and place him in circumstances in which recovery was more generally likely, but against that has to be placed the chance which he would face of infection from one of the diseases that the hospital would harbour. To prevent such infection properly trained nurses are needed, as also the segregation of infectious patients into special wards or special hospitals; but the life of Florence Nightingale shows how much in the proper training of nurses had to wait till after 1856; while, though there had been experiments in segregation in the eighteenth century and the practice was spreading in the middle of the nineteenth, it developed slowly and in many cases the construction of special fever hospitals had to wait till after the Public Health Act of 1875.[1] If the patient needed surgical treatment he would certainly find that in the eighteenth and early nineteenth centuries surgery was often extremely skilful; but it was surgery without anaesthetics, and without antiseptic precautions. These are necessary if when an operation does take place the patient is not to suffer severely from shock or to run the risk of fatal infection from the surgeon's instruments or from his clothes, or from the operating theatre, or the surgical ward. The first operation under anaesthetics in this country was not performed till 1846, and there is evidence that the practice did not spread at once to all hospitals.[2] Antiseptic surgery had to wait till Lister, and probably did not become at all general till after 1870. Before that the death rates in surgical wards could be very terrible, though probably surpassed by that in the worst

[1] W. M. Frazer *A History of English Public Health 1834-1939* (London 1950) pp. 152-3

[2] E.g. chloroform was not used in the Bristol Royal Infirmary till 1850, and even in 1851 there were doubts about it and its use seems at best to have been intermittent. G. Munro Smith *A History of the Bristol Royal Infirmary* (Bristol 1917) p. 320

lying-in wards in maternity hospitals.[1] Meanwhile the ordinary medical practitioner, inside or outside hospital, had not before 1850 very much to offer to the sick, and what he had to offer in those days of savage purgings and bleedings and sometimes very inappropriate medical procedures might not in fact lead to the prolongation of life.[2]

For all these reasons it does not seem at all likely that the extension of medical facilities in the eighteenth century made so great an impression on the death rate as to be a major cause of the increase in the population; indeed it seems probable that medicine was not likely to make any very great contribution to the saving of life at all till the second half of the nineteenth century.

A better case might perhaps be made for the improvement of the environment in which men lived as a factor in saving life. Men realized the importance for health of cleanliness, satisfactory drainage and pure water long before they realized why they were important, and before they had developed any other effective way of checking infection and curing disease. But it is difficult to see that this factor was likely to have had very significant results in reducing the death rate in the eighteenth century. Certainly in the eighteenth century a good deal of town improvement was going on. But this work was primarily urban in a population which was predominantly rural; it was often restricted to the better parts and main streets of a town, whereas the back alleys and slums were the most likely breeding places for disease, and it was normally limited in scope and object, particularly perhaps by the fact that as yet there was little realization of the need to provide sanitary drainage, a sewer being still merely a channel to carry off rain water.[3] In any case the eighteenth-century towns, such as they were, were to a very large extent overrun by the huge number of immigrants

---

[1] Sir Rickman Godlee *Lord Lister* (London 1917) pp. 120-42

[2] On this whole problem see T. McKeown and R. G. Brown *Population Studies* 9, 'Medical Evidence Related to English Population Changes in the 18th Century' pp. 119-41

[3] See E. P. Hennock *Economic History Review*, 2nd Series (1957) X, No. 1, pp. 113-20 correcting an article by Keith Lucas *Economic History Review* 2nd Series (1954) VI, No. 3, pp. 290-6 on 'Urban Sanitary Reform a Generation before Chadwick'. See also S. and B. Webb *English Local Government: Statutory Authorities for Special Purposes* (London 1922)—on Courts of Sewers, pp. 75-106, particularly p. 105, and on Improvement Commissioners, pp. 235-349, particularly pp. 314-49; and W. S. Holdsworth *A History of English Law*, Vol X (London 1938) pp. 214-19

who poured into them in the early nineteenth century and created large areas where there were no improvements at all. Yet the increase of population went forward unchecked and apparently uncheckable in spite of the fact that it was creating in the towns, and probably in the countryside also, conditions that were inimical to life.

The result of all this is exceedingly unsatisfactory for the non-expert general historian. Here is a movement which has revolutionized human affairs, not only in Britain but in Ireland, and not only in Britain and Ireland but in the continent of Europe too, and yet men do not know why it happened. What seemed to be a likely explanation has broken down and has been, as yet, replaced only by hints and possibilities and partial explanations of some elements in the situation. Fortunately, however, for present purposes it does not seem necessary to find an answer to the main problem. Whatever it was that started the increase of population it was well under way long before any date that might be conceived as having been the beginning of Victorian England, and the increase can be assumed as being something of which no doubt the results have to be considered, but without raising the awkward questions what began it, or by what mechanism, the increase in the birth rate or the decrease in the death rate, it originally proceeded.

In fact, for present purposes there would seem to be only one question to be asked; but that is all important. It is this. What conditions must be presupposed to exist in a society in which such an increase in the population is still going on? The answer seems to be that only two conditions must be presupposed. First there must be assumed to be a sufficient supply of the simplest food necessary to support life; and secondly it must be assumed that the society will not be attacked by a killing agent which will destroy on a scale extensive enough, in proportion to the size of the community in which it is operating, to cancel the natural rate of increase and even to reduce absolutely the numbers of the community. Such a killing agent might be an epidemic disease like the plague in the later Middle Ages, or a war which is sufficiently devastating in relation to the size of the population on which it is inflicted. If the killing agent is not sufficiently extensive in proportion to the size of the community, then, however terrible it may seem, it will not check the increase of population, as was apparently the case with the epidemics in Ireland in the early nineteenth century,[1] and also with warfare as it was waged in the eighteenth or early nineteenth centuries, at least when it was waged by professional soldiers and sailors on the other side of a sanitary cordon of sea water.

Of course, the increase in population may be caused, or accompanied, by other factors than these, and these factors may be such as to cause an increase in the wealth of the community or of the opportunities available to its members at the same time, so that with the increase in population there may also be a rising standard of life in the population. This is however clearly not inevitable, and even an increase in wealth or of opportunity, which has started an increase in numbers, may after a period come to an end or go into reverse. For instance, the traditional ratio between the numbers of a community and the land it occupied may have been destroyed by the development of industries which offered ways of earning a living not connected with agriculture, but in due course those industries might fail, as in the nineteenth century many rural industries did fail, and leave the district without the opportunities they offered. On the other hand, the development that effected the change, whatever advantage it might have had for others, might never have offered much, if any, additional wealth to the working man, while it certainly undermined his security. For instance, the disappearance of a subsistence economy might lead to the increase in the numbers of labourers' households depending largely on wages for their support without the security the possession of a holding might have given to them; and the increase in the numbers of families living as far as possible on potatoes alone could only lead to an increase in the number of people living miserably at the lowest level of subsistence.

If, however, the members of a community greatly increase without a comparable increase in the resources available or the opportunities offered, then there will be increasingly fierce competition for what exists and probably the driving down of standards of life. Such surely were the conditions which had prevailed in the more deplorable parts of the Irish countryside in the early nineteenth century where there was fierce land hunger among the peasants with, as the sequel, the extravagant

[1] K. H. Connell [op. cit. p. 69] 221-54

raising of rents and savage agrarian crime caused by the competition for holdings. And is it not possible that an increase in
the numbers the land had to support was one of the factors that
caused the troubles of farm labourers in England in the late
eighteenth and in the nineteenth century? Relief might be found
in migration. Naturally there would be many who would be
reluctant to leave their homes, for unless they were sent back
they would be unlikely ever to return, and in the days of
illiteracy and expensive postage they would probably be
venturing into the dark only knowing that others had gone in
that direction before them. At least before the days of railways
the journey inland would be slow and painful, probably by foot,
and the Poor Law authorities might make it difficult to settle
at the place to which they wandered. Nevertheless, it seems
clear that in the early years of the nineteenth century a good
many people from the country districts in England, Scotland
and Ireland were on the move.[1] Even so, this outlet does not
seem to have been sufficient to reduce the pressures of population on local resources, certainly it had not done so in Ireland.
What happened in Ireland suggests that if the only positive
condition necessary to permit the increase of population is a
sufficient supply of the simplest food necessary to preserve life,
then the population will increase to the limits which the supply
of that food will support at whatever cost to their standards in
other matters. Of course, if that supply fails a large number of
the people must go elsewhere, or they must die.

That catastrophe might very well happen in the ordinary
course of events; there seems to be evidence of such calamities in
other periods in history which suggest the probability of a kind
of cycle in pre-nineteenth-century societies. The conditions
necessary for an increase of population develop; a mass killing
disease like the plague disappears permanently or temporarily,
a destructive war comes to an end, there is an unusually long
period of political stability and the more robust members of
the community are kept under control, or essential foodstuffs
become available in unusual profusion produced by a run of
good harvests, the result of seasonable weather in recurrent
years. As a result the population increases up to the capacity
which existing conditions at their most favourable can support.

[1] A. Redford *Labour Migration in England 1800-1850* (Manchester 1926)

Then the luck changes, the weather breaks down, peace or political stability are lost, and the food fails, and many of the people must die or go elsewhere, probably to break down the stability of the societies into which necessity has projected them. There seems to be evidence of the population increasing and decreasing in this fashion in Sweden, where the accurate registration of vital statistics goes back further than in other European countries.[1] Or, to look further back, we could possibly understand the full importance of the part which this cycle has played in history if more was known than I believe is known what drove men from their homes in the various periods of folk wandering, such as that which led to the destruction of the Roman Empire in the West and of much of the ancient civilized world.

But there is no need to go as far back in time as the dark ages, or even as far away as Scandinavia, to observe this cycle in operation. It can be observed in relatively recent history within the compass of the British Isles. It is calculated that by 1845 the population of Ireland numbered about 8,250,000, not much less than the population of England at the time of the first census, and it is estimated that at the normal rate of increase it would have been about 9,000,000 at the next census in 1851. In that year, however, it was only 6,552,385, for in the autumn of 1845, and in 1846 and 1847, the potatoes which had made the increase of population in Ireland possible had been stricken by disease. When they were dug from the pits they proved to be black, rotten and inedible. It is calculated that in these years about a million of the Irish died and about a million fled overseas.[2]

Now, many must bear moral guilt for this horrible tragedy, and not a few of them are Englishmen. The English had wrecked Irish economic developments in the eighteenth century; they had imposed landlords on Ireland who were too often at best no more than a worthless encumbrance on Irish life and a drain on Irish resources. Partly as a result of this Irish land tenures were a museum for all that can be intolerable

---

[1] See H. J. Habakkuk *Economic History Review*, 'English Population in the Eighteenth Century', 2nd Series, Vol VI No. 2 (1953) pp. 117-33, and on Swedish statistics see H. Gille *Population Studies*, 'The Demographic History of the Northern European Countries in the Eighteenth Century', Vol 3, pp. 3-65

[2] *The Great Famine*, editors R. Dudley Edwards and T. Desmond Williams (Dublin 1956) p. 255

in land tenures and probably prevented the proper cultivation of the soil. The British Government did not do well in the crisis. Unfortunately the energetic policy of Sir Robert Peel in 1845 was sidetracked into a political crisis on an entirely English issue, whether the Corn Laws should be repealed, over which he was driven out of office. The Government of Lord John Russell which succeeded him lacked his force and his supreme administrative ability and they mismanaged the famine relief in the most critical period. They produced too little relief, and what was worse they produced it too slowly and on the wrong terms. But when all this has been recited the fact seems to remain that what happened was an example of the cycle which has been described. The cultivation of the potato had made possible a great increase of the Irish population with the result that a large proportion of the Irish population depended to a dangerous extent upon the potatoes alone for their sustenance. The potatoes failed and many of the people died or went away to avoid death.

They went, as is well known, to the United States, to Canada or to Australia, but they also came to Britain. Indeed, the passage from Ireland to England and Scotland was the cheapest and easiest line of escape open to them, and had long been so. In the 'twenties there had been a regular service taking passengers at half a crown a head, a rate which intensive competition reduced at one time to fourpence and fivepence a head for a passage from Ireland to England. Along this route came many refugees in the famine years, often starving, nearly naked and in many cases already smitten with fever. The impact came immediately and most markedly on Liverpool, South Lancashire and Cheshire, but the immigrants also flowed into Glasgow, South-Western Scotland, into Dundee and into South Wales, and then spread to other areas where there was unskilled work to be had.[1] As has been suggested, this was by no means the beginning of Irish immigration into England, there had even been earlier potato famines to drive them over. Engels' description of the *Condition of the Working Class in England*, published in 1844, two years before the great famine, gives a drastic account of the sordid habits of the Irish immig-

---

[1] A. Redford [op. cit. p. 74] Ch. IX, 131-156; see also p. 81 for cost of passage, and Map G for distribution of Irish-born residents

rants and the degraded conditions in which they lived.[1] But the years of the great famine, particularly probably 1847, immensely increased the numbers of the Irish in Britain. In the census of 1851 it is recorded that the numbers of persons who had been born in Ireland but were by that date living in Britain was 733,866, of these 519,959 were living in England, where they made up 3 per cent. of the whole population. Those who drew up the census calculated that 400,000 Irishmen and women had come into Britain between 1841 and 1851, but there are difficulties about this figure.[2] Not all of these had come to stay. These are years of very heavy emigration, and without doubt not a few of the Irish re-emigrated to the United States or to Australia when they had earned enough money to do so.[3] If, however, there were those who went away, their places must have been taken by others, for in 1861 the numbers of persons in Britain who had been born in Ireland was larger than it had been in 1851. In 1861 in England there were 601,634 people who had been born in Ireland, of whom 245,933 were living in Lancashire and Cheshire, 124,646 in the metropolitan counties, 50,664 in Yorkshire, 42,753 in Durham and Northumberland. In Scotland there were 204,003 people born in Ireland, less than the number in Lancashire and Cheshire, but yet 6·6 per cent. of the whole population, in Glasgow and Dundee alike they accounted for 15·6 per cent. of the whole population of those cities.[4] It was not till 1871 that the figures began to drop, probably because the original immigrants were dying off and were not replaced at an equal rate by new immigrants from Ireland.[5]

[1] F. Engels *The Condition of the Working Class in England*, edition and translation by W. O. Henderson and W. H. Chaloner (Blackwell, Oxford 1958); see references in index under 'Irish Immigrants'

[2] On this see J. E. Handley *The Irish in Modern Scotland* (Cork 1947) pp. 43-6

[3] Redford [op. cit. p. 74], 143-56. B. Thomas *Migration and Economic Growth* (Cambridge 1954) pp. 56-57 and 72-75

[4] Census of 1861. *Accounts and Papers 1863*, Vol LIII, Pt I, p. 40, and *Accounts and Papers 1864*, Vol LI, p. lx

[5] Census of 1871. *Accounts and Papers 1873*, Vol LXXI, Pt II, p. 70, Table 83. The figures there given are persons born in Ireland but living in England at successive census: in 1841, 290,891; in 1851, 519,959; in 1861, 601,634; and in 1871, 566,540. A movement which it might be interesting to compare with this Irish immigration is the immigration of Jews from East Europe between 1870 and 1905. See Lloyd P. Gartner *The Jewish Immigrant in England 1870-1914* (London 1960). But the number of Jewish immigrants seems to have been much smaller, Mr Gartner believes it to have been 'over 120,000' for the period covered by his book, and the social and economic impact of these immigrants was probably much less

These figures do not however represent the full size of the Irish community in England, Scotland and Wales. Apart from those who evaded the counts, they are necessarily defective at two points. They omit those Irishmen who came to Britain, lived in England or Scotland for a while and then died or emigrated before they could be counted, and what is much more important they omit the children born to Irish parents after they reached England. As a community they were often bitterly unpopular. They were of another race, they were mostly Roman Catholics, they were, poor things, desperately needy and as a result their standards were low, they were often disorderly and, worst of all, they threatened the wage rates of their neighbours. On the other hand as unskilled labourers and navvies they contributed much to the economic growth of Britain. But, as has been suggested, they were not the only people who were taking to the roads of England and Scotland in the first half of the nineteenth century. There were migrants from the Highlands and other rural parts of Scotland, and from Wales and from rural England, though these last seem to have been less mobile than the Irish and to have moved shorter distances, usually apparently towards the next town and probably without any very clear idea of what they would find there.[1] But it may very well be doubted whether many of the Irish had any very clear idea of what they hoped to find at the end of their journey; they only knew that they could not stay where they were and live, and that knowledge was enough to launch them out to join this great wandering of peoples which was to be so important a factor in the making of Victorian England.

III

They wandered from the countryside which could no longer support them, but to gain a chance to live they unavoidably wandered into the towns. The results were catastrophic. Between 1821 and 1831 the *addition* to the people in Great Britain who lived in towns with 20,000 or more inhabitants was 1,100,000 persons, between 1831 and 1841 it was 1,270,000, between 1841 and 1851 it was 1,800,000, and it seems clear

[1] Redford [op. cit. p. 74], *passim*

that others were at the same time coming to live in units which were definitely urban in character though smaller in size. Not a few of these were situated in what came to be very soon very heavily populated districts.[1] But the towns into which these millions were being drawn were singularly ill prepared to receive them. Suitable housing did not exist and the additional numbers were crammed into every nook and cranny from attic to cellar of old decaying property, or into cottages run up hastily in confined spaces with little or no access to light and air—in alleys, in rows placed back to back, in folds and folds within folds, in the backyards of existing houses or what had been their gardens. Water and sanitation were often not provided at all, and where they were provided there was often a judicious mingling of cesspools and wells with an occasional overstocked graveyard or active slaughter house to add to the richness of the mixture. Where the water for the town was drawn from rivers or streams they were often rivers and streams into which sewage and waste products were continually poured. The night soil deposited in privies and ash pits might be from time to time carried away by hand, but if it was removed it was quite likely to be dumped in one spot near to a street, or in a street, for a contractor who dealt in manure.[2] Since many industrial processes now needed coal furnaces, and by this time probably most domestic fires burned coal, from many towns, particularly in winter, a heavy sulphurous smoke cloud was emitted to combine with other atmospheric conditions to make the fogs which were such a feature of Victorian England, and which probably slew their thousands.

Such conditions were not new, nor probably were they inherently worse than what had existed before nor than what existed at the same period in the cities of the Continent such as Paris.[3] But as numbers increased so these evils increased in the area they affected, and probably certain factors in them, as for instance the problems of the provision of water and the disposal of sewage, came to be less manageable and more pregnant with danger. Certainly as numbers increased, and larger areas were overrun, often outside the limits covered by improvement acts,

[1] Clapham [op. cit. p. 16], 536. T. W. Freeman *The Conurbations of Great Britain* (Manchester 1959) *passim*

[2] Clapham [op. cit. p. 16], 539-40

[3] Ibid., pp. 316-17

it seems clear that the effects of most of what may have been done by eighteenth-century improvement must have been cancelled. In fact, it seems probable that the likelihood of death by disease in the great cities of Britain became greater after 1820, and not less.[1]

Nor was it easy to remedy these defects. Men did not know much about the causes of disease, and had they had adequate knowledge there would not have been at first adequate authority anywhere to apply it. In the early years of the nineteenth century central government was weak and suspect, and it can be compendiously said that by 1820 almost all forms of local government in England were inadequate for the task before them. They were remodelled after 1835 and a little later central government began to enter on its task. But even so the necessary physical equipment was lacking. If you destroy bad houses you ought to build better instead of simply pressing the people more tightly into other property as was done sometimes.[2] Where were these houses to come from? The prime necessity, however, was water. It has been calculated that to clean and supply a modern town 16·35 to 17·40 gallons of water per head per day is needed, and that in early nineteenth-century London at most 2 gallons per head a day were available for the poorer classes.[3] In some of the great provincial cities the amount available per head per day seems to have been rather more—say up to 8 gallons—but the gap must have been still very great between what was desperately needed and what could be had.

Some of the inventions which were necessary to collect this very large volume of water had come into existence in the eighteenth century and by the beginning of the nineteenth century were just coming into general use. For instance, it was obviously very important to be able to pump the water needed by power, instead of having to rely on its being brought by gravity, syphoning across valleys, and in the eighteenth century

---

[1] T. H. Marshall *Economic History Review*, 'The Population of England and Wales from the Industrial Revolution to the World War'. 1st Series, Vol V, No. 2 (1935) pp. 65-78
[2] See E. Hodder *The Life and Work of the Seventh Earl of Shaftesbury* (London 1886) Vol II, pp. 418-19, quoting from Hansard (3rd Series) CXXV, 400
[3] Sir Roger Hetherington, C.B., O.B.E., M.A., *Journal of the Institution of Civil Engineers* 1947-8 (Presidential Address) pp. 10-11. See also M. C. Buer *Health Wealth and Population in the Early Days of the Industrial Revolution* (London 1926) pp. 96-110

men had started to apply steam pumps for this purpose—one at York in 1784, one at Hull in 1793 and one at Chelsea in 1810. If you have pumps, iron pipes are necessary for driving water at pressure. They had been used in London in 1745, but they were only beginning to come into general use in the first ten years of the nineteenth century. Much that was essential had to wait till later on. For instance, the first effective sand filter to purify the water to be supplied was not invented till 1829, and it was not till much later that the engineers managed to collect the vast quantities of water needed for all purposes. In fact, much of the later nineteenth century was spent in the search for more and more water for the great cities, and some very remarkable engineering works resulted. But before these supplies could be won a great deal needed to be done, many local prejudices overcome, and many new techniques had to be learnt. For one thing men had to learn how to make large reservoirs. Probably the first large reservoir to be built was the Longdendale reservoir for Manchester. It was started in 1848, completed by 1851, but it was not until 1866 that the engineers dared to use it to its full capacity.[1]

At the other end of the cycle one important invention had been made when Joseph Bramah took out his first patent for a practicable water closet in 1778. But a water closet may be a source of danger if it discharges into an undrained sump from which the liquid can percolate into the surrounding soil, or if it discharges into an unsuitable sewer. Such sewers as existed in the early nineteenth century had only been constructed to carry away flood water, men had to discover what type of sewer could be relied upon to carry away more solid substances. In the early 1850s there was a lively controversy between those who advocated relatively small drainpipes egg-shaped in section made of pot and those who believed in brick culverts large enough to permit a man to enter and clean them.[2] The right answer was the egg-shaped drainpipe, but it needed time and practical experiment to prove this. Even when appropriate drains had been constructed there still remained the problem of how ultimately to dispose of the sewage. In London the

[1] A. Redford and I. S. Russell *The History of Local Government in Manchester* (London 1940) Vol II, pp. 171-204 and p. 333. On all these problems see F. W. Robins *The Story of Water Supply* (Oxford 1946)

[2] S. E. Finer *Life and Times of Sir Edwin Chadwick* (London 1952) pp. 439-52

solution of pouring it into the Thames was not a very satisfactory one, nor did it prove so profitable to sell as had been
hoped.

In fact, the task of maintaining even a modicum of decency
and health in the urban areas which developed in England in
the early nineteenth century required resources which were
not available, techniques which were not known, experts who
had yet to learn their job. To produce all these things time was
needed, but time was not given, never for one moment did the
human tide cease to pour into the cities. Small wonder that the
Thames in 1849 was more impure at Battersea Fields than it
had been in 1832 at London Bridge; the fact is significant of
what dreadful things had been going forward on its banks.

Such was the force which struck England in the first half of
the nineteenth century. After it had developed its full hurricane
strength it was clear that life must be lived on conditions and
in surroundings that were different from anything that had
existed in these islands before, and in the circumstances it might
well be that what was going to be offered to millions of men
and women was not going to be properly called life but was
merely to be a postponement, a short unhappy postponement,
of death. In fact, on one view of the condition of England before
1850 it might even seem to be possible that the old cycle of the
rise and fall of population was to be re-enacted. Unknown
conditions had caused the population to increase, and its
increase had inevitably created a situation in which by a slight
change of fortune that increase might be cancelled, if not by
starvation then assuredly by disease; or if that were not to
happen it might only be because no killing agent was likely to
be extensive enough to make an adequate impression on the
numbers now involved.

Such perhaps were the possibilities, but they were not to be
realized because of the intervention of two new factors. One of
them is the second basic factor which I have already mentioned,
and the other something of great importance which was invented to keep these blind forces under control. I shall discuss them
in my next chapter on the New Industry and the New State.

CHAPTER IV

The New Industry and the New State

It is often enough stated that certain movements, certain turns in human fortune have in fact settled the destiny of mankind, and no doubt that is often enough true. The destiny of mankind is no doubt being constantly determined by actions and chances which take place every day, many of them unnoticed by anyone. But there are some chances which are so noticeably important that it is tempting to emphasize them at the expense of everything else, and one of these is the chance—if it was chance, a matter which might be argued—that the increase of population in England combined with other factors to produce new methods of production of such great power that however large the increase it nevertheless produced in the end not greater poverty and a deterioration of standards but greater prosperity and greater and more widely distributed wealth; an achievement which was in due course repeated by other nations when their turn came.

The fact of this achievement can be seen in a comparison between the histories of Britain and Ireland in the second quarter of the nineteenth century. In Britain, as in Ireland, there had been this gigantic increase of population, to which had been added, particularly after the famine, the full weight of the Irish refugees. But there was not in Britain in those harsh years any catastrophe to parallel what happened in Ireland. There was very serious suffering in England and Scotland in the prolonged trade depression between 1836 and 1843, and a study of the inquests reported in newspapers suggests that men and women did actually die of hunger in those years, though this would appear normally to be as much the result of the brutal mismanagement of Poor Law officials as of the economic situation. But the situation is not remotely like what it was in

Ireland in 1847. More than this, the only hope available for many Irishmen was to leave Ireland; in Britain the situation was different, the depression partially righted itself in 1843, and though it returned in 1847-48, again things got better and many of the people, including many of the Irish immigrants, moved forward to prosperity such as they had never enjoyed before.

There were many reasons for the contrast between Britain and Ireland, not all of them creditable to Englishmen. Britain was the larger, more fertile, better stocked country; she had long been more fortunate. She had inherited much greater wealth, she had colonies, she was and had been for long at the centre of an extensive network of world trade. She had been her own mistress and not subject to the domination of another. But above all things she had been recently the scene of something unique in the history of civilized states, which as Professor Ashton pointed out in a passage that has become classic in the literature on the subject, made the decisive difference between Britain and Ireland; in Britain there had taken place the Industrial Revolution.[1]

Fortunately we are now permitted to use the phrase the 'Industrial Revolution' for what happened in Britain between about 1770 and about 1840. Economic historians in the recent past have been rather diffident about allowing us to use those words. They have had good reason for this. Very often in history when what seems to a superficial view to be a complete revolution is more closely studied it becomes clear that the change has been neither so unprecedented nor so complete as had been imagined. Many of the changes on which emphasis has been placed have either been anticipated, or have been preceded by even more critical changes sometime before the supposedly revolutionary period. Many of the conditions which the revolution was supposed to have abolished can be found enjoying an anachronistic but vigorous survival long afterwards. All this is true of the Industrial Revolution. Almost every element in it, if taken separately, clearly had a long history behind it, a history of which the period after 1780 was not, by any means, necessarily the most critical phase. The technological changes could not have taken place unless other technological developments had taken place in earlier times,

[1] T. S. Ashton *The Industrial Revolution* (London 1948) p. 161

and there had been other periods of rapid and crucial technological change, so much so that men have been tempted to talk
about the industrial revolution in the seventeenth or in the
sixteenth centuries, or in earlier centuries, going back to the
dark ages. Mass production in factories was not new in 1780,
nor obviously was industrial capitalism, however that word
may be defined. Certainly the accumulation of capital necessary
for the new developments was the work of a longish period
before 1780, so was the perfecting of the financial techniques in
banking and credit which rendered it readily available. A
world-wide commerce was probably one of the necessary
features of the Industrial Revolution, but such commerce had
been developing since the great discoveries of the fifteenth and
sixteenth centuries. A largely increased population, both to
provide a market and a labour force, was certainly a necessary
component of the Industrial Revolution, but such an increase
in the population had probably been taking place, with contingent results, at least from some undisclosed point early in the
eighteenth century and is still going on. If all these things were
operative factors in changing the industrial situation, why
choose forty-odd years with such particularity and call what
happened in them the Industrial Revolution? More than this,
a very great deal that might have been thought to be typical of
the world that existed before the Industrial Revolution, as for
instance industries in the hands of small craftsmen working
with perhaps little or no machinery and in their own homes,
survived the period which has been ascribed to the Industrial
Revolution, much of it survived till the end of the nineteenth
century, some of it survives today.

There is, however, a danger in thinking too analytically. I
suppose that when an explosion has taken place, it would be
possible to consider separately all the components which made
the explosion, to follow the processes by which they had been
manufactured, the history of the stages by which they had been
assembled, to record the moment at which they had been fired
and yet to gain no knowledge of the force and effect of what
happened after they had been combined and had been detona-
ted. The Industrial Revolution is not just one phase in the
history of the power loom or of the spinning-jenny or in the
development of the steam-engine, nor is it one period among

many in the process of the extension of a world market or of the development of the use of industrial capital, nor is it simply one particular point in the economic history of an expanding population. It is the moment when all these things combined, combining also with other conditions which I have not mentioned and possibly others that are not known, and the effect was explosive. It produced a new community with possibilities and realities different from anything that had existed before. One of the most recent writers on this has likened this moment in economic history to the moment when an aeroplane leaves the ground, in one moment it is running on its wheels and the next it is airborne, moving in a new way in an entirely new medium with new possibilities and no doubt with new dangers. This moment comes in the history of various countries at different times partly as the result of their own internal development, partly as a result of chain reaction from elsewhere. But it happened in Britain first.[1]

This sense that something revolutionary had happened, that they were living in a new world with infinite and unrealized possibilities for good or evil was indeed very strong among those who lived in Britain in the second quarter of the nineteenth century. They might view the prospect with almost unbounded hope, or with fear and dislike, the fear of the creation of an artificial society which might promise great wealth for a few but which for many meant only insecurity and oppression, and which had taken the place of an older more natural world of craftsmen and husbandmen, in which they dreamed men had been more happy and more secure. But whether they liked or disliked it they knew very well that a revolution had taken place. They had reason. Already there had appeared in the textile industry machines which could produce goods with a greater speed, in greater bulk and with less use of human muscle power and skill than ever before in the history of mankind. Hitherto the fastest speed which man could travel was that of a man on a galloping horse; now the steam locomotive has broken that limitation for ever. Hitherto man had needed the movement of the air or the water to carry his boats along, if he were not to do it with his own muscles or the muscles of an animal; now the

---

[1] W. W. Rostow *British Economy of the Nineteenth Century*, (Oxford 1948) and by the same author *The Process of Economic Growth* (Oxford 1953)

steamboat was beginning to enable him to move swiftly over the waters at his own behest in defiance of wind, or tide, or stream. Now he could light his cities and his houses by gas, what he was using must seem dim, smelly and inconvenient to us, but it is necessary to remember what it would mean to a world which hitherto had only been lit by lamps and candles. And in the 'forties men were already learning to send their messages by the electric telegraph in an instant of time.

In trying to measure the impact of these changes it is important to realize not only that they had all started within a comparatively short period of history, but that in such matters it is indeed the first step which counts. It is the first departure from immemorial habit, the first break through a barrier which had seemed to be a natural and permanent limitation on man's activities which is significant and bewildering. After that it is probable that further changes will be easier in themselves and that they will be assisted by changes going forward in other fields, and it is certain they will be less surprising. If thereafter the magicians do much more spectacular marvels that, after all, will be only what men have come to expect of magicians. It is important to realize this, because of course the machinery produced in the first half century of the Industrial Revolution was as nothing compared with what was to come, and the section of the life of the country which it directly affected, the number of people employed on the machines, the area of ground which the factories covered, the proportion of the wealth of the country which was directly derived from the new industries was relatively small, much smaller than I believe most people looking back on the period normally assume it to have been. But to contemporaries who saw one revolutionary change follow another in rapid succession, who saw industry drawing each year a larger section of the life of the nation into its grip, the change seemed portentous. And it was portentous, if a portent is the foreshadowing of notable and terrible things to come.

Indeed it had already brought good and evil gifts to men. It had created wealth, wealth not only to be enjoyed by the masters of industry but by many of those they employed and by many of the people in general. It had created opportunity, it had given intelligence and enterprise opportunities such as they never had had before and in truth have never had since. It had been a great social solvent, it had enabled a man like George Stephenson, an illiterate, to rise by sheer innate genius to a place among the highest in the land. On the other hand it had brought ruin to the hand-loom weavers, independent craftsmen whose work the machines took over; it had seemed to bring the harshest oppression to many of the children and women who worked in mine and factory. And it had brought insecurity to all; by 1840 the bounding prosperity which the new industry had conferred had very largely disappeared and had been replaced by deep depression and ruin and misery to those who had trusted to it for their living.

There were therefore good reasons for two sharply contested views about the Industrial Revolution in the early 1840s. On the one hand there were those who looked at the wonderful progress that had taken place since the beginning of the century and felt that if only the power that had done these great things could be liberated from the obstacles placed upon it by a stupid protectionist system, fit instrument of a selfish and parasitic aristocracy, particularly if the Corn Laws could be repealed, it would surely recover its old force and bring almost illimitable advantages to all humanity. On the other hand the Chartist, or the Tory, conscious of the revelations of the commissions of enquiry on child labour, repelled by the ugliness and inhumanity of the factory districts at any time and surveying the stricken field of Britain in the black depression that prevailed, not unreasonably took another view. Many of them felt that something evil had intruded itself into British life, something not only avaricious and cruel but dangerously reckless and unreliable as well. Many joined in a bitter attack on the mill owners, and even moderate men, who were not disposed to speak violently, read a very serious warning in what had happened.

For many men could not accept the statement that the depression had been caused by the obstruction of the Corn Laws. The Corn Laws were not new, they had been in operation all through the period of mounting prosperity; a more likely cause might well be the speculative activities of the manufacturers themselves. Trusting to the infinite possibilities of an expanding market, factory after factory had been built each equipped with ever more potent machinery. The result of this was to flood the markets of the world with British goods and to involve the manufacturers in cut-throat competition, to make them reduce the price of goods below what could possibly be remunerative and to bring down wages below starvation point. The end of this process was a situation in which the markets of the world had become glutted with unsaleable produce. Many of the manufacturers had been ruined, and the men and women they had employed reduced to unemployment and starvation or the tender mercies of the Poor Law bastilles, which a thoughtful Whig Government, with the support of the factory owners, had provided for them.

Taken with what other matter could be put on the charge sheet it was a formidable indictment and it was natural that a good many men should be impressed by it, as natural in fact as that others should be impressed by the tremendous potentialities of the new machines. The conflict of views is reflected in much that was written and spoken in the great battle over the Corn Laws and also in the controversy which seemed very important to men at the time but which has been rather neglected by historians, the controversy over the question whether the development of machinery brought advantage or disaster to mankind. It was a conflict which men on both sides were inclined to see in moral terms, as is normally the case with conflicts which are emotional and personal and likely to have an outlet in politics, for it is easier in such cases to conceive that an evil has been caused by the misbehaviour of people you know and dislike than that it is the result of impersonal historical forces which possibly no man can control.

The desire to assign personal responsibilities normally leads to a dangerous oversimplification of issues and it would have been as well if in due course so important a problem as the results of the Industrial Revolution could have been separated from its emotional context and more coolly and more objectively considered. This, however, was not likely to happen, for though the recovery of the 'fifties relieved many of the tensions of the 'forties, the issues that had been raised did not disappear. There remained much that was very wrong in the heart of the great cities and in the last twenty years of the nineteenth century they began increasingly to challenge the public conscience. Nor did the conflict between capital and labour disappear. On the contrary, after a period of relative quiescence it became more sharp, more important, more effectively pressed by better organized trade unions and became the reason for the existence of a new political party. All this affected the way men thought about the Industrial Revolution. The growth of a city like Manchester was clearly associated with the Industrial Revolution and therefore it was felt that its slums had been created in all their horror by the Industrial Revolution, the promoters of which ought to bear full responsibility for them. 'Industrialism', undefined or only vaguely defined, and the 'Industrial Revolution' were the creations and the tools of 'capitalism' and must share the same condemnation. As a result of this tendency the whole conception of the Industrial Revolution began to change, men began to think less and less of the usefulness and importance to mankind of its inventions, or of the human genius displayed in their development, and to consider it almost wholly as if it were an event in the sphere of morals to be judged, and condemned, according to the supposed motives of those who promoted it.[1]

Whatever truth there might be in this view, it has had unfortunate results for historical thought. It oversimplified the diagnosis of what have been the causes of suffering and cruelty in early nineteenth-century Britain and obscured the importance of two factors. One was the inherited tradition of callousness, brutality and degraded conditions which went far back into history, the results of which were now much more obvious because the nineteenth century had opportunities of learning what was going on which were denied to earlier centuries and humanitarians were teaching men to note these things and object to them. The other was the strain resulting from the rapid growth of the population. And apart from that, this view of the Industrial Revolution has suggested that it is easier than in fact it is to dogmatize with certainty about the motives of a large number of people who lived a long time ago and to compare their moral standards with those who lived before or after them. In fact, it is not easy to discern and describe with any confidence the motives of a man about whom there exists a great deal of evidence, and it is much more difficult to rest an

[1] For a discussion of the various ways of looking at the Industrial Revolution see R. M. Hartwell *The Journal of Economic History*, 'Interpretations of the Industrial Revolution in England: a Methodological Inquiry', Vol XIX, No. 2 (New York June 1959) pp. 229-49

argument on the presumed motives of men who have left very little direct record and to compare them satisfactorily with other men in other ages who have probably left behind even less. It would require more evidence than I believe is likely to exist to prove that the Industrial Revolution was caused by the fact that those who promoted it were more callous and ruthless than men who have lived before it happened or since, or perhaps that its conditions caused them to become so.

It is possible that the fast-developing conditions of the nineteenth century increased the opportunities for men on the make, themselves the product of harsh conditions, to indulge in such abuses as payment of wages in truck and to exploit cruelly those who worked for them, particularly when they were relatively defenceless women and children; it is possible that those conditions increased their temptation to do so. It is possible that the development of the factory system by dividing the great mill owner or capitalist from the artisan destroyed a natural sympathy which had existed between the small master and the man who worked at his elbow. But it is well to remember that probably the worst abused child labour in the country was that of the climbing boys, the wretched children apprenticed to chimney sweeps, small masters who were only too close to those they employed for they beat them when they would not go up flues in which they might be suffocated; or that the unhappy sempstresses, like the one celebrated in Tom Hood's 'Song of a Shirt', also seem to have been normally working for small-scale employers who were not mechanized at all. Even in the factories and mines the children were often not directly employed by the factory owner but by the worker himself, while some of the worst cruelties were inflicted by the overseer. This is not said to deny the responsibility of the factory owners, but it may suggest a reflection which any knowledge of the conditions of the time confirms, that neither the possession of capital nor the extensive use of machines was needed to make men callous and brutal in the early nineteenth century. Too many of them were like that by nature and had been so from time out of mind.

However, the worst result of the attempt to judge the Industrial Revolution primarily from a moral standpoint is that it deflects attention from what is after all the most important question, which is not a question of motive but of results. What matters most is the result of these developments in mechanization on the life which was offered to contemporary men and women. In fact, there can be little doubt that in very many cases these results were beneficial, sometimes immediately, sometimes ultimately. There is certainly a reasonably sharp controversy among experts whether in general real wages improved in the first half of the century. To one who is in no way an expert it would appear to be a controversy which it is not going to be easy to resolve, especially in so far as it refers to the actual lives of particular groups of workers. For one thing not enough would seem to be known about retail prices, which for those who live in the back streets of towns are probably the only significant prices. Moreover, there seems to be a doubt as to how frequently and how continuously what might be deemed to be the standard rates of wages were actually earned.[1] If, however, this issue is to be made a touchstone to test whether in fact the Industrial Revolution benefited or harmed humanity, another question must be asked even though it is one which cannot be answered. What would have happened to the wages of large sections of the working class if there had been no Industrial Revolution? This question should not only refer to those whose special skills and fortunate positions gave them peculiar opportunities to benefit by the Industrial Revolution, but also to humbler unskilled workers who got jobs for whom otherwise, as far as can be seen, there would have been no employment. What would have happened for instance to the Irish immigrant if there had been no railways to construct? Indeed this question might as well be extended over the whole century; it seems to be agreed by most people that in the second half of the century there was a general or continuous advance in real wages, it might be asked whether there would have been any chance of this if there had been no mechanization and industrialization on the scale achieved in the early nineteenth century. The answer here surely is No.

Nor did the Industrial Revolution only benefit the working

[1] On this see Clapham [op. cit. p. 16] 536-602. T. S. Ashton *Journal of Economic History* Supplement IX, (September 9, 1949) pp. 19-38. E. J. Hobsbawm *Economic History Review*, 2nd Series, Vol 10, No. 1 (1957) 46-48. S. Pollard *Economic History Review*, 2nd Series, Vol 11, No. 2 (December 1958) pp. 215-226. R. M. Hartwell *Economic History Review*, 2nd Series, Vol 13, No. 3 (April 1961)

classes as wage earners, it benefited them as consumers also. As the century went forward it produced even for poor people, if they had any money to spend at all, goods in a profusion and a variety which would have been beyond men's wildest expectations in earlier ages. The hastiness and carelessness of the manufacture of so much that was put on the market, the poorness in design, materials and workmanship which are often so painfully evident in what has survived, the silliness of a great deal of the reading matter which the new steam presses ran off, the obvious discomforts of a cheap railway excursion, all these considerations may make one forget how much was being added to the richness of life. And when such things as washable clothes and soap are provided for those who would have had in the past little chance for such luxuries, the advantages to health and comfort are incalculable.

Yet none of this establishes the fact that the Industrial Revolution was a benevolent movement designed by far-sighted philanthropists for the good of humanity. It probably should be considered as nearly as void of moral significance as a change in the weather which happens to produce in some year a good harvest; probably the human agents who promoted it were in many cases as innocent of any far-sighted visions for humanity as the human agents who caused the increase in population. It was in fact morally neutral. It was not directed with any certainty to any particular end. It might bring good and might bring evil. Indeed, as men realized from the beginning, it did bring good and did bring evil to different people or to the same people at different times, and if it were to be made safe for humanity its propensities for evil must be brought under control or compensated.

It cannot be said that the attempts to do this were at first strikingly successful. As has been seen, one of the dangers which the new forces at work produced was that of recurrent financial crises producing ruin and widespread distress and unemployment. Even through the period of greatest prosperity men remained aware of this danger, in fact they experienced it in such years as 1847, in 1857 and in 1866. But it cannot be said that they discovered any satisfactory way of dealing with it: probably their understanding of the issues at stake were too limited and their monetary mechanism too clumsy to enable them to do so. Fortunately the buoyancy of the economy in the middle of the century seems to have been always strong enough to pull them out of the difficulties which they encountered. Nor did they prove themselves to be more capable of dealing with the very difficult problem of technological unemployment, the problem of those skilled craftsmen whom new mechanical developments have put out of business. They investigated the lot of the hand-loom weavers at considerable length, but they could do nothing more for them. At first they were almost equally unsuccessful in the attempt to control conditions in the factories and to protect the overworked factory children. Up to 1833 the legislation passed on the subject was largely inoperative and very little was done. Even after 1833, as Lord Shaftesbury was to find, the way of the factory reformer was hard and very frustrating, he had to face excessively bitter opposition and often enough the sickening experience of success being forfeited when it had seemed to be assured.

But the Act of 1833 was a turning-point, not because it gave the factory reformers what they wanted, it certainly did not do that, it was only passed after Shaftesbury's motion for a Ten-Hours Bill had been rejected, but because it contained provision for the appointment of a board of inspectors with executive powers to put it into effect and to report on the way it worked. Both functions were important; on the one hand the reports were evidence of the inspectors' growing specialized knowledge of the problem in hand upon which all future legislation was in part necessarily based, on the other hand the discretionary power confided to the inspectors looks forward to the immense delegated powers which were to be given in the twentieth century to ministers to be in fact exercised by civil servants. Indeed, the lesson seems to be this. Though the tremendous power which was being developed by the Industrial Revolution could and did work for the good of humanity, there could be no security that that was what it would do unless it was brought under conscious discipline, and that discipline could only be imposed by the assumption by the public of constantly increasing discretionary powers to be exercised under the direction of experts who would draw upon the growing experience which only work in that particular department of government could give. It was a lesson pregnant with importance for the future.

II

The same lesson was very soon to be repeated in the history of the cities and towns of Britain in the first half of the nineteenth century. Something has been already said of the flood of humanity which was pouring into them and of the conditions they created when they got there. The force at work here was the increase of population, not the Industrial Revolution. As I have observed, it is often said that the cities of early nineteenth century Britain were what they were as the result of industrialism, but it is important to think carefully what those words can mean. The condition of nineteenth-century British towns was very largely the result of the incursion of a very large number of poverty-stricken immigrants. Industrialism had not called these people into existence, nor had it made them poor. They were born so. It is not even clear that it was, at least in many cases, industrialism that drew them into the towns. They flocked into non-industrial towns such as Brighton and they seem in many cases to have come to the towns for no better reason than that they had nowhere else to go. After all, a town is most likely to be where the displaced or surplus countryman will end, he is less likely to find a permanent resting-place in another countryside unless it is an empty one that he can colonize. The city offered the chance of survival to many who would otherwise not have survived, and possibly life in a cellar in Manchester was better than death by the roadside in Connemara, though not much better. At the least, while there was life there might be hope, and there would be hope if the industrial development of the country was to go forward with unchecked speed and force.

However, even though in due course industrial development might give them employment and a place in the community, it would not by itself make the cities of nineteenth-century Britain places in which human beings might live with self-respect or even perhaps live at all for long. As a matter of fact, the actual lethal character of what was happening in Britain has apparently been exaggerated. It is a remarkable fact that the death rate in England in the first half of the nineteenth century seems

on the whole to have been a good deal lower than what it was
in countries which were as yet less mechanized and less urban-
ized.[1] It is possible that part of the cause of this as far as England
—not of course Scotland—is concerned was the existence in
England of a Poor Law which however badly administered did
at least reduce the possibility of death from starvation. But it
suggests also that the new cities which were coming were at
least not more deadly than what had existed before. This,
however, should probably not be counted to the credit of the
new urban areas, but as a measure of the badness of conditions
in the old cities, and often enough in the countryside, old or
new. There are enough accurate descriptions of what it was
like in the worst sections of the towns in early nineteenth century
English cities to make it clear that as far as such areas were
concerned, whatever the force behind it, their extension in size
meant merely the extension of large suppurating masses of
degradation and disease. Perhaps if such were to remain forever
the living conditions of large numbers of people in Britain it
would after all have been better if nineteenth-century developments had led not to life on such terms, but to more merciful
death.

It is true that industrial development might produce what
was necessary to improve these conditions. It produced the
steam-pumps and iron pipes which were necessary to convey
such water as was necessary for a civilized life; it might help to
train the civil engineers to make reservoirs and drainage systems;
it might, but this was in the future, produce the local transport
needed to spread the congested populations; above all things
it would produce the wealth without which all urban improvement is impossible. But without conscious direction privately
directed industrial development was not likely to do any of
these things. There would be exceptions, of course, there would
be model areas planned by benevolent factory owners, but left
to itself though industry might produce wealth some of
which might even be enjoyed by the working classes, or sections
of them, to the terms on which their life would be lived in the

[1] See Sir John Clapham [op. cit. p. 16] 316-17, and also the *Fiftieth Annual
Report of the Registrar-General of Births Deaths and Marriages in England* (reports from
commissions, etc., 1888, Vol XXX), pp. lxxvii-lxxxviii, Tables 39-56. (It was
Mr. R. J. Lambert [see p. 104] who called my attention to the significance of
these tables.)

areas in which it was most active its main contributions would be smoke and dirt and haphazard congestion in ill-built and brutally utilitarian streets. Power and knowledge to discipline and to direct and utilize these forces was needed if life was to be lived in tolerable conditions, let alone to improve in quality. That power could only be developed and directed to the right ends by the public authority.

At first sight it might not seem likely that in Britain in the first half, or even in the third quarter, of the nineteenth century any such development would take place. This period has been called often enough 'the age of *laissez-faire*'; the description is inaccurate if it implies that a coherent economic doctrine was generally accepted by every man, or if it implies that the great classical economists were so rigid or so uncompromising in their objections to State intervention in economic and social matters as the phrase is sometimes held to imply. But there was nevertheless a very widespread objection to all Government interference and all necessary Government expenditure, not only founded on theory but also on a belief that Government interference was likely to be interested and incompetent and Government expenditure likely to be corrupt, which was one of the natural legacies of the eighteenth century. Behind this there was a dislike of paying rates and taxes which is common to humanity and a profound reverence for the rights of private property. To these natural feelings men added a distaste for what was called 'centralization', that is, the assumption by some central organ in the State of the power to meddle and fuss and to impose common standards on the whole country.

With such formidable obstacles in the way it might be conceived that nothing could be done, or if anything was done the opponent powers would be effective enough to frustrate and possibly to cancel it. Indeed, it is often held that that is precisely what happened. I have already referred to the story of public health and it is well known.[1] It starts with the enquiry in 1838 instigated by Edwin Chadwick, then Secretary to the Poor Law Commissioners, by three doctors into the conditions in the East End and proceeds through the committee of enquiry set up by

[1] The two most important modern books on this section of the subject are S. E. Finer [op. cit. p. 81], R. A. Lewis *Edwin Chadwick and the Public Health Movement* (London 1952).

the House of Lords to the Royal Commission on the health of towns. All these activities enabled Chadwick to reveal the situation which existed in the towns to the public and to excite opinion on the subject. As a result, in due course the Health of Towns Act of 1848 was passed, an adoptive Act which could, however, be applied without local consent in extreme circumstances. Under this Act a directive board of health was established on which Chadwick and Shaftesbury served. Their service was vigorous and devoted but not universally appreciated, indeed they tried to do too much, and so in 1854 the forces of dirt and decentralization triumphed, Chadwick was driven into resignation, Shaftesbury followed him in disgust and in 1858 the Board of Health itself was brought to an end.

And if that was the whole story there might seem to have been little chance that the necessary public authority would have appeared to do what so urgently needed to be done either in the first half, or the third quarter, of the nineteenth century. But it is not the whole story, and it omits some very important elements which went to the making of Victorian England; for as often received it suffers from two defects, it concentrates too much on the actions of the central authority and it concentrates too much on the fortunes of Chadwick, supremely important as he was. In fact, the story should be started some time before the days of Chadwick or even of those of Bentham.

The eighteenth-century physicians might be ill-equipped to cure disease, but the best of them had developed one supremely important habit. They observed, carefully and accurately recorded their observations, and tried to interpret them systematically. They used this method to try to study the correlations between disease and the conditions in which people lived. There are in fact many notable works which are examples of this, as for instance Richard Mead's *Short Discourse concerning Pestilential Contagion and the methods used to prevent it,* published in 1720, or the *Observations on Diseases of the Army,* published in 1752 by John Pringle, physician-general to the British Army, while James Lind and Gilbert Blane did comparable work for the Navy. Clearly the development of this type of study was a very important preparation for the scientific analysis of social conditions and their relation to disease upon which any effective attack upon the problem of public health must be based. Indeed, such studies engendered a habit of mind which was relevant to other problems than those of public health and the wide distribution throughout early nineteenth-century England of intelligent medical men, often enough trained in Edinburgh and Glasgow, is a factor the importance of which has not yet been fully recognized.

As far, however, as public health was concerned it mattered a good deal that important exponents of this systematic method were to be found in Manchester and Liverpool and their districts; in Manchester the most important pioneer was Dr Percival, whose dates were 1740-1804, with whom should be associated Dr Ferriar, 1761-1815, and in Liverpool it was Dr Currie, 1751-1805, with whom can be placed Dr Haygarth of Chester, 1740-1827.[1] This was a critical area. Of all towns in England, with the possible exception of London, Manchester and Liverpool were to face the problems of urbanization at their most savage. They were both great cities on their own account: Manchester was the centre of the new cotton industry, Liverpool had become one of the greatest ports in the world. But what in this context is even more important, they were to become, with perhaps Glasgow, the chief cities of refuge for the unhappy immigrant Irish. With such strains coming upon them it was going to matter a good deal that they should each have a local tradition which led to the early adoption of a systematic and scientific consideration of the problems of public health. Quite early in the 1830s each city showed that that tradition was intelligently alive. In 1831, at the time of the cholera, a voluntary board of health was set up in Manchester which instructed Dr S. P. Kay, afterwards Sir James Kay-Shuttleworth, to investigate the causes of the disease, and shortly after this, in 1833, the Manchester Statistical Society was founded with Kay as one of its joint secretaries. It did very important pioneer work in the systematic study of social conditions.[2] In Liverpool the effective movement towards sanitary conditions was started in the middle 'thirties by Dr Duncan, Physician to the Liverpool Infirmary, and Samuel Holme, a local builder and Chairman of the local Trademen's Conservative

[1] For short descriptions of these doctors see Delmege [op. cit. p. 69] 149-56
[2] Redford and Russell [op. cit. p. 81], Vol II, p. 130 ff. T. S. Ashton *Economic and Social Investigations in Manchester 1833-1933* (London 1934)

Association. From 1840 till 1846 we are told that there was in Liverpool continual agitation on the subject.[1]

If, however, the origins of this movement, both in Liverpool and in Manchester and probably elsewhere, can be traced back to eighteenth-century medical men, that is no reason why that tradition should not have been influenced in due course by the thought of Bentham; in fact, in such men as Dr Kay-Shuttleworth and Dr Southwood Smith the two traditions were probably conflated, together in the person of Dr Southwood Smith with another tradition which was going to be curiously important in the history of the improvement of towns, the tradition of Unitarian idealism. Chadwick himself had been first drawn to the systematic study of disease as a social factor from his study of life insurance. He also had been drawn into the orbit of Bentham and thereafter it might not be easy to say how much of his ideas and policy really derived from Bentham and how much came from his own thought and experience. What cannot be a matter of controversy is the supreme importance of his initiative and influence in the critical period between 1838 and 1854. Even where there was a strong local tradition the impetus derived from Chadwick seems to have made all the difference. It might be argued that the infirmities of Chadwick's temper, the badness of his manner and in some cases the rigidity and narrowness of his mind at times came near to ruining the cause of public health, but it is quite certain that without his enterprise, his initiative, his genius and his dogged courage a national health policy would not have come as soon and as effectively as it did.

Yet it is important to remember that he had intelligent allies, and that it seems doubtful that he would have been able to do anything if they had not been in existence when he started. They supplied him with trained observers, with expert witnesses to appear before Parliamentary committees and Royal Commissions and also with skilled assistants. They also probably helped to stir up and direct public opinion in the country when the time came. No doubt much of the interest excited was stimulated by Chadwick's reports, particularly the report of 1842 which was a best seller. But, as has been pointed out, in

[1] Brian D. White *A History of the Corporation of Liverpool 1835-1914* (Liverpool 1951) pp. 33-8

Liverpool and Manchester and elsewhere there already existed men who had given much attention to these problems before Chadwick started, and that must have helped to consolidate opinion. Certainly the speed and effectiveness with which public opinion was mobilized is very remarkable. In December 1844 a Health of Towns Association was formed to support Chadwick, and in the months that immediately followed it developed branches in no less than fourteen towns, most of them considerable ones.[1] After the Act of 1848 had been passed there was even more practical evidence of widespread local interest. By February 1850 the Board of Health had received requests for the application of the Act from 192 places with a total population of 1,969,915 inhabitants and the Act had been introduced in 32 places; by July 1853 petitions had reached the Board from 255 places, 164 of which had been brought under the Act.[2] No doubt the personal force of Chadwick was behind all this, but this achievement would have been impossible unless there had been in a great many places a large public prepared to co-operate and local leaders prepared to stimulate action. A study of local politics and of the history of the various local sanitary associations would reveal more clearly than we know now what kind of people these local leaders were; a very superficial consideration of the materials suggests the importance of the influence of the local medical men, and also of the tradition of public service to a man's own town or neighbourhood, particularly among the Unitarians.

Liverpool and Manchester had not waited for the general Act to be passed in 1848. By that time Manchester had already started to sewer the city; by its Police Act of 1844 it had started to control housing and in 1845 it followed these things up with an important Sanitary Improvement Act.[3] As has been said, in 1848 Manchester started to build the first large reservoir in the country. In 1846 and 1847 Liverpool had obtained a Sanitary Act, and in 1847 had appointed the first borough engineer in the country, Mr Newlands, and the first medical officer of health, Dr Duncan, the man who had played a considerable

---

[1] R. A. Lewis [op. cit. p. 97] 111-16. The towns included Edinburgh, Liverpool, Manchester, York, Halifax, Derby, Bath, Rugby, Marlborough, Walsall, Plymouth and Worcester.

[2] Ibid., pp. 290, 339-40 and 364

[3] Redford and Russell [op. cit. p. 81] Vol I, p. 363, Vol II, pp. 154-6

part in the agitation of the problem of public health in Liverpool. In 1848 the City of London appointed as its medical officer, the second medical officer of health ever to be appointed, an even more important figure in the history of public health, Dr John Simon. The fact that all this was the result of independent local action does not of course mean that it had been unaffected by the stimulus of Chadwick. On the contrary, it would appear that the stimulus of his activities was very great, even in communities which preferred to act on their own. But it does mean that in such places and indeed all over the country there were men who were still prepared to take the initiative when he was driven from the scene in 1854. As the movement for public health had not started with Chadwick, obviously it did not end with him.

Indeed, it is possible to exaggerate the importance of the defeat in 1854, and to misunderstand the significance of the Act of 1858.[1] The local opinion that had become anxious for sanitary reform had not been snuffed out, there is still evidence that many people in different places were very anxious for guidance from the centre, and also that the work was extending into places which Chadwick himself had found to be recalcitrant. For instance, Chadwick had fought an angry indecisive frustrating battle with the authorities in the metropolitan area of London. Immediately after he disappeared that area was taken in hand. In 1855 the Metropolitan Board of Works was erected, in 1858 an Act was passed for the disposal of London sewage, by 1865 the main sewers were complete, by 1875 new roads had been cut through some of the worst parts of London and the river was embanked. The work was significant. G. M. Young called 'the conversion of the vast and shapeless city which Dickens knew—fog bound and fever haunted, brooding over its dark, mysterious river—into the imperial capital, of Whitehall, the Thames Embankment and South Kensington' the 'still visible symbol' of what he calls 'the mid-Victorian transition'.[2] It was a transition which was taking place all over Victorian England. It was certainly piecemeal and imperfect, leaving many dark and smelly places for future ages to clean up,

[1] See Robert M. Gutchen's communication in the *Historical Journal* 'Local Improvements and Centralization in Nineteenth Century England' Vol 4, No. 1 (Cambridge 1961) pp. 85-96
[2] G. M. Young *Victorian England, Portrait of an Age* (London 1936) p. 82

but it was letting in light air and pure water where they were sorely needed. The initiative was very largely local. Indeed, it seems probable that the real importance of the Act of 1858 was not so much that it abolished the Board of Health but the fact that it gave new possibilities of action to local authorities. And some local authorities were extremely enlightened in the matter. Liverpool still seems to have retained the lead, Manchester for some reason seems to have become less progressive in this period, but important work seems to have been going forward in Bristol. In some cases, however, the city fathers had to be prodded from behind by public opinion often organized in a sanitary society in which often the local medical men were active, and sometimes they had to be shamed by the disgrace of a peculiarly high death rate. In small towns and country districts often the initiative was taken by a local clergyman or landowner or again perhaps a local doctor, and a situation possibly developed such as is reflected, with melodramatic trimmings, in Kingsley's novel *Two Years Ago*.[1]

Piecemeal and local as it was, it would be too tedious and too complicated to attempt to give an account of what was going forward in these years. Sometimes the dates at which a medical officer of health was appointed are cited as giving a rough index of the progress of the movement, for Leeds appointed one in 1866, Manchester in 1868, Birmingham in 1872 (Birmingham was by no means the pioneer in these matters that it is sometimes claimed to be), and Newcastle (normally in these matters a laggard) in 1873. But this is an unsatisfactory index, for it was possible to appoint a medical officer and then do nothing more, and much could be done and was done without such an appointment. Nor would it be satisfactory to attempt any other index until more is known of the local history of Victorian England.[2] There is, however, one further important point to be made.

It has been said that the work was largely the result of local

[1] *Two Years Ago* appeared in 1857. For an example of action by a clergyman in a country district see Esmé Wingfield-Stratford *This was a Man* (London 1949) pp. 191-4

[2] On Birmingham see Asa Briggs *History of Birmingham* (Oxford 1952) Vol II, *passim.* On Newcastle see S. Middlebrook *Newcastle upon Tyne: its Growth and Achievement* (Newcastle 1950) and W. L. Burn *Archaeologia Aeliana*, 'Newcastle upon Tyne in the Early Nineteenth Century', Vol XXXIV, 1-13. On Sheffield see S. Pollard *A History of Labour in Sheffield* (Liverpool 1959) pp. 93-105

initiative. It was not entirely so. Chadwick's place at the centre of the movement had in fact been taken by one whose contribution was to be as great, or greater, but who perhaps fortunately was in temperament a complete contrast to him. He was Dr John Simon, originally medical officer of health for the City of London; he was first attached to the Board of Health in the fateful year 1854, and then when the Board of Health was abolished in 1858 he was transferred to the medical department of the Privy Council. Simon recognized the greatness of Chadwick but was also determined to avoid his mistakes. Where Chadwick had tried to force men's assent, Simon persuaded, greatly preferring to stimulate the initiative of others than to appear to take it himself. Chadwick was notoriously, flagrantly so for a civil servant, the author of the policy he was pressing; Simon preferred to remain in the background, to appeal to the unimpeachable voice of science speaking through the findings of some high-powered Government committee or in his own profoundly important reports and to work so effectively behind the scenes that only nowadays are scholars discovering the full extent of his activities. He had his reward; so effectively did he work that twelve years after Chadwick's defeat the Government was able, without serious opposition, to impose a reasonable sanitary standard on the whole country by means of that remarkable Public Health Act of 1866 in which, to use Simon's own words: 'The grammar of common legislation acquired the novel virtue of the imperative mood'. This was the beginning of the consolidation of the position. That Act was followed by an important Royal Commission, by more legislation ending with the important consolidating Acts of 1871 and 1875.[1]

By a tragic and ironical redeployment of power those very Acts brought Simon to the effective end of his official influence; like Chadwick he too suffered the fate which luck, as reflected in politics or in the chances of administrative life, so often deals out to able and devoted men who are trying to do urgent and important things for their country. At what seemed to be a

[1] Upon Sir John Simon (who should apparently be pronounced with a short *i* and a long *o*, sounded as if there were an *e* at the end of his name) I have received valuable help from Mr R. J. Lambert, who will, I hope, publish valuable work on this phase of the history of public health. Simon's own book *English Sanitary Institutions* (London 1890) is also of the greatest interest. See also W. M. Frazer [op. cit. p. 70] (London 1850) esp. pp. 77-125, and Sir Arthur Newsholme *The Ministry of Health* (Whitehall Series, London 1925) pp. 1-49.

critical moment his power to influence matters was taken from him, but unlike Chadwick he had really completed his work. The country had been provided with a reasonable sanitary system, the tide of humanity had flowed in full force into the cities of England, and yet what had happened had not brought men to disaster or to the brink of it. On the contrary, the battle against death and disease seems to have been gradually turning in the right direction. In the years 1846 to 1850 the mean annual death rate per 1,000 living persons was 24·1 for males, 22·6 for females, between 1871 and 1875 it was 23·3 for males and 20·7 for females, between 1896 and 1900 it was 18·8 for males and 16·6 for females.[1] General death rates are perhaps clumsy tools to use since they cover too many varying circumstances; perhaps more significant of what was happening in the matter of public health was the decline in deaths from infectious diseases, deaths which had caused one death in three in the years 1848-1872.[2] This decline seems to become marked between about 1870 and about 1880. There is no serious cholera epidemic after 1866, after 1870 the deaths from cholera become negligible. There is a serious smallpox epidemic in 1871, but even so the smallpox killed less in that year than in 1838, and after 1871 the deaths from smallpox diminish very sharply indeed. The death rate from typhus seems to go down rapidly from a little before 1870, from scarlet fever from a little after that year and from typhoid from a little after 1875. In 1851 the death rate from tuberculosis was 3·6 per thousand of the population, in 1861-5 it was 3·3 per thousand, it fell to 2·9 in 1871-5 and thence by reasonably steady stages to 1·9 in 1896-1900.[3]

This is, of course, only intended to be a very general statement of a very complicated problem, and if a closer discussion of the matter was desired before proceeding from facts to

[1] W. P. D. Logan *Population Studies*, 'Mortality in England and Wales from 1848-1947' Vol IV (Cambridge 1951) p. 134, Table 1

[2] Logan [loc. cit. p. 105], 141; this rate is to be compared with that of one male death in 14 and one female death in 17 caused by infectious diseases in 1947

[3] For the annual standardized death rates see *The Registrar-General's Statistical Review of England and Wales for the Year 1925* (New Annual Series No. 5) (London 1926) Tables, Part I, Medical, p. 3, and ibid. p. 35 for average annual deaths for various diseases, and also the *50th Annual Report of the Registrar-General* 'Annual Death Rates from the Principal Zymotic Diseases'. [op. cit. p. 96] LVIII, Table 18. See also the graphs on pp. 4-7 of Hetherington [loc. cit. p. 80] and that on p. 178 of W. M. Frazer [op. cit. p. 70]. Frazer's Chap. 4 pp. 163-87 is on the epidemic situation. See also M. C. Buer *Health Wealth and Population in the Early Days of the Industrial Revolution* (London 1926) p. 137 ff.

explanations, a good many difficult problems would have to be faced, such as those presented by the ambiguities of registration and diagnosis before certain dates in the nineteenth century. Even then the explanations must necessarily be extremely complex; they must necessarily take into account such factors as the improvement during the century in real wages, the changes in the average age of the population, the vagaries of infectious disease—the incidence of epidemics, the changes in virulence in certain diseases, the ecology of the carriers, and so on and so forth. But even when all these possible complications have been considered, it still seems that here, in these figures, is the result of a quarter of a century's work on public health, the work of those who had been responsible for such things as the general vaccination against smallpox that had been attained by the 1870s, who were gradually providing for the isolation of patients with infectious diseases, who had destroyed rookeries and controlled nuisances, and above all those who had provided the people with water pure enough for them to drink, abundant enough for them to wash their clothes and clean their bodies to free them from disease-carrying vermin and readily available to scour their streets and flush their drains, and incidentally who had provided them with drains to flush.

Very much remained to be done; there were still terribly large slum areas, very bad urban, and for that matter very bad rural, conditions remained everywhere, many of them till the twentieth century, many of them till now. There was much ignorance and a lack of expert help where expert help was desperately desired, and, partly as a result of this, infant mortality stayed at a distressingly high figure. Nevertheless, may it not be said that a corner had been turned? This is a result which should be put alongside the effects of the Industrial Revolution. The great increase of population had taken place, but it had not been necessary to pay the penalties. Instead of men becoming poorer they became richer, instead of life becoming more precarious it slowly became safer. Human beings had been assembled in great masses, and yet the likelihood of death from infectious disease had decreased and, what was more important, was going to go on decreasing.

It would seem that in general this improvement came too late in the century to be the original cause of the increase of population, indeed it seems probable that when it became really marked the birth rate was going down. It may have prevented that increase from being cancelled by some epidemic of overwhelming proportions, but the possibility of that seems doubtful. But that is not the most significant point. What it must have altered effectively were the terms on which life was offered, and the chances of individual disaster. Indeed, it must always be remembered that disease does not necessarily strike at the unfit or the useless, it can also impartially cut down the active, the potentially vigorous, the individuals of great social importance, such as the breadwinner in a family or the house mother; and it not only kills, it mauls, reducing the able bodied to shadows of what they might have been.

III

If all this is true, an important point had been passed in the history of humanity. There had started, probably in the eighteenth century, a mysterious and overwhelming increase in population. Upon the reasons for this increase the experts are at present undecided, but, as far as can be seen, the fact of this increase does not presuppose any conditions but the sufficient supply of the simplest food necessary to support life and the absence of some killing agent effective enough to cancel the increase. It seems clear from what did happen in certain areas and at certain periods that the result of this increase could mean the ever-increasing competition of a growing population for other resources which were, at best, not increasing at the same rate. At best this might lead to a stable situation in which men's standards did not improve, but it might lead to a deteriorating situation and it might end in disaster, as it did in Ireland. This did not happen in Britain, and it did not happen in other countries which followed in the road of Britain, because of what is called the Industrial Revolution which enabled men to convert the new masses of the population into a source, not of poverty, but of affluence. To this, however, as a powerful auxiliary was added the methods of public hygiene which could control the dangers which the new teeming urban populations were likely to create, or even perhaps produce in their stead conditions more favourable to human life than had ever normally existed before, even in the countryside.

But there was an essential difference between these two agents. The Industrial Revolution was to a large extent a blind force, almost as blind, as unconscious of its results for humanity, as the increase in population. It could be promoted by a large number of people pursuing their own immediate objectives without thought, or with only secondary and passing thought, of what the effects of their activities on the community in which they lived or on the people through whom they worked might be. The struggle for public health was unavoidably teleological, it was the conscious pursuit of a social ideal, and it could only be developed by imposing on the community an ever-increasing body of rules to secure that men's actions should be consistent with the realization of that ideal. In this it found its parallel with the development of a code to control the ways in which labour was treated in mine or factory, and in due course in a good many other matters as well. In fact, it was proved early on that if the standards of humanity and well-being attained in the new mass-populated industrial community were to be compatible with the increasingly humane standards demanded by nineteenth-century society, increasing social discipline was necessary which must be imposed by some public authority. There were many who intensely disliked this conclusion, but circumstances made it unavoidable.

The sanction behind this development was public opinion, often, as in the case of the factory children or as in the case of the health of towns, public opinion whipped up by an agitation over the revelation of particularly outrageous conditions. But the work had to be done by officials who would supply the continuous executive activity which would alone convert a pious aspiration embodied in legislation into something which really happened in the world of dirty streets and of suffering men, women and children. This executive activity unavoidably required both discretionary administrative action and the making of regulations. In theory, no doubt, both the power to perform these actions and make these regulations might be placed in the hands of a minister of the Crown, though at first even this was not by any means always done; but practically of course both executive and legislative power were necessarily exercised by officials under the mantle, not in the first stages always very complete, of the ministers' responsibility. More than this, since unavoidably very soon the officials got to know more about the subject-matter in hand than anyone else, future legislation was necessarily founded upon their expert knowledge. In fact, in the second and third quarter of the nineteenth century, at the very time when private industry was putting on the strength of a giant, when men were prating of the benefits of freedom and of the dangers of Government interference, unnoticed, unplanned and certainly as far as most men were concerned absolutely undesired, the modern State with its delegated powers imposing on the community the rule of experts and officials was beginning to take shape. It was to play its necessary part in the making of Victorian England.[1]

The relation of this development to public opinion was equivocal. Many men, even intelligent men in a position to know such as journalists or members of Parliament, did not realize what was happening, and when they came upon traces of it they were angry. They had sometimes willed the end but they had seldom willed the means by which alone it could be reached. There were often fierce controversies in which, because the doctrines of ministerial responsibility and official discretion had not as yet been adequately developed, the experts in the Civil Service took an open part which nowadays would be thought to be intolerable.[2] This was most notorious in the history of public health in the days of Chadwick, Simon was consciously more discreet. He worked in the background and as far as he could he used public opinion and did not try to master it. The public opinion he used seems, however, to have been the rather specialized public opinion of enthusiasts and experts in the country, the odd member or minister of the Crown who happened to be interested, in Parliament. The policy he developed was not the result of the conscious policy of any particular political party and it would be hard to say

[1] See Oliver MacDonagh *The Historical Journal*, 'The Nineteenth Century Revolution in Government' (Cambridge 1958) I, pp. 52-67 [loc. cit. p. 19]; and also David Roberts *Victorian Origins of the British Welfare State* (Yale University Press 1960). I obtained this book after I had finished my work, when it was too late to use it

[2] On this see G. Kitson Clark *The Historical Journal*, ' "Statesmen in Disguise": Reflexions on the History of the Neutrality of the Civil Service', II, 1 (Cambridge 1959) pp. 19-39

it was a response to the demands of public opinion in general. This indeed was no more than was to be expected for the period 1854 to 1866 when the policy was being developed piecemeal and locally and politics were still suffering from the frustrations of House of Commons government. But it might have been thought that since the transition to the period of consolidation and general legislation which starts with the Act of 1866 and goes on to 1875, corresponds so closely with the passage of the second Reform Bill, the change must have the same impetus which was reviving party politics and causing the approach of democracy. It may be so, the pattern is tempting, but in truth it is not clear that either the renewal of party politics, or the approach of democracy had very much to do with the matter. The critical Act was passed in 1866, the year before the Reform Act of 1867. It would not seem that after the general election of 1868 the call for public health measures became much more insistent because of the new classes that had been enfranchised. Nor apparently had party politics much to do with what happened. This policy was pressed forward continuously whatever party was in power, and the claim of Disraeli and the Conservative party to some special initiative in the matter does not appear to be substantial.

It was in fact a policy devised by experts, appealing to experts, to be executed by experts. Parliament could hamper or expedite it, politicians and other administrators could frustrate its promoters, as in the end John Simon was frustrated, or they could grant the powers desired, as powers had been granted at Simon's request. But in the last resort the initiative could only come from those who possessed the special knowledge that Simon commanded. It was a foretaste of what was to come as the work of the State grew more technical, and Simon was the forerunner of other men, like himself unusually able and unusually devoted, who were to play their part in making both Victorian and post-Victorian England from behind increasingly effectively closed doors.

They were to play their part in making it, but not all the work could be done in that way. There were some reforms which needed the afflatus of public opinion, and if Britain was to develop from the aristocratic House of Commons government of the mid-century towards something like a democracy, it was necessary for men and women outside the charmed circle of those who had had political influence to be able and willing to act more effectively than so far they had done. And to understand how that was to happen it is necessary to look more closely at the people whom the increase of population had largely brought into being, whom the migrations had regrouped and upon whom the Industrial Revolution was to have its effect.

CHAPTER V

The People

In my last two chapters I touched on two, or rather three, of the factors which helped to make Victorian England. The first was the increase of population, the second the increase in productive power, and my third was the development, as yet the very partial and imperfect development, of that power in the community which was needed to control those two blind forces. My main example of this third factor was the development of sanitary legislation and the authorities to enforce it; but this was only one example of the new power which the State and society would need to assume in order to master not only the new dangerous energies which were daily developing but also some very ugly things which had been inherited from the past.

There is, however, a danger in talking too glibly about factors and forces as if they were inhuman elemental energies like earthquakes or whirlwinds tossing about a mass of indistinguishable human material without individual feelings and personalities. This would, of course, be wrong. Most of what happens in history is in some measure the result of the decisions of the human will, probably of a great number of human wills, directed to a greater or less extent by the human intelligence. Often, in fact, it is the result of the decisions of the human will intent on some immediate object of personal importance to the actor but forgotten by history. Men act as individuals in history, they think as individuals and, what is more, they suffer as individuals. In order to understand something of what has happened to people it is necessary to produce all the paraphernalia of wage rates, of prices, of index figures carefully worked out and properly weighted by statisticians; but in using these things it is important to remember that they present averages and that the average is the life lived by no man. What a man actually receives may be better than the scales suggest, or it may be worse, perhaps much worse, since it is difficult to take into account a man's spells of unemployment or short time, or for that matter the possibility of sickness, or the probability that, though in his full strength his rewards may be reasonable, when his strength fails he may very well come to the workhouse. Yet these things matter a great deal to the man or woman into whose face they stare.

All statistics, all generalizations about classes, all tables of real wages, all index figures are, then, unsatisfactory general statements describing human beings about many of whom perhaps the most important fact is the extent to which they differ from the generality. But it is necessary to use them, in order to get some sort of plan of a community about which one is thinking.

II

In order to get a general picture of Victorian England it is therefore probably as well to start with the census at the beginning of my chosen period, the census of 1851. In that year the population of Britain (not of England and Wales only) was 10,224,000 males and 10,736,000 females, of whom 7,616,000 males and 8,155,000 females were of 10 years old and upwards and therefore may be considered as potential wage earners. It is significant that in this labour force the two largest groups were agriculturists—farmers, graziers, labourers, farm servants —who numbered 1,563,000 men and 227,000 women, and domestic servants who numbered 134,000 men and 905,000 women. It would seem, therefore, that the leaven of the Industrial Revolution had not yet transformed the whole community. A very large section of the population had not yet been drawn into the towns, nor had the work upon which it was employed yet been mechanized. In contrast to this should be placed the workers in the textile industry, which of all industries had in 1851 been most closely concerned in the Industrial Revolution. There were 255,000 men and 272,000 women cotton workers (of all kinds) and 171,000 men and 113,000 women wool workers. To these perhaps might be added linen and flax workers, 47,000 men and 56,000 women, and silk workers, 53,000 men and 80,000 women. Some of all these, however, still worked on the hand loom and not on the machines in the factories, nor would all those working in factories be highly skilled.

It would, however, be impossible to say of anyone in the England of 1851 that he was untouched by the Industrial Revolution. It had affected different people in different ways. It had been the tragic fate of many hand-loom weavers to face the competition of the machines which the Industrial Revolution had developed, but in other cases even where a man or woman's work had not been mechanized, the needs of mechanized industry might have created, or greatly increased, the demand for their labours. This was clearly the case with the 216,000 men and 3,000 women employed in the coal-mines who were active in producing the fuel for machines, who used mechanized lifting and pumping gear, but in the actual work on the seam used nothing but their muscles. In something of the same case were 144,000 merchant seamen and pilots still very largely working in sail who carried the products of the machines abroad, the blacksmiths 112,000 men and 592 women, and the labourers unspecified 367,000 men and 9,000 women. Even the men and women in those trades which did not directly supply the needs of industry would nevertheless be profoundly affected by the fact that they were confronted by the demands of a much larger and in many ways a much wealthier population, as was obvious in the case of the large numbers employed in the building industry, 442,000 men and 1,000 women, with the milliners, dressmakers, seamsters and seamstresses who were 494 men and 340,000 women, with the shoemakers who were 243,000 men and 31,000 women, the tailors 135,000 men and 18,000 women and the washerwomen who numbered 145,000.

What can, however, be said of such people and of several of the other smaller groups enumerated in the census is that though their lives were affected by the Industrial Revolution their actual methods of labour were not dictated by the demands of the new machines, that they probably depended for their livelihood on pre-industrial skills and that they were likely to have been working in pre-industrial conditions; for instance, a great many of them, particularly of the milliners, tailors, shoemakers and blacksmiths, were working on their own premises, or in relatively small establishments. Indeed, it would seem to be clear that by 1851 the process that had drawn the people into towns had gone further than the process that was to lead them into factories, certainly into big factories, and that in general the urbanization of Great Britain had preceded its mechanization.[1]

Even so, urbanization did not yet by any means dominate the whole island. In 1851 about half the population still lived in what were called 'rural conditions', and as has been seen the largest single group of workers still worked on the land. Industrial conditions attract so much attention from those who think about mid-nineteenth-century Britain that it is possibly difficult to realize that about half of the picture ought still to be taken up by the countryside and the people who lived there. They lived there on varying terms and in circumstances which present some very marked contrasts. Conditions differed very noticeably even in different parts of England and still more widely if the special circumstances of parts of Wales and Scotland are included. Moreover, this large group in the census is in no way uniform in social status and function, and even if it were practicable to isolate the agricultural labourers in England and to disregard the rest it would still be dangerous to generalize about the terms on which life was offered to them, for these varied not only from district to district but from village to village. There seems, for instance, to have been a considerable difference between the earnings of agricultural labourers in counties where industry had developed to compete for their services and the miserable pittances which were too often what they got where there was none. Even within the same county the standard of living would depend on a large number of different things about which it is not always easy or possible to get evidence—the rent of cottages, the readiness of farmers to allow labourers to take home unwanted foodstuffs, skim milk, surplus potatoes and the like, the customs of the estate on which they might live, the chances there might be of cultivating a potato patch, or of gathering fuel, or of raising a pig, and the chance of poaching.

Since this is the case, any simple general statement about the

[1] Clapham *Economic History of Great Britain*, 'Free Trade and Steel', Vol II (Cambridge 1932) pp. 23-25 in the text. I have used the figures as cited in Clapham, and anyone familiar with his book will realize how great is my debt to him. For a careful list of the numbers in the more numerous occupations see *Census 1851 Population Ages and Occupations* etc., Vol I, p. c, Table 41.

lot of agricultural workers at this period, unfavourable or favourable, must be suspect. But there can be no doubt at all that in many parts of England the picture must be a grim one. In some counties the wages of agricultural labourers were unbelievably low, so low that it is difficult to see how they could have lived and brought up families upon them, whatever auxiliary sources of income they had, and in many cases they seem to have had no auxiliary resources. The hours of labour were intolerably long, while the food upon which a long day's work sometimes had to be done seems to have been both monotonous and unattractive and also insufficient. Rural cottages could be very bad, sometimes with earthen floors and with no ceilings or attic overhead, but open rafters or rafters only covered with a cloth nailed beneath them. Sometimes there was only one sleeping apartment for all ages and sexes, often no sanitation. In such conditions it was hard to maintain cleanliness, or the most rudimentary decency, while the damp almost inevitably led to the tortures of rheumatism in later life. To make the improvement of such conditions more difficult it is clear that in a good many different parts of the country there remained much ignorance and superstition, as there was obviously much habitual violence and brutality, while the affrays between poachers and gamekeepers could become battles in which lives were sacrificed.

To such depths rural life in England and Wales could fall, or from such depths it had never risen; the distinction may be a significant one because it is probably important to know the heredity of these conditions, to what extent they were inherited from remote antiquity, or to what extent they represented a decline from the conditions that had existed in the English countryside in the first half of the eighteenth century. It seems probable that much had come down from remote antiquity. For instance, it would seem that the housing of which such justifiable complaint was made was traditional; in many areas a good many of the huts, cottages or bothies in which some of the people had lived may have been worse in the past, certainly they had not been better. Indeed, so ingrained were the habits of some people that some of them found it difficult at first to adapt themselves to better houses when their landlords built them for them, though it is clear that many of them were very anxious for more decent conditions, particularly the women.[1] Ignorance and neglect were no new factors. The quarrel over game between the lord of the land and those who worked it was not new either; it stretched back through centuries of cruel laws and harsh punishments. Indeed, the situation had been improved a little by the modification of the game laws in 1831 and the prohibition of man-traps and spring guns, though the law was still oppressive enough and the quarrel contested with sufficient bitterness to be a source of profound division in the countryside. Apart from this, endemic and widespread violence and brutality in remote and country places certainly went back into the remote past. As was said earlier, the forces which would curb these things were being developed, but they were developing slowly and would do so while men deluded themselves with the belief that it was an economy not to have a sufficient force of rural police.

The legacy of the past, therefore, was bad enough; but it also seems clear that in many parts of England in the last half of the eighteenth and in the first half of the nineteenth century things had got worse for the country labourer. It had possibly become less likely that he would have secure possession of a separate holding sufficient to support himself or to make a considerable addition to his wages, in many districts real wages had declined and rates had gone up, and too often a man and his family had to be supported in some way by the Poor Law if they were to live. There are several obvious reasons for this decline: there was a run of bad harvests, the revolutionary and Napoleonic wars drove prices up and put a strain on the economy, and men suffered from whatever social results came from the enclosures of the eighteenth and the early nineteenth century and the breakdown of a subsistence economy;[2] but in addition to all these things there was another factor which has possibly not quite received the attention which is its due. As in Ireland, so in England it seems that by the turn of the century the population living in the countryside had increased greatly, possibly beyond the numbers that the land could support in tolerable decency; and in the early nineteenth century it was still increasing. Of course, the situation was relieved by migration into the towns,

[1] See J. C. Atkinson *Forty Years in a Moorland Parish* (London 1891) pp. 19-26
[2] On this breakdown see W. G. Hoskins *The Midland Peasant* (London 1957)

and in the nineteenth century by migration overseas, but even by the middle of the century it does not seem that the numbers migrating had been large enough actually to reduce the population living on the land.

If, however, the rural population was not in the first half of the century being actually reduced, from the very beginning of the century the urban population was increasing very rapidly. It was probably mainly into the towns that those who represented the natural increase of the countryside migrated, and the towns were also the recipients of the huge immigration from Ireland. Moreover, as the century proceeded new industries developed in what had been the unsullied countryside creating urban conditions where all had been rural before, while in due course the definite depopulation of parts of the countryside would begin. As a result of all these things the time was certain to come when the balance would inevitably swing over decisively and the town dweller would come to outnumber the countryman and agriculture come to seem much less important than industry and commerce. But this had not yet happened by 1851; indeed, the general lesson of the state of affairs in 1851 would appear to be this. The characteristic processes of the nineteenth century, the urbanization, the mechanization, the development of factories had begun, but they had not penetrated as deeply into the life of the community as perhaps we are apt to think. Very much that existed in the Britain of 1851 was in fact closely akin to what had existed in 1800; it is worth while, however, to remember that there had been one decisive change since 1801, the population of the country had nearly doubled. England had also received the addition of about half a million Irishmen.

III

So far, those of whom I have been speaking would probably be considered to have been unquestionably working class, but what about the middle class? This, however, raises the old awkward and difficult question, Who were the middle class? It is difficult not only because so many and such various people were considered to be middle class, but also because the conception of the middle class seems so often to have been subjective. It might almost be said that the best definition of the middle class is that it was made up of those people who thought themselves to be middle class and were allowed by their neighbours to be so, or were accused of it. At the time, however, the conception was deemed to have more definite roots in fact than that, and more concrete tests were applied by contemporaries, as for instance whether a man's income came within certain limits or rather above a certain limit, because, though it might reasonably be held that a man could not aspire to be middle class unless his income reached a certain figure, he might be as rich as you like and yet not be conceded to be, or perhaps not desire to be, anything else. Certain trades and functions were considered to be definitely middle class, but unfortunately opinion on this point altered as the century went forward, and for instance certain functions became in due course possible for gentlemen and not specifically middle class. Moreover, at any particular period this was a matter in which circumstances could alter cases. Whether a man might be considered to be middle class might be decided by the education he had received, by the style of his life, by his manners, by the district in which he lived, by whether he went to church or chapel on Sunday, by the way he dressed, or by any number of possible tests some of which it would be quite impossible to recover. In fact, the conception is too important and significant to be abandoned, and too indefinite and subjective to be used with any comfort.

It may, however, help to divide the class into two and to concentrate for the moment on those who are obviously of the 'people', that is those who came to be called the lower middle class, leaving out everyone in the higher income groups or in important professional commercial or industrial positions. The minimum annual income for this lower group might be given in the second quarter of the century as about £60 a year and its uppermost income might be considered to be £150 or £200. Neither upper nor lower figure is satisfactory, for it is never satisfactory to define a social group in terms of income alone, and in this case it seems certain that some people who were considered to be middle class, poor clerks for instance, had less than £60 a year, and less than quite a number of people who were palpably not middle class at all. Bob Cratchit in Dickens' *Christmas Carol* published in 1843 earned only 15s. a week. This is of course fiction, but in such matters as this Dickens was normally a good observer, and there seems to be evidence from elsewhere that such very poor clerks existed. If so, it might be a little difficult to see in what way they were differentiated from the working class. They would have to be more literate and probably to be more formal in their behaviour and dress, though in fact Bob Cratchit in the story could not afford an overcoat and had to be content with a muffler, and a top hat, such as he most certainly wore, would be worn at that time by many people who were not middle class at all. As he is described, Bob lived in considerable poverty with recourse from time to time to the pawnbroker; his daughter worked in a shop and he himself probably had to work harder for less money and lived in less comfort than many working-class folk. Indeed, the claim of such a man to be middle class might seem to mean singularly little, and yet it might be all-important to someone who claimed it. To turn from Bob Cratchit to his creator and his creator's father, old John Dickens as a clerk in the Navy Office was a member of the middle class if a singularly unsuccessful one, and for his son Charles the descent from the possibility of some sort of middle-class education to manual labour in a blacking factory was a descent into the nethermost hell, the denial to him of everything that made life worth while, an injury never to be forgotten and never to be forgiven. Indeed, it would seem that the more uncertain the frontier, the more thin the partition between a middle-class family and the working class, the more passionately its importance might be estimated, which is of course natural and to be expected.

There were a good many different kinds of clerks, and the incomes of some of them would be very much greater than Bob Cratchit's; indeed, it is clearly Dickens' intention to describe Bob as unusually poorly paid while he worked for the unconverted Scrooge. The whole number of clerks seems to have been in 1851 smaller than that of most of the large working-class groups, though it is considerably larger than some of the socially significant groups higher up the scale. Charles Booth in an interesting article on the census figures between 1801 and 1881 gives for 'Commercial Clerks Accountants and Bankers' the figures 44,000 in 1851, 67,000 in 1861 and 119,000 in 1871.[1] To the 44,000 commercial clerks in 1851 should presumably be added the law clerks who numbered 14,013, and perhaps smaller categories like the commercial travellers who numbered in 1851 8,538. But the really large numbers in this section of the community were in all probability those of the retail shop-keepers. Here, as with the commercial clerks, the numbers were rapidly increasing. Booth notes that between 1851 and 1881 those who came under the head of 'dealing' had increased by 69 per cent. as compared with the 39 per cent. increase of the population, an increase which he said was due to multiplication of small shopkeepers and street sellers. The numbers he gives for these are 547,000 in 1851 and in 1881 as many as 924,000.[2]

These are very large figures, and as evidence of the size of what should be called the middle class they must be scaled down. Booth himself points out that they are unsatisfactory because they fail to distinguish 'dealers' from 'manufacturers', for clearly a craftsman living on his own premises and selling what he had made would not necessarily be called middle class, nor would a street seller with a barrow and without a shop. Even a shop could vary from a relatively large establishment to the front room of a cottage where an old lady sold sweets and pickled onions. There is also another difficulty in using the figures available. They do not seem to differentiate between the shopkeeper and his assistants, and it is not easy to see which was which in the relevant figures in the 1851 census, as for instance in the case of the 52,672 tailors, or the 85,913 grocers with the addition of 14,320 greengrocers and fruiterers, or the 67,691 butchers, though, presumably, each of the 75,721 inn-keepers was master of his house. The figure given in the 1851 census for 'masters' seems to be too indiscriminate for use.

Yet with all these deductions all the evidence seems to suggest that a large, and growing, section of society was composed of retail shopkeepers. It is an impression which seems to be con-firmed by the number of shops that have existed in any street or section of a town whose history one tries to reconstruct. They are only exceeded by the very surprising number of public

[1] C. Booth *Journal of the Statistical Society*, 'Occupations of the People of the United Kingdom 1801-81', Vol XLIX, pp. 314-444
[2] Booth [op. cit. p. 121] 335

houses, to which should be added the beer shops which must mostly have disappeared without trace.[1] Since the needs of the population which are now supplied by multiple shops and large stores would then be supplied by smaller retail shops, and the magistrates and brewers had not gone far in their chosen work of devouring public houses, this is not surprising. But it probably means that in trying to form a mental picture of Victorian society it is always necessary to allow the retail shopkeeper and public house keeper a very much larger section of the canvas than he would possess now. There would probably be actually more of them in proportion to the rest of the population in the country than now, and they would be a very great deal more important for they would be more likely to be literate, though not well-educated, and reasonably sure of themselves in a population in which there would be a great many people who were still illiterate or relatively illiterate and very humble. The shopkeeper would also be more likely to have a Parliamentary vote in a population in which such a distinction was rare.

If this is so, it would account for much in the tone of the country, possibly in its general religious habits and culture, certainly in the general attitude to any expenditure which might come on the rates. In national politics shopkeepers would be only likely to play a secondary rôle not as candidates for election to Parliament but as voters, or as helping to form the public opinion to which candidates had to appeal; but they would be more likely to come into their own in local affairs, in borough councils, but still more in such bodies as vestries and boards of guardians. Indeed, in the descriptions of such bodies in action shopkeepers are often prominent, and the impression that they leave is not always pleasant, for they could be very anxious to avoid expenditure, rather self-assured, and very hard on the poor.[2] As well as this they are to be found in all political parties, they are to be found in all religious denominations, but it must be remembered that in these matters

---

[1] *Reports from Committees 1852-3*, 'Select Committee on Public Houses and Sale of Beer', Vol XXXVII. Committee on Public Houses p. 615 (627) gives numbers of licences, and the Select Committee of the Lords on the Sale of Beer, 1850, p. 33 (821) records that the number of houses for the consumption of intoxicating liquors had risen to 123,396

[2] An example can be found in the proprietor of an à-la-mode beef shop who was Chairman of the Strand workhouse at the time of Dr Rogers. See *Joseph Rogers Reminiscences of a Workhouse Medical Officer*, ed. Prof. Thorold Rogers (London 1889)

shopkeepers had to be very careful. Voting was open, and the way in which a man voted was known by his potential customers, who would vary their habits accordingly, as they would also take count of where he went to worship on Sunday morning, or whether he went anywhere, so that shopkeepers were inclined both in politics and religion to take protective colouring from their surroundings.

IV

Taken in rather general terms, and realizing how many exceptions there always were, this stratification into classes supplies something of a guide to the way men behaved in politics and still more to the way men thought about politics. From fairly early on in the century men recognized the political importance of what they called the 'middle class'. When they used those words they did not often define clearly whom they meant and probably did not realize the great difficulties of any such definition, but they knew in general whom they were talking about and they talked about them a great deal. The middle class were respectable, they were hard-working, they were, if you disliked them, grasping, narrowminded and uneducated, but it was recognized increasingly as the century went forward that their opinions mattered. Indeed, one of the main objects of the Reform Bill of 1832 was to admit them to the electorate, partly because it was thought to be necessary to take account of their wishes and partly as a prophylactic against demands from the people below them, to whom it was felt that it would be dangerous to give a vote.

This calculation did not necessarily appeal to all members of the middle class themselves, nor to their leaders. After all, the concession of a vote in a limited Parliamentary system heavily dominated by the 'proprietary classes' might not be of great value. It was probably of greater value than John Bright sometimes asserted, but it was a reasonable calculation that it would be of greater value if large numbers of the working classes had also been admitted to the electorate. This was, indeed, in the eyes of men like Bright, no less than the right of the working classes, but it would also probably supply a middle-

class leader with allies who would help him to make head
against the power of the aristocracy; for to many of the middle
class the essential division in the community was not that
suggested by the reformers of 1832 between those who had
some stake in the country as property holders and those who
had none, but between the old privileged classes and the
'people'. It was very natural to feel this. No doubt individually
a great many members of the middle class were peculiarly
anxious not to be confused with the lower orders, and certainly
sections of the working classes came to hate the 'middle class'
more than they hated any other people in the State. But the
most natural, and for many the only real, division in the State
was what divided the nobility, the gentry and the established
Church from all the rest. The gulf fixed here was very wide even
if it was in fact repeatedly if surreptitiously crossed by individual
descendants of Dives. It was therefore to be expected that men
who were not gentry, who were probably Dissenters in religion,
who conceived themselves with some reason to be sufferers
from the system of privilege which was, so they believed, the
inheritance of an iniquitous past, should feel a sense of unity
with all who were outside the ranks of the aristocracy and wish
to bring them into the Parliamentary system.

This sense of social solidarity would be likely to be at its
strongest in those areas where there were no marked social
distinctions and where economic divisions were not as yet very
deep. In an industrial area like Birmingham or Sheffield, where
industry was still in the hands of relatively small concerns, there
would be no great social or economic distinction between the
small master whose factory was also quite probably his home
and the retail shopkeeper and the artisan who made goods and
sold them on his own premises.[1] Nor where the concern was very
small would there probably be any great difference in life or
outlook, or even necessarily in interest, between the small
manufacturer and the assistants who worked at his side. There
would be social unity and therefore probably there would be
political unity. If there were grievances, they would be charged
against the State and the classes who governed the State, men
who as landowners or royalty owners were the recipients of

[1] On conditions in Birmingham see Briggs [op. cit. p. 103] and in Sheffield see
Pollard *Labour in Sheffield* [op. cit. p. 103]

much unearned increment, who were responsible for the Corn Laws and who used their position as the manipulators of patronage to bleed the national exchequer of very large sums indeed, or so it was believed. For such troubles the remedy which would rather obviously commend itself would be the extension of the power of the 'people' in the constitution—however the conception of the 'people' might at that moment be construed. To adopt a convenient label, it may be useful to describe what resulted as the 'politics of popular radicalism'.

The classical example of the politics of popular radicalism lies in the history of the Birmingham Political Union. Thomas Attwood, the founder and leader of the Union, was not at first in any way an advanced politician, but he became convinced that the policy that had secured the return to cash payments and a gold-based currency in 1819 after the Napoleonic Wars was disastrous, and when the Government were recalcitrant on the point he turned to political agitation and organized the famous Birmingham Political Union. In that Union all classes in Birmingham seem to have co-operated, and it played an important part in the battle for reform in 1832. The first Reform Act and its immediate sequel failed to satisfy Radical opinion; 1837 in Birmingham as elsewhere saw a renewal of agitation and in 1838 the Birmingham Political Union promoted a national petition which may reasonably be held to be the beginning of the Chartist Movement. The Charter itself was a programme of advanced political reform which was drawn up at the same time by an association of London working men who were mainly small craftsmen.[1]

The flaw in popular radicalism, however, lay in the fact that it assumed a greater uniformity of opinion and interest among the classes who were not aristocrats and not committed to the old system than was likely to exist, while in fact in the mass of the middle and lower classes there were not a few potential fissures among those classes which would open dangerously when the right pressures were applied. There was, for instance, the old difference between town and country. The Anti-Corn Law League liked to believe that the farmer was a man of the

---

[1] See Asa Briggs *The Cambridge Historical Journal*, 'Thomas Attwood and the Economic Background of the Birmingham Political Union', Vol IX, No. 2, 1948 (IV) 190-216, and ibid., 'The Background of the Parliamentary Reform Movement in three English Cities', Vol X, No. 3, 1952 (IV) 293-317

middle class, and like themselves a victim of the aristocracy, and they rather eagerly reported meetings at which they were able to explain to the farmers that their attack on the Corn Laws was in the interest of the farmer as well as of the townsman. But independent reports of the meetings which they described together with accounts of ones they did not mention and of the tenant farmer's own activities give a very different picture. Certainly tenant farmers very often had serious grievances against the aristocracy over such matters as rents, or compensation for improvements, or the game laws; but when it came to the retention of the Corn Laws their views were often far more uncompromising than those of their landowners, and, if that were possible, more hostile to the League. In this matter there can have been no real communication between many of the farmers and the members of the League, and it would seem also that in many cases the town agitator found it difficult to penetrate into the dark world of the agricultural labourer. But you did not have to go as far as the countryside to find barriers which cut off man from man quite as effectively as did the difference between the world of the hedgerows and that of the streets.

There was for instance one line which ran right through Victorian society, the line which divided those who were respectable from those who were not. It is very unfortunate that the whole subject of Victorian respectability, particularly of Victorian prudery, has been considered more as the subject for satire, or humour, or indignation, rather than as a matter for serious historical analysis. It seems probable that the development should be considered as a chapter in a history that clearly goes back in time long before the Victorian epoch or the nineteenth century and is essentially part of the history of the battle for refinement and civilization, and above all the better protection of women, against the promiscuity, animalism, brutality and grossness which had been common even in the eighteenth century. Unfortunately it seems that this battle wherever it is fought seems normally to cause the development of an etiquette which becomes in many points otiose and extremely cumbersome, the encouragement of taboos which are at best ridiculous, and the imposition of a code which can be extremely cruel; it can lead to the overweighting of morality at certain points and the miserable distortion of religion. But when these things are to be judged it is only fair to remember also the circumstances in which they developed and the evils which they were intended to control, evils for the continuance of which into the nineteenth century there is adequate evidence in what might happen in Victorian streets, and in railway trains and elsewhere.

The same consideration is relevant to the passionate attack on the use of alcohol. It would be hard to say why historians have not rated the effect of strong drink as the significant factor in nineteenth-century history that it undoubtedly was. Its importance stands out from every page of the contemporary record. The most prominent factor in every disputed election was bestial drunkenness, which the candidates were expected to subsidize by expending what were, considering the cheapness of liquor and the smallness of the population involved, very large sums.[1] Drunkenness caused endless trouble to the employers of labour, as for instance the builders of the railways found to their cost.[2] The results of strong drink were patent in disgusting forms at the appropriate times in most of the streets and market places of Britain. The drunken women he saw in the streets of Manchester and Liverpool horrified Emerson when he visited England in 1847. 'Woman is cheap and vile in England', he told his wife, and he might have been stirred to say as much about the men and women that he could have seen in some streets in every town in England on every Saturday night in the century.[3] In the background there was always present the degradation, the cruelty, particularly to the weak and defenceless, which resulted from drunkenness. The cause of its prevalence was no doubt an unfortunate historical tendency made much worse by intolerable living conditions. In many cases indeed the terms on which life was offered is a complete explanation of any drunkenness there was: for instance the Irish were often held to be the most drunken and rowdy section of the working class; if this is so, it would seem that the cellars and slums and holes in which the Irish were expected to live

[1] For examples of this expenditure see G. Kitson Clark *Transactions of the Royal Historical Society*, 5th Series, Vol I (1951) pp. 109-126

[2] L. T. C. Rolt, *George and Robert Stephenson* (London 1960) pp. 228-9

[3] *Journals of R. W. Emerson*, ed. E. W. Emerson and W. E. Forbes (London 1913), Vol VII, 354

offer every excuse, and without doubt the proper remedies for their drunkenness and the drunkenness of others would have been to provide better houses, better wages, better education and more chances of rational enjoyment. That is however not the way in which men normally thought in the nineteenth century; and indeed any wide experience of drunkards, and it must be remembered that men in the middle of the nineteenth century saw much more of them than any normal person does now, would excuse a man for thinking that sobriety must come first, if the results of any other reform were not to be thrown away. In the 1860s Samuel Morley said that 'the Temperance cause lay at the root of all social and political progress in this country', and the opinion though excessive was not in fact absurd.[1]

The result of this feeling was an agitation into which an enormous volume of emotional force, of intelligence, of time and of money, and of what else was disposable, was poured by devoted people throughout the nineteenth century, and which apart from everything else was going to be of considerable political importance. It has to be confessed that as a movement it was often hysterical, arrogant and intolerant, and heavy with self-righteousness. Its adherents too often assumed that the proper test of the reality of a man's Christianity was whether he was a total abstainer and not whether he was charitable, or even just, to his opponents, or merciful to the fallen. But in order to be just to the people who felt like this and to understand the emotional force behind the movement it is necessary to try to see clearly the world in which they lived and the way in which they saw it. This is not in fact difficult. It can be seen in the pictures of drunkards which George Cruikshank drew in his latest, his reformed phase, or in the grim stories of the fate of the disorderly, even in this world, which the virtuous left in every imaginable place for the unregenerate to read. It was normally stated in these tracts that the stories were either true, or to use a favourite phrase 'founded on fact', and it is quite probable that these statements were often justified.

This struggle in Britain divided the nation into two, the desert and the sown so to speak, the respectable and the disreputable, those who accepted the Victorian taboos and those

[1] Edwin Hodder *Life of Samuel Morley*, 3rd ed. (London 1887) p. 153

who did not. It was a division that cut through all the classes in the country from the nobility, among whom there were some very odd characters, down to the poor whom men sorted out into the deserving and the undeserving poor, the last class being the group about whom Mr Doolittle speaks with such insight and sympathy in Shaw's *Pygmalion*. The standards imposed and the way in which men and women viewed those who did not accept them seems to have been different in different social classes, and it seems probable that the tensions became greater and the rigidities among the godly stiffer in the lower half of the social pyramid. This is not surprising. In all probability even the more virtuous among the nobility had a more established tradition of indulgence towards the uncontrolled characters of their order; certainly the wealthy and well-connected had more elbow room. Among the upper class the temptations to drink and debauch were probably not so continuously present to those who wished to avoid the sight of them, and the penalty for those who did not were not so severe. A disorderly life could be concealed behind the various defences of gentility, but for a shopkeeper or a working man, or the son or daughter of a working man, it might mean ruin with consequences upon which the writers of religious fiction or moral pamphlets dwelt lovingly. To people in the lower middle class and in the working classes their respectability was therefore a matter of great moment to be defended by strict conventions and with much prejudice. These conventions were apparently sometimes insisted upon for others by those whose own lives did not strictly abide by them. For instance, to judge by their behaviour in the various Anti-Irish riots the opponents of the Irish were not themselves noticeable either for their sobriety or their peaceable conduct.

Those clashes were however probably abnormal. The more normal tension seems to have been between the respectable, who were often but by no means always Nonconformist, and their less strict and censorious neighbours, who often expressed a general if confused allegiance to the Church of England. Possibly the sharpest skirmish between the godly and the unregenerate was the violent election which Samuel Morley fought at Nottingham in 1865. On other occasions the tension was no doubt less overt but nevertheless present beneath the surface in politics. It was no doubt intensified by the identification of many Liberals with temperance legislation; but the effect of this factor has been exaggerated particularly by one eminent historian who seems to have believed that it provided a turning-point in politics before the general election of 1874.[1] It is not clear upon what direct research into elections he was relying, and subsequent research has not borne him out. Nevertheless, as the element of nonconformity developed in the Liberal party an element of Puritanism developed in it also, and it was also present in the Labour party when that appeared. It seems, significantly, normally to be an element in English and Scottish popular movements.

There was, however, an even more important, even more significant source of division among the classes that inhabited the English towns. The assumption behind popular radicalism was that there was a natural community of interest among all those who were not members of the old privileged classes. Let the people combine and break the power of privilege, remove monopolies, abolish artificial restrictions and distinctions and curtail the extravagances which the aristocracy had invented for their own corrupt purposes, and a common prosperity would be enjoyed by all. It was a natural deduction to make when society had only half emerged from the trammels of the old régime, but it was not the only possible analysis of the situation at any time. It was always possible for a man to trace his troubles from foes much nearer to his home than the aristocracy were likely to be—from the shopkeeper who raised prices on him, from the landlord who squeezed him for rent, or from the master who employed him, folk who might themselves be Liberals and Dissenters and also in nominal revolt against the old régime. And as the Industrial Revolution developed, the possibility that the employer or the men who financed the employer might appear to be the chief enemy increased. The size of factories increased and the old fellow-feeling between master and worker as men working on the same tasks with the same tools began to die away and an endemic rivalry between employer and employed took its place; and as men reflected on the condition of England in the birth pangs of the new order many of them began to believe that the power which raised the

[1] R. C. K. Ensor *England 1870-1914* (Oxford 1936) pp. 20-3

factories in reckless speculation, which sweated the women and children, which drove the small skilled craftsman out of business, was the main source of evil, and not the aristocracy or the legacy of the past.

This obviously could create a new pattern in politics. The large manufacturer and his allies who were quite probably Liberals might become the enemies of the people and the Tory, the parson or the aristocrat might even be conceived to be their friends. Since this pattern is so different it is probably desirable to give the politics that derived from it a different name to distinguish them from the politics of popular radicalism. They might be called 'the politics of class conflict', because the predominant cause is the conflict of classes in close contact because they are in close contact, and it is a conflict that need have nothing to do with the old grievances springing from the traditional organization of society. The cause of such conflict is most likely to be more or less directly economic and therefore the desired cure is likely to be some economic readjustment. A radical reform of the old system which does not offer that readjustment will not suffice, and if there is to be a radical reform it must be extreme enough to circumvent the power not only of the aristocracy but of the middle class, otherwise the desired economic readjustment would not take place.

Now, the rapid growth of the Industrial Revolution effected by the power of capital and enhancing the power of capital and emphasizing its dangers and defects was likely to develop in Britain the classic pattern of class conflict, the conflict between capital and labour. That did not, however, mean that the politics of class conflict speedily or completely or inevitably replaced the politics of popular radicalism. On the contrary, popular radicalism became in the later nineteenth century the creed of one of the two parties of the State, the Liberal party, in which wealthy manufacturers and capitalists combined to support a Radical policy. The political principle of popular radicalism, that is political democracy, became the orthodox doctrine of the State, and the very progress of the Industrial Revolution brought wealth and power to the men who were likely to put all their force behind a Liberal or Radical programme. Even before 1850 the agitation against the Corn Laws shows how powerful a movement men who had made their money in the Industrial Revolution could already produce.

Those who wished to press the grievances of the working class against the middle class had no such resources. They had no direct representation in Parliament, they had little money to spend in organization, if they pressed their claims too hard they were liable to frighten all other classes into resistance and might in their impatience bring the whole force of the State down on their shoulders. Perhaps the best, perhaps the only way for them to gain anything at that moment was through the means of industrial warfare, using the natural instrument of class warfare the Trade Union. After the repeal of the Combination Acts an attempt had been made to procure extensive reforms by means of Trade Unions, but it had failed egregiously. Certainly there were still Trade Unions in existence. They were craft unions, normally the organs of highly skilled artisans, men whose skills were required by the new industries or by an old handicraft that was still important. Such men often commanded an income which exceeded that of the lower-paid members of the middle class, while they seem often to have enjoyed a security of employment which ordinary members of the working classes looked for in vain. In fact, in any plan of the social stratification of the country in the first half of the nineteenth century this aristocracy of labour should be grouped with the middle class many of whose prejudices about keeping down the rates and maintaining social order they probably shared, and a large gap should be marked between them and the mass of the skilled or the semi-skilled, or those unfortunates whose skills no longer commanded a market, like the hand loom weavers. On the working-class side of that gap men were too poor, too uncertain of their position, to organize Trade Unions which had any great chance of effective survival; on the other side of the gap Unions were developed that were largely societies of specialists anxious to protect their professional privileges and standards of remuneration, interested in a number of friendly society activities, not willing to indulge in strikes because they wasted their societies' resources and not in the least likely to be militant in class war or to lead an assault on the embattled middle class.[1]

---

[1] See E. J. Hobsbawm in *Democracy and the Labour Movement* ed. J. Saville, pp. 201-237. 'The Labour Aristocracy in 19th Century Britain' (London 1954) pp. 201-39

Nevertheless, in spite of these difficulties the pattern of class conflict did develop in Britain in the politics of the second quarter of the nineteenth century. It was helped to do so by the nature of the first Reform Act, which not only left most radicals dissatisfied so that it was followed by an immediate resumption of agitation, but to working-class radicals seemed to be the result of a betrayal. It was constantly repeated in the next twenty years that the Act had been gained by an agitation of the whole people, but that it had only enfranchised the middle class, who had dropped their more humble allies as soon as they had got what they wanted. It was not perhaps a very fair accusation, because it is difficult to see that the middle class had had any great choice in the matter; but it helped to emphasize the pattern. Meanwhile the pressures in the new factories had led to the agitation for the protection of the factory children and for the Ten Hours Bill, an agitation in which factory operatives, led to a large extent by Tories Sadler, Oastler and Lord Shaftesbury and assisted by Conservative members of Parliament and the Clergy of the established Church, attacked master manufacturers who were normally Liberals and Radicals. In 1837 this agitation developed into the violent attack on the new Poor Law which showed much the same pattern; and then in 1838 and 1839 under the lowering skies of the trade depression this was followed by the most notable example in the first half of the nineteenth century of the pattern of the class struggle, the Chartist agitation.

The agitation for the People's Charter was, as has been seen, largely started by Radicals who had not much idea of the class struggle, and the document itself is a purely political manifesto enumerating points many of which had been put forward by Radicals from time to time since the reform agitation had begun in the eighteenth century. It was pre-industrial and had no direct reference to the problems of the manufacturing districts. But the Chartist Movement would never have had the importance it has had in British history in the hands of its first sponsors. But it changed hands; in 1838 the feeling that had been gathering head in the manufacturing districts poured into the agitation and it was from that boiling mass that it gained its force and its tragic significance. Unfortunately this development also meant the passing of the lead of the movement into the

hands of Fergus O'Connor, who had made himself the spokes-
man of the manufacturing districts and who was unworthy of
the trust which they so strangely reposed in him. He was an
egoist who spent much of his time consolidating his own
position and eliminating other leaders of whom he very early
became jealous, and he was a braggart, a man who used
rhetoric about force without clearly understanding what the
words meant, and as a result under his inspiration the movement came to be conspicuously ill led. Probably this did not
matter very much; however well led or however ill led, the
Chartist agitation was without question doomed to failure.
Their petitions were bound to be rejected, their half-hearted
attempt at something like a general strike, ill prepared and ill
supported, was a complete fiasco, and their threat of force such
as could be contained by the Government with the greatest of
ease. They could in fact do nothing, and their significance lies
not so much in what they did as what they were, and in what
they said; for what they said discloses what they were, the
symbol of the potential revolt of labour against the manufacturers which might make nonsense of the whole radical
pattern in which middle class and working class were supposed
to be allies.

Perhaps the best and most effective exposition of their
position was Fergus O'Connor's paper the *Northern Star*, which
in spite of the fact that it is too often the vehicle of O'Connor's
feuds was nevertheless a paper written with considerable ability.
As it appears in that paper the pattern is unmistakable. As
Chartism developed into a demand for revolutionary constitutional change it unavoidably forfeited all chance of a Tory
alliance, though there are obviously rather pathetic hopes in
that direction until Lord Ashley made it clear at the beginning
of 1842 that Peel would not support the Ten Hours Bill. But
the alliance with the Tories had always been adventitious,
significant as evidence that the old pattern had been discarded
but not necessary for the new pattern that took its place. What
was most significant in the new pattern was the conflict between
one section of the working class and the employers and capitalists and the middle class in general, certainly in the *Northern Star*
there was unceasing attack on the manufacturers, for whom the
singularly inelegant word 'millocrats' was coined, and on the

shopkeeping class, who were given the even uglier hybrid 'shopocrats'. The old accusation that the middle class in general and the shopkeepers in particular had betrayed the people at the time of the Reform Bill of 1832 was of course continually repeated, as was the accusation, which was probably more fair, that the shopocrats favoured the new Poor Law to keep down rates.

But the fiercest attack was reserved for the millocrats and their works. The people were continually warned not to be the catspaws of the Anti-Corn Law League. The object of the League was to repeal the Corn Laws in order to bring down wages. It was true that the repeal of the Corn Laws could be of advantage to the working class, but it would only be so if before repeal Britain had come under working-class control through the adoption of the People's Charter. Without that safeguard the operations of the Anti-Corn Law League would only, to repeat words used by O'Connor on this occasion, 'make the rich richer and the poor poorer'.[1] The extension of commerce on which the commercial classes set such store held out no hopes for the working classes; its agent was speculative capital developing more and ever more undertakings each with a larger mass of expensive machinery, and as a result there would be cut-throat competition, the continuous reduction of prices and of wages alike, and in the end the flooding of the markets with underpriced goods and ruin for all. What the Chartists desired was no doubt to return to a society of small masters and skilled craftsmen, or at least a stay to the development of large factories and high capitalism, a desire which was as impracticable as their proposal to plant out the surplus population in colonies of smallholdings on the land. But it did not matter what the Chartists proposed or desired—they would in their generation get nothing at all except hard knocks and prison sentences and scant sympathy; their significance was for future generations when the conflict which they revealed might alter the whole shape of British politics and perhaps of British life.[2]

---

[1] *Northern Star*, 19th February 1842. O'Connor's message

[2] For the relations between manufacturers and Chartists see *Chartist Studies*, ed. Asa Briggs (London 1959) particularly: I 'The Local Background of Chartism' (Asa Briggs), IX 'National Bearings' (Asa Briggs) and XI 'The Chartists and the Anti-Corn Law League' (Lucy Brown)

V

It was not, however, likely that either the class struggle or, for that matter, the battle for popular radicalism would decide the shape of politics in the early years of the Victorian interlude. After 1848 the pressures behind both of them died away, Chartism flickered out, the agitation for factory reform died down, it had gained something though what it had gained was neither satisfactory nor complete, and the attack on the new Poor Law largely ceased, though it is hard to see that that had gained anything at all. As conditions became easier, the tension between the middle class and the working class seems to have slackened and they appear to have learnt to co-operate and to live together in the great cities which they had formed.[1] Meanwhile popular radicalism was at a discount. When the Corn Laws were repealed the Anti-Corn Law League was dissolved and though John Bright was still anxious to lead the assault on the battlements of privilege he could never get enough determined followers to give him much chance to make an impression.

But, as has been suggested, it is wrong to believe that broken water and foam are the only signs that the river is running fast. In fact, the very prosperity that in the 'fifties and 'sixties damped down conflicts and removed pressures was probably producing such fundamental changes in the structure of society as would in due course make political and constitutional changes inevitable, changes which the old alarms and excursions had failed to effect. That prosperity affected a very large sector of the population. For instance, if the successive census figures mean anything, what might be called the lower middle class—the clerks, the shopkeepers, the minor officials—were growing in numbers, and there seems to be evidence that many of them were growing in prosperity and wealth as well. Unfortunately what happened to the wealth of the shopkeepers must remain a matter of speculation. The obvious source of evidence about the growth of incomes is the income tax returns, but it seems

[1] See Trygve R. Tholfsen *The Historical Journal*, iv 'The origins of the Birmingham Caucus', II, 2 (1959) pp. 161-84

to be impracticable to work out the size of individual incomes from the returns for Schedule D of the income tax—which relates to profits from business, etc.; however, the income tax returns seem to establish that there was a general increase in the number of those paying tax under Schedule E—that is in respect of office and employment—and a general progression up the ladder of income by the lower-salaried workers.[1] This evidence of increasing prosperity seems to be supported by the increased demands of consumers in different classes and also by the general growth of suburbs and the kind of houses erected in them in the third quarter of the century, which present a picture of fairly widely diffused solid comfort.

This general improvement was not confined to the kind of people you might find in suburbs, it extended to sections of the working class. Sir John Clapham gives as the general result of the statisticians' calculations the conclusion that real wages in 1850 bore to wages in 1874 the proportion of 100 to 156, though they fell in the years after 1874 which were years of depression.[2] This improvement was least marked among those who were already relatively well paid, like the old skilled working men, and was most marked among those who had left ill-paid employment, probably in many cases agricultural, and had entered other industries that were expanding. A comparison between the census of 1851 and that of 1881 suggests what was taking place. There had been a relative decline in the importance of textiles and in the old trades in consumer goods and a rise in heavy engineering metal work. There had been a decline in domestic work and an increase in factory work and in particular an increase in the number of women employed in factories. There had been an increase in the numbers engaged in transport and in coal-mining. In 1851 miners, seamen, railwaymen, carters, etc., numbered about half a million: in 1881 this group numbered about a million and a half.[3] In fact, the Industrial Revolution had developed and a larger section of the population had been sucked into industrial occupations.

[1] See J. C. Stamp *British Incomes and Property. The Application of Official Statistics to Economic Problems* (London 1916) Chap VI, pp. 170-262, Chap VII, pp. 263-73. And on p. 318 see Table G 4 for the taxable income in the country at different dates, and J. A. Banks *Prosperity and Parenthood* (London 1954) pp. 103-12 and p. 221 and *passim* for the increasing demands of consumers

[2] Clapham [op. cit. p. 115] 446-56

[3] Hobsbawm [loc. cit. p. 132] 213

Since the railways and the coal-mines were two of the great agents in this change, they had been sucked not only into the old larger cities but also into new populous areas, as for instance areas where coal-mining was being developed or relatively new towns coming into existence, like the railway towns of Crewe and Swindon.[1]

It seems possible that in this period fewer of these migrants had been drawn from Ireland. In 1871 the number of people living in England but born in Ireland was actually less than it had been in 1861, but there seems to be evidence that people were being drawn in considerable numbers from the English countryside, particularly from the deep countryside, those parts furthest from industry, a movement the railways may have facilitated. At first this does not seem to have meant an absolute decline in the numbers living in the country; indeed, Sir John Clapham points out that a careful enquiry in the 'eighties seemed to reveal the fact that between 1851 and 1881 in 15 of the most purely agricultural of counties there had only been a decline of 1 per cent. in the 'rural' population if one definition of the word 'rural' was used, or 2·1 per cent. if another was used.[2] What had probably happened was that at first before 1851 only the natural increase of the country population had been drained off. Then after 1851 this reduction in the increase was gradually converted into an absolute decrease of the numbers living in the country, which became steady after 1881.[3]

In fact, the force of the Industrial Revolution had altered the stratification of English society. Instead of there being this relatively empty gap between the relatively prosperous middle class and highly skilled artisans on the one hand and the large numbers of unskilled or semi-skilled labour on the other there was now more continuity in good fortune. The middle class were, it is true, larger in numbers and still more prosperous than ever before, but there was also much nearer to them a large body of what was technically semi-skilled labour drawing better wages than they had enjoyed in the first half of the century,

---

[1] T. A. Welton *Journal of the Royal Statistical Society*, 'Distribution of Population', Vol LXIII (1900) p. 527 ff. For Swindon see reference on p. 242 below

[2] Clapham *Free Trade and Steel*, p. 252

[3] T. A. Welton [loc. cit. p. 138] 538. See also J. Saville *Rural Depopulation in England and Wales 1851-1951* (London 1957)

indeed possibly very much better wages if they had been Irish immigrants or English agricultural labourers. This improvement had penetrated into the countryside itself, particularly perhaps where the railways had brought alternative employment and new ideas about life. Even the labourers still engaged in agriculture had enjoyed some improvement of their condition, if this had not gone very far and if it was in danger because of the dangers that were overshadowing British agriculture. It is probable that this change ought also to be attributed largely to industrialism, for it is interesting to speculate what the lot of the agricultural labourer might have been if there had been nothing beside agriculture to draw off his surplus numbers into the towns, or to give him alternative employment in the country.

It would, however, be as well not to exaggerate the well-being of any of the working classes at any point in this period. There remained much severe poverty; when Charles Booth came to work on the population of East London in the late 'eighties and 'nineties he apparently came to the conclusion that his three most depressed classes, the 'poor', the 'very poor' and the 'lowest', contained 30·7 per cent. of the whole population and 40 per cent. of the working class, and apparently estimates from other places yield much the same proportion.[1] Even when the mid-nineteenth-century working men and women were reasonably well paid they were living by a chasm into which any one of them might fall, into which many must fall in the end. As Sir John Clapham points out, a year of bad employment in the middle of the nineteenth century could be very hard indeed on large sections of the working classes; such a year was 1858, such were 1862 and 1863, the years of the cotton famine during the American Civil War; and apart from such general disasters there was always the possibility of the ordinary private disasters, illness, accident or bereavement, and for those who lived so long the certainty of old age. Many of the working class do not appear to have saved much, but to have spent up to the limits of their weekly income, as who shall blame them for doing so; at least that is the evidence of the accounts of the savings banks, in which it appears that domestic servants, and rather strangely agricultural labourers, managed to save

[1] Hobsbawm [loc. cit. p. 132], 214

much more than semi-skilled artisans who were getting better
money, but it is probable that against this must be put what
such people saved through friendly societies, and their Trade
Unions.[1] And at the bottom of the abyss lay the workhouse.
No doubt workhouses in the 'sixties and 'seventies were better
than the very terrible places that had existed in the early years
of the new Poor Law. In particular the treatment of the sick
poor had in many places improved after the activities in the
1860s of Mr Thomas Rathbone and the heroic sacrifice of Miss
Constance Jones in Liverpool, and the activities of Miss
Nightingale, Mr Villiers and Mr Farnall about the same time
in London; but even a well-administered late nineteenth-
century workhouse could be a very dreary and degrading place,
a cruel end for a hard-working and meritorious life, while the
stigma of pauperism was often felt very sharply indeed.

Even in their times of wealth and strength the lives of many
of the working classes still lacked much in dignity and amenity.
There was still a great deal of heavy drinking. In 1871, out of
397,495 summary convictions in England and Wales not quite
a third, that is 130,785, were for being drunk and disorderly.[2]
The streets could still be the scenes of brutal and unchecked
violence, as the Salvation Army found when it started operations in the 'eighties, and Rudyard Kipling as a young man in
1889-91 living in lodgings near St Clement Danes noted 'the
shifting shouting brotheldom' which filled the district from
there to Piccadilly every night at any time after 10.30 p.m.[3]
There was still much illiteracy in spite of all the efforts of all
the societies, and when a new industry like coal-mining extended itself into a rural district the standards of literacy seem to
have been reduced as it was in County Durham.[4] It is true that
the sanitary engineer and the administrator were in the 'seventies beginning to win their battles against both disease and
degradation in the great towns. But there was still a long way
to go; there were still very large slum areas, many authorities
had done singularly little to provide decent housing, and when
private enterprise had built new and sounder working-class

[1] H. Oliver Horne *A History of Savings Banks* (Oxford 1947) pp. 93-100 and
pp. 228-36. S. Smiles *Thrift* (London 1875) p. 130 and pp. 157-8
[2] Accounts and Papers 1871 LVIII p. 227
[3] R. Kipling *Something of Myself* (London 1937) p. 87
[4] Hobsbawm [loc. cit. p. 132] 238

houses, they were too often dull brick houses arranged in dreary row upon dreary row with their doors flush with the roadside in an atmosphere that carried enough dirt to daunt the most resolute of housewives.

Nevertheless, again it may be said that a corner had been turned. The working class was moving into a position in which it could compete as a class for its position in society, soberly and effectively, and not as a body of picturesque rebels to be pitifully defeated. The signs of the change are to be found in the development of those institutions which more than anything else have been the practical agents of the working-class challenge, the Trade Unions. As has been said, the first really practical Trade Unions were craft unions and normally relatively small affairs devoting themselves to wasteful internecine warfare with other unions. But from the beginning of the 'fifties some men saw the practical need for larger and more effective units. The first important step in this direction was taken, significantly enough, by the engineers, probably the most technologically advanced of all trades, who formed in 1851 under the guidance of William Allan the Amalgamated Society of Engineers. This was the amalgamation of 121 distinct societies and branches of unions connected with engineering. It began with about 12,000 members in 1851, rising to 33,000 members in 312 branches in 1868.[1] It was a portent of what was to come, and ten years later another very important amalgamation was built up with the advice of William Allan by another important Trade Union organiser Robert Applegarth, the Amalgamated Society of Carpenters and Joiners founded in 1861.[2]

Trade Union history is very complicated in these years, and one union never covers a whole industry; there were other reasonably strong engineering unions outside the A.S.E., and indeed a rival carpenters' union to compete with Applegarth. But there was a good deal of development going on, and in the late 'sixties and early 'seventies there were signs that Trade Union organization was spreading beyond the old aristocracy of labour. It was a symptom of the change that had been reflected in the improvement in wage rates and in the census, and as was to be expected is reflected in the development of

[1] Clapham *Free Trade and Steel*, pp. 159-60
[2] Clapham ibid., p. 157

Trade Unions among the miners and the railwaymen. Apparently there had been a good many attempts in the past to develop unions among coal-miners, but they had always failed; however, in the late 'sixties, largely under the inspiration of Alexander Macdonald, they began to succeed and it was claimed by that time that there were actually 200,000 miners 'in union'.[1] The claim is probably unjustified, and if that number was ever reached it was very soon lost. Indeed miners' unions still found it difficult to survive the storms that beat upon them; nevertheless, the miners and their unions remained important; indeed, in 1874 the miners supplied the two first Trade Unionist members of Parliament, Thomas Burt for Morpeth and Alexander Macdonald for Stafford. Meanwhile in 1871 there was founded the Amalgamated Society of Railway Servants, and in 1872 came perhaps the most interesting developments of all, the effective formation of Trade Unions among the agricultural workers.[2]

A new shape was forming in society. In the depressed and divided mass that had formed so much of the lower half of the section of the social life of England there was forming an organized and coherent body of workers, relatively prosperous, helping to form a body which was already an obviously important element in the State. In 1868 to advertise the position of this group the first Trade Union Congress was called together by the Manchester and Salford Council.[3] Between 1867 and 1869 the whole position of the Trade Unions in the State was in fact reviewed with the assistance of Trade Union officials, and in the 'seventies, after a certain hesitation, the Trade Unions appeared to have achieved what they wanted in the definition of their legal position, though in fact a dangerous pitfall had been, through inadvertence, allowed to remain, which was going to cause trouble later on.

Of course, if this was the politics of class conflict it was indeed something very different from the emotional desperate half-revolutionary agitation of the 'forties: so much the progress of Victorian England had ensured. Indeed, it is difficult to see it as the politics of the class struggle at all. The Trade Union

---

[1] Clapham ibid., p. 163
[2] See Rex C. Russell *The 'Revolt of the Field' in Lincolnshire* (Louth Lincs 1956)
[3] Clapham ibid., pp. 171-2

leaders at this time were often sober, practical men, in no way attracted by Utopian dreams; in politics they were normally Liberal or possibly in Lancashire Conservative, and would not have had any desire for a separate working-class party. It was their primary object to serve the interests of their members and to do so as far as possible without having recourse to strikes, which wasted the funds of their unions. Yet to understand what was moving in Britain it is necessary to recognize all this for what it was. It is the proper object of a Trade Union in any class of society to sell the services of its members at as high a value as it can, and it is the object of those who use those services to obtain them as cheaply as possible. The point was put with admirable simplicity by William Allan of the Amalgamated Society of Engineers to the Royal Commission on Trade Unions in 1867. 'It is in their interest', he said of the employers, 'to get the labour done at as low a rate as possible and it is ours to get as high rate of wages as possible.'[1] And that after all is the quintessence of the class struggle however soberly, practically and even amicably it is being carried on.

In fact, the class struggle was to have increasing importance in the next fifty years. The immediate future was, indeed, to be frustrating. In about 1873 the prosperity of Britain partially broke and with it the prosperity of the Trade Unions. In the late 'seventies and early 'eighties the movement was at a stay or in retrogression. But when it started again the situation had changed; not only the semi-skilled but the unskilled workers had come into the picture; there was more militancy, more conscious socialism, and men were moving towards the foundations of an independent labour party.

VI

The Labour party is, however, beyond my field of vision. Indeed, from the vantage point of 1875, or even of 1880, it would not have been possible to say with assurance that an independent Labour party would develop in the form that it

[1] Quoted from L. G. Johnson *The Social Evolution of Industrial Britain* (Liverpool 1959) p. 112. The whole of Chapters IV and V of this work are worth reading for an understanding of the working class at this period

did, much less that it would displace the Liberal party. Even if an increasing insistence on the politics of the class struggle was likely there could be no certainty that events would take the particular course that they did take, especially under the impact of the peculiar circumstances of the years 1914-18. And in the years between 1860 and 1880 the current of events seems to favour the dynamic development of popular Radicalism. The most formidable political fact at that moment was the progressive development of the national Liberal Federation with its headquarters at Birmingham and its natural leader Joseph Chamberlain. This was, indeed, the full flowering of popular Radicalism; at this time advanced Liberalism was prepared to accept the lead of manufacturers such as Chamberlain and Mundella and yet to be able to gain the alliance of important sections of the working class, for the first Trade Unionist members of Parliament entered the House of Commons under Liberal auspices. Capitalist, shopkeeper and working man could still unite in the same cause. There was to be a greater emphasis on social reform than there had been in the past, but the cause was fundamentally the same as that for which Radicals had struggled in the 'forties, certainly the enemy was the same, the 'titled and proprietary' classes against whom Bright had been fighting for twenty years.

Now, however, the battle promised greater hopes of success, and probably at least part of the reason for this was the greater diffusion of wealth through the country. The prosperity of the 'fifties and 'sixties had not only benefited sections of the working class, but to a much greater extent had enriched the various middle classes above them; the clerks, the shopkeepers, the business men and the directing and employing classes, all these had prospered and multiplied. The result was to facilitate changes which men had desired before 1850 but had not obtained. Before 1850 there had been the politics of distress and uncertainty, the difficulties of the late 'thirties and early 'forties had made many men very angry with the position claimed by the old governing classes; but their anger had effected little and then, after 1850, prosperity had developed to dull its edge and dissipate the attack. Now, however, the prosperity had worked its own changes, the numbers and wealth of those who were securely inside the old establishment had increased but the wealth and numbers who were not sure of their place in it had increased still more. Consequently it became difficult for the old privileged classes to retain their old position. The habits by which they had controlled the constituencies became increasingly inoperative, the leading positions which they claimed as their right began to be increasingly challenged, and new men or at least men using with new effect the appeal to the people began to emerge on the Liberal side of politics. In fact, the growth of the country under the continual influence of the blind forces of the increase of population and the Industrial Revolution had in the end created a country which could not be ruled in the old way.

To that development I must return later, but it is as well to make the point here that these political changes were not the only results of the greater diffusion of wealth, as for that matter the greater diffusion of wealth was not the only cause of these political changes. It is important to keep in mind the social as well as the political results of what was happening. The period from about 1860 onwards seems to have seen the gradual development of a popular culture for a large group in the lower half of society which was the result of the new conditions and may have served to replace what may have been lost through the increase of population, the folk wanderings and the growth of urban desolation. There was the development of county cricket and association football, in due course of professional association football as a spectacle, the progress of the brass band movement, the extension of Cook's Tours and development of the popular seaside resorts like Margate and Blackpool and above all things the development of the Music Hall which offered so important a commentary on late Victorian England.[1] A most significant development was the elimination of the second class on English railways and the admission of third-class passengers to all the amenities that the railways provided, or were about to provide—upholstered carriages, express trains, lavatories, corridor trains, refreshment cars, etc. This process started with the actions of the Midland Railway between 1872 and 1875; the other lines protested but had to

---

[1] See J. A. R. Pimlott *The Englishman's Holiday: a Social History* (London 1947). G. Green, J. R. Witty and H. V. Usill *The History of the Football Association* (London 1953). R. C. K. Ensor [op. cit. p. 130] 164-169. John Pudney *The Thomas Cook Story* (London 1953)

follow suit, and between 1880 and 1914 the Great Eastern managed to recover its finances by becoming deliberately and explicitly the 'Poor Man's line'.[1] For those who were slightly higher in the social scale the gain was greater. Some were assuming the trappings of gentility, others who could hardly be said to have reached that level seem to have been at least securing a standard of comfort to which the number of domestic servants in the census in 1871 or in 1881, and the kind of houses still to be seen in what were then the slightly better streets of English and Scottish towns alike seem to testify.

But the buildings in these streets seem to testify to something else. There are in them a surprising number of what are, or what once were, places of worship, and there have been more. Indeed, a student of this period will find it worth while to note any chapel, or church, in a street through which he passes, to note the date of the building or rebuilding, the denomination which it serves or has served and to try to see whether he can guess the social status of the group which built it and, or, worshipped in it. All this may tell him something about one of the important movements in nineteenth-century England, the revival of religion. This revival of religion was also to give its impetus to the political changes which took place after 1867; but it had wider results than that, and since it is important in its own right I will turn to it in the next chapter.

[1] On the change in the railways see J. Simmons *The Railways of Britain* (London 1961) pp. 25 and 26

CHAPTER VI

The Religion of the People

If Victorian England was subject to the blind forces of the increase in population and the Industrial Revolution and with them to the turbulent powerful political forces of the time, there was also another power at work in the country almost equally dynamic; it was the revival of religion. This also pervaded all society, challenged men and women of every level of society or of education and became fused with the objectives of most political parties and the hopes of every class. However, to understand its most extensive effects it is, I think, desirable to look at it from a rather different angle of vision from that which historians most often use. Since the religious history of the nineteenth century presents a series of extremely important and extremely interesting intellectual problems it is natural for historians to place those problems in the foreground and to consider most carefully the very remarkable men who became involved in them. But viewed from, so to speak, more nearly the ground level of the ordinary not very intelligent, not very erudite, human being the scene changes, the intellectual issues raised—the problems propounded by biblical criticism or the question of the whereabouts of authority in religion or even the challenge of evolution—fade into the background and other equally important problems take their place. From this angle perhaps the most interesting problems presented by the history of the Roman Catholic community in England in the middle of the nineteenth century are not those which start with the reception of John Henry Newman and develop through his relations with his fellow-convert Henry Manning, but those caused by the arrival in England of half a million destitute Irishmen. Or when considering another large section of the populace it is necessary to think of the years which followed 1859 not as years of an acute crisis of the mind but rather as the years of the great religious revivals among people who were probably little troubled by Darwinism and had certainly never read *Essays and Reviews*.

It is a whole nation that must be considered, and if we look at it from our chosen point of vantage it seems at first sight to be a very religious nation. These were indeed intelligent agnostics and for that matter militant atheists of the artisan or small shopkeeper class, and they caused considerable alarm, but after all they were the exception. The bulk of the nation still seems to be at least nominally Christian; it was dangerous to attack religion in public except before a highly educated audience. Much public discussion was religious, or at least pietistic, in tone, and popular literature and drama had a rather obtrusive, if sentimental, Christian background. The standard of church-going was high. It was this indeed that impressed the foreigner. A foreigner arriving, like Hippolyte Taine in 1862, would probably be impressed by the forest of masts in Liverpool, or in London river and he might be impressed, alas, by the sordidness and the drunken women, the evident poverty and misery, in the streets behind the water front. 'I have seen', said Taine of Shadwell, 'the lowest quarters of Marseilles, Antwerp and Paris: they come nowhere near this.'[1] But sooner or later he would come into conflict with the English Sunday in a large city with the bells mercilessly calling, all forms of reasonable recreation forbidden and myriads of sober-faced men and women with children in tow pouring into church, chapel or conventicle of every style, size or religious variety.[2] Not everyone appears to have found this an attractive or pleasant experience, but it seems to have been impressive. Here was a nation at prayer on the one day which intervened between weeks of what was for many people almost unremitting toil.

In fact, it was normally not as much as half a nation in prayer. That fact was proved by one of the most remarkable documents of the nineteenth century, the religious census of 1851. On Sunday, 30th March 1851, the worshippers were counted at each of the services morning, afternoon and evening by whoever was in charge, if he were willing to do so, in every church or chapel in the land. From these figures an estimate

[1] H. Taine *Notes on England*, translated with an Introduction by Edward Hyams (London 1957) p. 29
[2] Taine [op. cit. p. 148] 8-13

was made to make allowance for those who had attended twice, or three times, and a total was made to compare with the number of the whole population. As a result it was calculated that whereas the population of England and Wales was in 1851 17,927,609, only 7,261,032 had attended some service. Of course, there were obviously those who could not have gone to church, the sick the very young and those who had to tend them, those employed in public transport and other necessary services; but even when allowance was made for all these it was concluded that there still remained 5,288,294 who could have gone to church and had not done so. The reliability of the census was attacked, and the figures were attacked; indeed it is as well to remember that in part they do rely on estimated uncertainties. Nevertheless, it seems reasonable to accept the census as on the whole a reliable guide to the religious condition of the country at the half century.[1]

The result was profoundly shocking to contemporaries, to realize how shocking it was it is necessary to remember how generally it was assumed that at least one visit to some place of worship every Sunday was the normal custom of anyone who claimed to be a respectable Christian. Nowadays the number of those who actually attended some service that Sunday would seem to be remarkable, but then it was otherwise and contemporary instinct was right to be shocked. There were many things which kept the poor out of service. For many there was no church or chapel within reasonable distance for them to attend, in many cases no doubt these were deterred by the appropriation of pews in church or chapel, or they found the atmosphere repellent, or the state of their clothes forbade them to come, which seems to have been a very real source of trouble. But in very many cases the master reason seems to have been this: many people had had no religious instruction at all and had had no contact with any Christian body.[2]

---

[1] Census of Great Britain 1851. Religious Worship England and Wales. *Parl. Papers 1852-3* LXXXIX. On the method of taking the census see K. S. Inglis *The Journal of Ecclesiastical History*, 'Patterns of Religious Worship in 1851', Vol XI, No. 1 (April 1960) pp. 74-86. This also contains a valuable appraisal of the results

[2] On some or the obstacles which prevented working-class people from going to church or chapel see Asa Briggs [op. cit. p. 28] 465-8. He cites an unpublished doctoral thesis by Mr K. S. Inglis on the 'English Churches and the Working Classes' which I have not yet read

This disclosure was not novel. Public enquiry among factory children had shown that the only knowledge of Christianity which many a child possessed was a horrific mixed hash of misapplied holy names. Serious reviews had uttered solemn warnings about the state of the cities and the 'vast multitudes, ignorant and excitable in themselves and rendered still more so by oppression or neglect' who had been 'surrendered, almost without a struggle, to the experimental philosophy of infidels and democrats'.[1] Many of the clergy had realized with distress the immensity and impossibility of their responsibilities: 'When, then, in 1842 I was instituted to the cure of the souls of the parishioners of S. George's, East, as Rector, the number of such souls nominally entrusted to my charge was about 38,000.'[2] Many Nonconformists seem to have been conscious of the large areas of heathendom all round them; indeed the condition of the great towns, particularly of London, was patent to anyone who walked their streets and was not blind and deaf. 'In no foreign city are such scenes to be witnessed as every night disgrace the principal thoroughfares of London. To whatever extent vice may prevail in other countries it does not there obtrude itself as with us.'[3] That is a clergyman in a note to a sermon on the need for Church extension preached rather later in the century, but that there is every reason to believe that things were quite as bad and quite as obtrusive at any earlier period.

But though men had known the lesson which the religious census taught for some time before it happened, yet it seems clear that the figures of the census gave the lesson a new force, a new particularity and a new certainty. Indeed, it may seem to us to raise an important question. England has always claimed to be a Christian country; the phrase is of course ambiguous, it might mean a variety of things, but there is one rather obvious meaning which might be appropriate to it. A Christian country might mean a country of at least nominal Christians. If that is so, however, it is not clear how far the title

[1] *Quarterly Review* No. CXXXIII (1840). The writer was Lord Ashley, afterward the 7th Earl of Shaftesbury

[2] The Rev. C. F. Lowder *Twenty One Years in S. George's Mission*, p. 226, the Rev. Bryan King to Lowder, 1877

[3] The Rev. J. Sandford, D.D. *The Mission and Extension of the Church at Home*, *Bampton Lectures, 1861* (London 1862) p. 226

might rightly be claimed by a country in which there were a number of people with no contact with any Christian Church and no knowledge of the rudiments of the Christian faith.

II

This was, however, not the only issue which the census raised. Of those who did go to service, the proportion of those who attended the services of the Church of England to those who went elsewhere was calculated to be in the proportion of 52 to 48. It was this fact which caused the most bitter controversy, since the Dissenters declared that a Church which could only manage to attract a little more than half of those who went to church had no right to claim to be the Church of the nation and the Churchmen answered sharply, among other things impugning the accuracy and fairness of the figures. It was not a very fruitful controversy, but it was true that without doubt something of what had been wrong in the nation in the past had been due to the failures of the Church of England, and much that was bitter and harsh in mid-century was caused by the truceless war between the Church of England and Dissent.

It would be harsh to impute the blame to one generation of Churchmen. Upon few institutions in the country had the course of history worked so much harm as upon the Church of England. Ecclesiastical appointments had suffered, as had all other appointments, from the low view which in the late seventeenth and the early eighteenth century most men had taken of all patronage and from the exploitation of all appointments, if politicians could get their hands upon them, to meet the ever-present demands of electioneering. But the abuse of Church patronage was not confined to party politicians and did not start with Parliamentary politics. Church patronage was being exploited to meet the needs of the well connected and of people useful to government right back into the Middle Ages; and in the English Church medieval abuses were peculiarly likely to survive, for, though in the sixteenth century the English Church had been reformed in liturgy and doctrine, administratively her institutions had been left very much as they were. They had not been recast as much as they would have been if they had fallen into the hands of the continental reformers or come under the decrees of the Council of Trent, and this naturally facilitated the survival well into the early nineteenth century of such ancient abuses as clerical absenteeism and its companion vice, the holding of livings in plurality.

Indeed, the figures in the second quarter of the nineteenth century are sufficiently startling. In 1827, of 10,500 beneficed clergy about 4,500 were absent from one living which they held; by 1838, of 10,570 clergy about 3,100 were absent; in 1842, of 11,000 about 2,700; by 1848 the number of absentees had been reduced to about 2,000.[1] In the eighteenth century and before where the incumbent had been absent the duty had been done by the neighbouring clergy, by a curate who came into the parish to do duty, or by a resident curate. Two Acts of 1813 and 1817 enforced the duty of maintaining a curate, and in a parish whose value was over £300 a resident curate; they also tried to secure that except in poor parishes a curate was paid a minimum salary of £80 a year.[2] But it remained a constant struggle to secure that all curates were in fact paid a reasonable stipend, and even where a resident curate was appointed it still very often meant that most of the money provided for the endowment of the parish was being spent elsewhere.[3] In mitigation of this situation it should be remembered that there were no clerical pensions or provision for sickness and therefore if an incumbent became too old or ill to serve his parish the only thing he could do short of resigning his living and facing penury was to get leave of absence. But it was palpably true that many of the absentees were not notably old, or in any way ill. They were absent because they preferred to live in some watering place in England, or in Italy, or in the South of France, or because they held another living elsewhere. In 1831, for instance, 2,268 clergymen held two or more livings; in fact, of these, 352 held three livings, 57 held four and 3 held five.[4] It was sometimes said that pluralities were necessary because some livings were so small that they had had to be

[1] Figures supplied to me by Dr G. F. A. Best, who is soon to publish a history of the Ecclesiastical Commission

[2] 53 Geo. III, c. 149, and 57 Geo. III, c. 99 (clauses XLVIII onwards)

[3] For a valuable study of the problems of non-residence, pluralism and the provision of curates as they affected one group of clergy see Diana McClatchey *Oxfordshire Clergy 1777-1869* (Oxford 1960) pp. 13-79

[4] Figures communicated by Dr Best

combined with others in order to yield an income on which a man might live. This was probably true in some cases, but not in all. In those days, when a curate or a dissenting minister could be expected to live on £80 a year or sometimes less, £200 a year could be considered to be a reasonable income. Of these 2,268 pluralists, 643 held livings each of which was over £200 per annum and 711 held two, one of which was over £200.[1]

These practices had flourished from time out of mind. Indeed, it would hardly be possible to name a century when it had not been considered that one of the natural uses of the endowments of the Church was to maintain a number of gentlemen in the condition to which they were accustomed, which obviously would be denied to them if they had to live in places where no gentleman could be expected to live, or on one meagre endowment. However, in the increasingly harsh light of the nineteenth-century conscience the genial tolerant mist which had cloaked these practices began to dissipate. From the beginning of Victoria's reign effective legislation was passed against them,[2] and the episcopal jurisdiction became more and more unsympathetic. In what was really a remarkably short time a considerable change seems to have been effected. In 1854 Selwyn, who had been Bishop of New Zealand, when preaching at Cambridge was able to say, 'a great and visible change has taken place in the thirteen years since I left England. It is now a very rare thing to see a careless clergyman, a neglected parish or a desecrated church.' He was specially thankful for the multiplication of schools and for the more religious character of the universities and public schools: he even thought the Cathedral system was putting forth signs of life which would of course surprise everyone.[3] There is evidence to bear him out, at least as far as the country districts are concerned. For instance, Bishop Wilberforce's visitation returns for the Archdeaconry of Oxford for 1854 seem to demonstrate both the activity and

---

[1] Figures communicated by Dr Best

[2] The effective Acts seem to be, against non-residence, 1 and 2 Vict., c. 106, and against pluralities 13 and 14 Vict., c. 98. See Sir Robert Phillimore, D.C.L. *The Ecclesiastical Law of the Church of England* (London 1873) Vol 2, p. 1149 ff. and 1170 ff.

[3] The Rev. G. A. Selwyn, D.D. *The Work of Christ in the World, Four sermons preached before the University of Cambridge on the four Sundays preceding Advent in the year of Our Lord 1854* (Cambridge 1855) p. 7

the relatively small number of absentees by that time.[1] This must have made a considerable difference to the countryside; indeed, there is evidence of this from Dissenters who did not entirely relish the change. Even so, it clearly took a considerable time to deal with all the absentees, particularly when the episcopal administration was perhaps less ardent or more old fashioned than that of Wilberforce. William Thomson became Archbishop of York in 1862 and he found that when he visited the diocese of York there were still 47 non-resident incumbents, 22 on grounds of ill-health, 18 because they held another living, 7 for other reasons. Some of the non-residents had been absent from very important posts, for instance the Vicar of Hull had been absent for fifty years and at Middlesborough the incumbent of St Hilda's never resided.[2]

These, however, were not the only results of the fact that the machinery of the Church of England had not been recast since the Middle Ages. As a medieval institution the Church was in many ways a network of rights, privileges, traditional duties, with, normally, circumscribed powers for its officers who had often to act judicially rather than by direct administrative act. This had some of the advantages which such medieval freedom often confers. The security of the parson's freehold could protect the intellectual independence and so the moral integrity of the incumbent against the tyrannies of party rule and spiritual bigotry in high places; unfortunately it could also protect sloth, incapacity, eccentricity to the point of madness, an immoderate addiction to foxhunting or liquor, in fact almost anything except open immorality, complete neglect of duty or absence without leave; and where there was a possible case against an incumbent the proceedings could be expensive and uncertain. Nor was much that the law secured of any possible spiritual value. Many of the personal rights and privileges in the network were no more than an incumbrance to the work of the Church; in fact in many cases they were the private property of irrelevant laymen, like lay rectors, lay patrons of livings or lay owners of the pews which often cluttered up the whole floor of the church squeezing the poor to the sides or the back and even

[1] Transcribed and edited by E. P. Baker (1954) *Oxfordshire Record Society*, Vols 35-37
[2] H. Kirk-Smith *William Thomson, Archbishop of York, his Life and times 1819-90* (London 1958) p. 17 ff.

insolently spanning the chancel arch. More than this, so rigid was the constitution of the Church that until 1818 it was very difficult to do what it was urgently necessary to do if the Church was to deploy its powers to serve the new swarming population, that is to create new parishes out of the division of parishes far too large ever to be worked properly. There was no ordinary legal provision for the division of parishes before 1818. Before 1818 a new parish had to be formed by Act of Parliament which could be opposed by those who thought their rights to fees and dues were impaired. Indeed, so great were the resistant powers of vested interests that as long ago as 1710 and 1711 an attempt to provide adequately for the more crowded parts of London had been to all intents and purposes thwarted. Under the Queen Anne's Bounty Act it was possible to turn curacies into perpetual curacies, and it had been possible to make chapels of ease. Even so, it was always open to the tithe owners, patrons or incumbents of any living that might be affected to obstruct the foundation of any chapel that might infringe on the monetary returns that they might expect to gain from their parish. Such opposition could be successful, while the immense complication of the law which was developed to reconcile the needs of Church extension with existing private rights shows how extensive and various were the obstacles to any advance.[1]

Yet advance there had to be; men had realized that fact from long before the religious census had pointed to the danger and disgrace of the situation, and something had been done. From early in the century the Evangelicals had begun to revolutionize Church life in particular parishes, and to consolidate their position by the purchase of livings. On the other wing Joshua Watson and what was called the 'Hackney phalanx', pre-tractarian High Churchmen, became active. In 1811 they helped to found the National Society for providing Church Education, in 1818 the incorporated Church building society came into existence and in 1818 Parliament was persuaded to hand £1,000,000 over to the Church Commissioners to build churches in populous districts. This was the beginning of the flood of money to be poured into church building, at the same

[1] On the difficulties of building a chapel for the Church of England see A. B. Webster *Joshua Watson, the story of a layman* (London 1954) pp. 59-60. On the legal position see Phillimore [op. cit. p. 153] Vol 2. pp. 2167-88

time some £200,000 had been privately subscribed, and in 1824 Parliament was persuaded to add another £500,000 to what they had already granted.[1] Apart from the money it granted, the Act of 1818 is very important because it began that alteration of the law which facilitated the creation of new livings. But unfortunately in its nature and provisions the Act of 1818 looks back as well as forward. Its authors clearly conceived that the ministers of the new churches could largely be paid out of pew rents, and only provided that not less than a fifth part of all sittings should be set aside as free seats for the poor;[2] and it was an Act which could only have been passed in the days of the Church of England's unchallenged security. At no moment after 1832 would it have been possible to use a grant from the national exchequer for Church extension, though ardent Churchmen refused for a long time to learn that lesson. However, the Church had large endowments which it could redeploy, and in 1835 by instituting the Ecclesiastical Commission Sir Robert Peel began the very important process by which this redeployment could be taken in hand and the Church gradually re-fashioned till it was much more nearly able to meet the pressures and demands of nineteenth-century England.

The actual legislation by which the delayed reformation of the Church of England was partially affected was passed by his Whig successors in office between 1836 and 1840, but the initiative had been that of Peel. In 1841 he became Prime Minister again and in 1843 he put through another important measure to further the spiritual care of populous districts, which proved to be of peculiar importance because it made possible the creation of Ecclesiastical districts and the appointment and endowment of a clergyman to serve them before the expense and elaboration of building a parish church in them had been attempted.[3] Indeed, it is an arguable proposition that if any one man saved the Church of England it was Sir Robert Peel. His was the initiative in the most important legislation; as Prime Minister he followed Lord Liverpool in making much more responsible use of ecclesiastical patronage and he gave freely from his own large fortune for Church extension. The

---

[1] Webster [op. cit. p. 155] 64
[2] See 58 Geo. III, c. 45 clauses LXXV and LXXVII
[3] 6 and 7 Vict., c. 37, clause ix

point is important for the light it throws on the moral forces at work in the country. The salvation of the Church is often put down exclusively to either the Evangelicals or to those inspired by the Oxford Movement or to both seriatim. Peel was of neither party. To the evangelical Lord Ashley he seemed hard and cold and worldly, while he seems to have found the high Church principles of his favourite political pupil W. E. Gladstone mainly unintelligible. Indeed, in many ways the motives which prompted him to do what he did do might seem to the ecclesiastically minded to be strangely secular.

In fact, at first sight he seems normally to be no more than a secular statesman responding to the exigencies of politics, or a Conservative affected by the fears of the time. In 1835 he launched the Ecclesiastical Commission because the attacks upon the Church had made it clear to him that it could no longer be defended when it contained such outrageous anomalies and did its work in many cases so ill. The legislation of 1843 was directly inspired by the Chartist disturbance of 1842. It would be easy to caricature Peel's motives in both cases and to say that in 1835 he only abolished abuses because they could no longer be maintained, and that in 1843 all that he wished to do was to use religion as an opiate to prevent severely wronged men from demanding their rights. To anyone who has bothered to read Peel's letters it must be clear that neither diagnosis is just. If in 1835 his attention had been called to the state of the Church by the sharp attacks upon it, it is clear that as he studied the matter he became consumed with anger at the abuses he saw, and inspired by a great desire to ensure that an institution which he revered should serve the purposes for which it was intended. In 1843 his feelings were probably deeper and more poignant. He had been Prime Minister through the terrible winter of 1841-42. He knew what men had suffered and, this is quite clear in his letters, the thought had bit deep. It is quite true that he had feared what might happen, but it is also true that a much stronger feeling was distress at what human beings were going through and a great desire to help, mixed with the ugly feeling that there was little he could do. In the Act of 1843 he was not just trying to give the poor what he believed would make them more disposed to orderly conduct, but also what would make for their best happiness. His motives were the same as when he tried to give them cheap bread; only the other was, if he had risked so emotional and revealing a phrase, the bread of life.

It is desirable to make this point because many of the ruling classes seem to have been undergoing something of the same spiritual development. Peel was unusually intelligent, unusually sensitive and, beneath a very formal façade, unusually passionate. But in the minds of much duller men a like change was taking place. How much it was caused by the fear of revolution, how much by the need to answer the insolent attacks of radicals, how much by that mysterious factor the atmosphere of the time, it would be impossible to say; but certainly through all the governing classes, who had in the past lived comfortably off the old abuses without a thought to disturb them at night, there was a readiness to accept or even to initiate reform, and it was to be found among men and women who were by no means strict Evangelicals and did not draw their inspiration from Oxford. If it had not been so, the reform of the Church in the middle of the century would not have been so relatively thorough and so unexpectedly quick, and the Church would not have rallied so effectively from the attacks made upon it at the time of the Reform Bill.

That rally was, however, the last thing which many Englishmen desired, what they had wanted was not the reform but the extinction of the Church, at least as an establishment. Part of the unfortunate legacy of the past was the hatred entertained for the Church of England by many of those who dissented from it. If hatred in ecclesiastical matters can be justified this would seem to be justified, justified by the remaining disabilities which Dissenters still had to suffer, and justified by the general social pressures which Dissenters had suffered from the oppressive weight of the classes that made up the establishment.

Probably these pressures were heaviest and hardest to bear in the countryside. In the countryside the Church of England was largely the instrument of the rule of the gentry, the farmers and others such as lawyers associated with them. The Dissenters made up the natural opposition to them. They can probably be divided into two groups. There seem to have been knots of Dissenters with a longish tradition behind them often enough associated with an old chapel of seventeenth-century foundation, often independent or congregationalist. These groups merit further investigation, but I believe that in many cases they will be found to be associated with a group of freeholders or men whose tenure rendered them immune from interference by landlords or with a country village large enough to be a small town and perhaps support some industry. In addition there seem to have been in the early nineteenth century wandering Methodists whose appeal was very often to the farm labourers. They were often disliked and persecuted by the authorities, for they were often rude and unlettered men and it was felt to be impudent and wrong for such men to undertake religious instruction, and they were suspected, probably without much reason, of being Jacobins. It was these men who felt most heavily the weight of the Conventicle Act and the Act which replaced it, and the laws which prevented men preaching without a licence or preaching in the streets or public places.[1] But it is likely that even well-established or respectable Dissenters in the country districts felt the weight of the Church and the gentry to be pretty heavy upon them; but till 1880 or thereabouts there was very little that they could do.

In the towns things were different. In the eighteenth-century towns there seems often to have been a local ruling aristocracy normally associated with the parish church, and well represented on the local bench of magistrates. The members of this aristocracy do not always seem to have been very exalted in station or very different in manner of life and education from many of those who were not members of it and were possibly attached to an old-established Dissenting chapel. Such a chapel had often in the seventeenth century been Presbyterian but had turned Unitarian in the eighteenth century, and in the nineteenth century in provincial cities the aristocracy of Dissent was often Unitarian, or possibly Quaker. There were, however, other traditions. The strongest *political* tradition seems often to have been among the Congregationalists, who by their own account were often shopkeepers; in the background there were congregations with a much humbler background like the grim little congregation of weavers among whom Silas Marner

---

[1] 52 Geo. III, c. 155. H. B. Kendall, B.A. *History of the Primitive Methodist Church* (London 1919) (revised ed.), on p. 62 reports that there were 30 cases of arrest among Primitive Methodists in the period ending 1843

passed his youth, or the group of whom the wife of Mr Weller Senior was a distinguished member; while after 1800, if not before, the towns were being invaded by Methodists of various brands. If, however, at the head of urban society there might be no great social distinction between Church and Dissent, the political division was likely to be marked. For the operation of the Corporation and Test Acts excluded Dissenters from many offices in the town and very often the nature of the constitution of the borough emphasized the position by confining power to a small self-perpetuating oligarchy, who were necessarily Church of England.

The historians of English borough government are of opinion that in many places these local groups served the places they governed reasonably well according to their lights, which may not have always been very good ones but were not outrageous according to the general standards of the eighteenth century. At the end of that century, however, trouble started. During the panic produced by the French Revolution and the social troubles that followed the wars the local oligarchies—Corporations, Clergy and the local magistrates—seem at times to have lost their heads and acts were done or permitted—like the burning of Priestley's house and laboratory, the prosecution of James Montgomery, or the activities of the local magistrates and yeomanry in St Peter's Fields, Manchester, on 16th August 1819—which caused bitter resentment at the time among those who suffered or were in danger of suffering from them and were not forgotten by them when their opportunity came.

After 1819 that opportunity was approaching rather quickly. No doubt there were many reasons why these urban oppositions were increasing in strength in the 'twenties. The Industrial Revolution was increasing power and wealth in new hands, the Evangelical revival was increasing the number of Dissenters, the swing towards liberalism inclined men's minds to enquire what the city fathers were up to, how ancient charities were being administered and what was spent in dinners. But it is not necessary here to decide which causes were the operative ones, suffice it to say that in not a few towns by the middle of the 'twenties the pressure on the old oligarchies was increasing, and under pressure some of them began to do silly things to defend themselves, as when in 1826 both in Leicester and Northampton they used the corporate sources to finance Tory candidates.[1] This in the circumstances made things worse, and in 1828 came the first of a series of events by which the position of the old groups was finally lost. In 1828 the Test and Corporation Acts were repealed, in 1832 the first Reform Act was passed which took from the old closed corporations their political power and confirmed in power a House of Commons and a government inimical to the old local oligarchies; therefore in 1835 the English Municipal Corporation Act was passed and in most places the opposition came into office, and then, to fill the cup of bitterness to the brim, Lord John Russell began to fill the local magistrates' benches with Liberals and Dissenters. Many steady people were not in the least surprised when during the Chartist troubles of 1842 some of these radical magistrates seemed not to be able, or not to want, to protect the public.

It was in fact a real revolution in the social background of government, much more complete than anything which the Reform Bill had achieved in the membership of the House of Commons. Its extent can be suggested by the number of Unitarian mayors who achieved office after the Municipal Reform Act of 1835, for after that Act the first mayor of Manchester, the third mayor of Liverpool, the first mayors of Leicester, the first mayor of Derby, the second mayor of Leeds and the third mayor of Birmingham were all Unitarians; but the list could be extended by including not only mayors but councillors and aldermen and not only Unitarians but Independents, Baptists and members of the Church of England who were not in accord with the old oligarchy.[2] In many cases it was a lasting victory, but it did not normally mean that the remnants of the old oligarchy had been destroyed. In Leicester, for instance, they continued the battle with great bitterness using

---

[1] A. Temple Patterson, M.A. *Radical Leicester* (1954) pp. 146-164, for Northampton see Owen Chadwick *Victorian Miniature* (London 1960) p. 17. I have no doubt there are other examples

[2] R. V. Holt *The Unitarian Contribution to Social Progress in England* (London 1938); Temple Patterson [op. cit. p. 161] 214-21. The 42 councillors elected in Leicester in 1836 together with the 14 aldermen were distributed as follows: 16 Churchmen, 12 Unitarians, 12 Baptists, 10 Independents, 3 Quakers, 2 Wesleyans and 1 Huntingdonian, only 4 were Conservatives. The whole matter requires further research particularly perhaps into the part played by the Congregationalists and the Baptists. The first mayor in Leeds, Sir George Goodman, was a Baptist, the ruling denomination in Manchester seems to have been Congregationalist rather than Unitarian

the weapon of Church rates to castigate their opponents. As a result a Congregationalist draper named William Baines was cast into prison for refusing to pay Church Rates, and as a sequel his friend and pastor E. T. Miall started a campaign for the disestablishment of the Church of England which in due course played an important part in national politics.[1]

This counter-attack in Leicester was almost certainly purely factious and without doubt there were all over England groups of disappointed Tories who were anxious to get their own back for the reverses of 1836. But in the last years there was a revival of Church of England activity and influence which had more respectable objectives. For instance, both in Manchester and Liverpool evangelical clergymen made successful attacks on secularized education which shewed sincerity and zeal even if the results were unfortunate. Under a rather better inspiration first in the West Riding and then in Lancashire a large number of the parish clergy supported the agitation in favour of the factory children.[2] This last movement was in fact completely, or almost completely, non-political, and indeed several of their allies were in fact radicals, but a political motive was suspected. In fact, by the second quarter of the nineteenth century religion had received so political a shape, or politics so religious a shape, that it was for many people almost impossible to separate the two. They became obsessed by this quarrel between Church and Dissent, and referred everything back to it. For instance, when the Conservatives won the general election of 1841 one of the reasons given for their victory by that leading Liberal newspaper, the *Leeds Mercury*, was the recovery of the Church of England, though in fact Church issues had not noticeably played much part in the election.[3] On the other hand, many deeply religious people found it difficult to think of a direct moral issue like factory reform, or education, without bringing it into the terms of this unhappy quarrel and the politics which sprang from it. It was therefore to be expected that when the

[1] Temple Patterson [op. cit. p. 161] 247-55
[2] On education in Liverpool see James Murphy *The Religious Problem in English Education* (Liverpool 1959) and G. R. Balleine *A History of the Evangelical Party in the Church of England* (London (new ed.) 1933) pp. 200-5. On the activities of the clergy on the question of the factory children see J. C. Gill *The Ten Hours Parson, Christian social action in the eighteen-thirties* (London 1959). It is hoped that Mr J. T. Ward will produce a comprehensive study of this problem
[3] *Leeds Mercury*, 24th July 1841

returns of the religious census became available men should scan them eagerly to see how far they substantiated the claims of either party.

III

It would, however, do mid-nineteenth-century opinion an injustice to suggest that they only read the religious census to see how many people went to church and how many to chapel, most of them seem to have known well enough what was the most serious issue that the religious census raised. It was the problem of what Bishop Selwyn called in 1854, 'the dark masses of our uninstructed people'. How vast those masses were the census had not only suggested by recording the numbers who did not go to church, it had also suggested where they were and who they were. The worst proportionate attendance at church was in Bethnal Green, where of a population of 90,193 only 6,024 attended service, but there were bad spots elsewhere and in the industrial areas north of a line between Gloucester and Grimsby only 6 out of 37 towns contrived to reach the national average of a 58 percentage of church attendance.[1] In fact, the most obvious absentees were the urban working class, particularly in those great conurbations into which the great human tides of the early nineteenth century had carried them.

In spite of this it would be a mistake to think of the absentees as a uniform group, presenting a single problem. In fact, they were very diverse, their problem was complex, and different observers saw different parts of it. For instance much attention has been paid to the review of the whole matter by the Congregationalists in 1848 and to their confession that they did not seem to be able to attract the working class.[2] 'Why', asked Mr Wells, one of the ministers whose task it was to report on the matter, 'do our new built chapels gather congregations of tradesmen, but never of artificers?', and he gave a number of very interesting and carefully analysed answers, the gist of which was that the atmosphere of Congregational chapels had become too essentially middle class, and also too polemical on the political issues which specially interested the Congregationalists.

---

[1] For comparison of the figures see K. S. Inglis [loc. cit. p. 149]
[2] *Congregational Year Book*, 1848, p. 83 ff.

It was a problem that continued to trouble the Congregationalists, in 1853 they are still recording the fact that 'it with
us is a matter of deep regret, and not less of astonishment . . .
that the artisans and working men of England are so rarely
drawn within our circles',[1] and they had considered the matter
in the intervening years. They seem to have been reasonably
clear about the kind of people whom they had in mind. They
were, so Mr Wells said, 'great readers', but would not read
Congregational literature. They were class conscious, they
were anxious to gain the franchise and they were inclined to be
atheists. 'Apart from the religious portion, our population
generally may be divided into two classes mainly. The one
consisting of those who are given up to low sensual indulgence,
the other, of those marked by a sceptical activity of mind,
disposed to question everything. A spirit of infidelity is observ-
able, strongly working in the undercurrent of society, and
festering in the workshops of our operatives.'[2]

Altogether the picture of the working men the Congregationalists appear to have had mainly in view is not that of
people who were spiritually and intellectually destitute, nor
probably at the bottom of the economic scale. They were not
only literate, they must have been capable of appreciating a
reasonably advanced argument, for their infidelity must have
derived from Holyoake or Bradlaugh, or the other secularists;
there was, it is true, a cruder atheism to which the blasphemous
orators in the parks seem to have appealed, but it does not
sound as if the Congregationalists were referring to people who
indulged in that, for they make no reference to direct blasphemy
or obscenity.[3] They also had a clear idea of their position in
society, and knew what they wanted. In fact, it seems clear that
the Congregationalists were referring to a section of society
familiar to contemporaries under the name of 'intelligent
artisans'. It is really a cultural group which should not be
defined in terms of economic status or function, though in the
middle of the century it was probably mainly recruited from

[1] *Congregational Year Book*, 1853, p. 85

[2] *Congregational Year Book*, 1851, p. 11

[3] For a short discussion of working-class secularism see the Rev. Adam Storey
Farrar, M.A. *A Critical History of Free Thought in reference to the Christian Religion*,
Bampton Lectures 1862 (London 1862) pp. 440-2. Possibly the references in the
notes to this passage are more valuable than the text though the epitome is not
unfairly done

the craftsmen or skilled workmen. It was an important section of society and it was to grow in importance as wealth, stability, education and social consciousness extended among the working classes. From it were to come the early Trade Union leaders and the pioneers of the Labour party.

If, however, this diagnosis is correct, either a change must have taken place by the time the Labour party was formed, or the Congregationalists must have been mistaken about the extent of working-class atheism, or irreligion. When the pioneers of the Labour party emerged, they were most of them Christians and often lay preachers in some Nonconformist chapel, often one of the Methodist chapels. In 1929 information was collected about the religious beliefs of 249 Labour members of Parliament, and among them apparently only 8 confessed to be atheists.[1] This is perhaps no very conclusive argument, a man may for political purpose accept a religious label which does not mean much to him, but it is supported by the known personal histories of a large number of Trade Union leaders and Labour members of Parliament, and for very many of them the starting-point seems to have been the chapel and not the teaching of the secularists.

Moreover, there were already in existence when the Congregationalists were analysing the situation some fairly large groups of Christians in this class for whom their picture makes no allowance, groups such as the Primitive Methodists which was largely a working-class body and various congregations of Baptists; and there were the Irish.

Perhaps the Irish generally were lower in the social scale than these others, certainly they increased the number of absentees from church on census Sunday. As has been said, the census in 1851 recorded the fact that at the time 519,959 living in England had been born in Ireland. It has been estimated that of these 75 per cent. were Roman Catholics, and that adding Irishmen of the second generation and native Roman Catholics the whole Roman Catholic population in England at that moment was 679,067.[2] Yet on census Sunday, only 252,783 Roman Catholics attended Mass. But the reason for this

---

[1] Quoted in E. J. Hobsbawm *Primitive Rebels* (Manchester 1959) pp. 141-2. The whole chapter 'The Labour Sects' pp. 126-49 is important

[2] These are the estimates of Fr Philip Hughes from his article on 'The English Catholics in 1850' in *The English Catholics 1850-1950*, ed. by G. A. Beck, A.A., co-adjutor Bishop of Brentwood (London 1950) pp. 42-85, esp. p. 45

deficiency seems fairly clear. There was nowhere for them to go; as it was, the number of those who attended greatly exceeded the number of sittings provided, which was the opposite to the situation in most large communions,[1] but for many Roman Catholics there can have been no church and no priest within any reasonable distance, for it is recorded in *The Catholic Directory* for 1851 that there were as yet only 597 Roman Catholic churches and 826 Roman Catholic priests in England and Wales.[2]

Most of the Irish in 1851 were probably desperately poor, but many of them lived together in rather closely settled communities and it was going to prove to be possible to recover very many of them for their Church, though it was no doubt to require heroic efforts to do so in a Church in which the hierarchy had only just been established and in which in many districts there were relatively few wealthy people—twenty-five years later than 1851 it was said that in the populous bishopric of Salford there was no Roman Catholic wealthy enough to keep a carriage.[3] Obviously they constituted a distinct group in the block of working classes different in many ways from the rest. No doubt there were other distinct groups as well. But outside and beyond all these there was obviously a large mass of people with no clear opinions, whom the tides of the nineteenth century had carried far from any religious teaching or observance with which they, or their parents, or their grandparents might at some time have had contact. They were not intelligent artisans, they were not Roman Catholics, they were not atheists unless to have no coherent creed and to use crude blasphemies whose words mean nothing to you is atheism; in fact, what went on in their minds probably ought not to be included in an account of coherent opinions.

It was this group who provided in all probability many of the people who were in the words of the Congregationalists 'given up to low sensual indulgence', or in other descriptions to 'mere animalism'. Since 'mere animalism' is a moral condition it might be found, indeed it is clear it could be found, in every class; but it was likely that 'mere animalism' would become more pervasive as the ties of respectability or tradition

---

[1] Only 186,111 sittings were available. [2] *The Catholic Directory*, 1851, pp. 106-8
[3] *English Catholics 1850-1950* [op. cit. p. 165] 63

got less strong, conditions harder, and there was less to illuminate and instruct the intelligence. The section of society in which these conditions were likely to predominate probably stretched in mid century from the borders of the skilled workers and reasonably successful craftsmen out into the darkness. In this section there would be semi-skilled and the unskilled workers and their families, there would be skilled workers who had fallen on evil days either through age, or illness, or drink, or because their trade had failed them. There would be the casual workers, dock hands, longshoremen and lightermen and the people in sweated trades. There would be the flotsam and jetsam of society, the people with no trades or with very odd ones such as many of the people whom Mayhew interviewed. There would be wretched women in the streets whose misery and numbers appalled observers like Taine, and there would be the brothel keepers and public house keepers who preyed on the sailors at the ports and presumably many of the sailors on whom they had preyed.

Some of the more wretched sections of society can be seen in the records of people like the ritualist slum parsons of the 'fifties, or of missions such as that which turned into the Salvation Army. Indeed, Christian missionaries of a good many styles of Christianity had very great success in the desolate areas in which many of these people lived, but there is always the sense that there were more people beyond in the shadows with whom no contact had ever been made.

IV

This situation challenged all religious denominations alike, and all responded to it alike.[1] But the nature of the response in each denomination necessarily differed with the peculiarities of its position. The Church of England had the greatest resources, it had also the burden and the privilege of almost unlimited direct responsibilities. It suffered from the intense hostility, sometimes deserved sometimes malevolent, of those outside it

[1] E. R. Wickham *Church and People in an Industrial City* (London 1957) gives a most interesting account of the history of the various religious bodies in Sheffield in the nineteenth century, which should be studied by any concerned in the problems discussed here. It is very desirable that other local studies of the same sort should be produced

and the very sharp divisions of its members within, divisions which grew almost to hysteria when the ritualist developments began after about 1850. It was still hampered by its clumsy constitution; but with certain outrageous exceptions the evils of non-residence and plurality had by the mid-century been mastered and the general standard of attendance to duty on the part of the parochial clergy was very much higher than it had probably been for centuries. Two ancient abuses remained. One was the appropriation of the Church into private pews. Many of the clergy expended a great deal of time and energy fighting this, but they were not only hampered by the tenacity of the pew holders but by the fact that the endowment of the clergy was in certain cases supposed to come from pew rents, as in the case of the churches built under the Act of 1818. Moreover, it has to be remembered that the system was one to which most people were accustomed, it prevailed in very many Nonconformist chapels, and many of the working class when they came to church were apparently anxious for an appropriated seat and would pay a small rent for one or tip the verger to get a free seat kept for them. The other ancient abuse was the continued existence of parishes so large that no clergyman could work them properly.

These parishes were naturally at their worst in those areas into which the tide of humanity had flowed with greatest volume, such as London and the industrial districts. It was reported in 1860 that in three Metropolitan parishes there was a population of more than 35,000 persons, in four more a population which exceeded 30,000, in five more one which exceeded 25,000, and so on.[1] But conditions in London were equalled and indeed surpassed in the crowded North. In Bradford the situation was made worse by the extent to which private pew holders had contrived to appropriate for their own use the space of the parish church. The result was fantastic. In Bradford the population connected with the parish church was reckoned as being 78,332, the accommodation available for them there was about 1,400 sittings, of these, however, only 200 were free, others however had been freed by the action of

---

[1] *The Times*, 16th April 1860, quoted in Sandford [op. cit. p. 150] 344. For the most comprehensive information on this subject see the report of a select committee of the House of Lords of July 1858. 'On the means of Divine Worship in populous Districts' *Parl. Papers 1857-8*, Vol IX.

the Vicar and Church wardens.[1] There were also three school-rooms licensed for service. Possibly Bradford was the most extra-vagant case, but there were also very bad conditions elsewhere, as in some notorious cases in Manchester and Liverpool.[2]

Strenuous efforts had been made since the beginning of the century to remedy this situation. There had been the two Parliamentary grants and much money had been raised by voluntary subscription. In 1858, in fact, it was asserted that during the last half-century 3,150 churches had been built at the expense of £11,000,000 raised by voluntary subscription.[3] Later, in 1876, it was recorded, in a return to Parliament of the number of churches built or restored since 1840, that 7,144 churches had been restored and 1,727 new churches had been built and that the amount of money spent on the restoration of churches and cathedrals and the building of churches had been £25,548,703. Not all of this was voluntarily subscribed, part of the money came from the Ecclesiastical Commissioners, the Church Commissions or was raised on the security of Church rates; but in fact the amount received from these sources was much less than that voluntarily subscribed, for instance the amount spent in the diocese of London was £2,708,613, of which £2,536,629 was subscribed from private sources.[4] In fact, it seems probable that the figure for the build-ing of churches is an underestimate, as is probably the figure given for the number of new churches.[5]

---

[1] House of Lords Select Committee 1858 [op. cit. p. 168] 417, evidence of the Rev. Dr Burnet

[2] For Liverpool see House of Lords Select Committee 1858 [op. cit. p. 168], evidence of A. S. Tomlin, p. 397 ff.

[3] House of Lords Select Committee 1858 [op. cit. p. 168] 14-15, evidence of W. Cotton, Esq.

[4] 'Returns [for House of Commons] showing the number of churches (including cathedrals) in every diocese in England, which have been built or restored at a cost exceeding £500 since the year 1840.' *Parl. Papers 1876*, Vol LVIII, pp. 553-658

[5] The following figures have been communicated to me by Dr Best. They are only approximate, but they are of interest:

[a] Parishes divided and Districts assigned to Churches, etc.
   (i) by Church building Commissioners 1818-1856 . . . 1,077
   (ii) by Ecclesiastical Commissioners 1856 to Autumn 1861 . . 235
   (iii) by Ecclesiastical Commissioners under Peel and Blandford's
        Act 1843-60 283
[b] New Parishes and Districts set up by Ecclesiastical Commissioners probably with a new Church
   (i) Autumn 1861—Autumn 1866 397
   (ii)   „   1866   „   1868 174
   (iii)   „   1868   „   1880 744

Churches are, however, no great use without clergy; to serve these new parishes a greater number of clergy was necessary. It was therefore a matter of importance that the numbers of the clergy of the Church of England went up from 17,320 in the 1851 census to 19,198 in the 1861 census and 21,663 in 1881. This, however, in itself created additional needs. It was no longer considered that a general degree course at Oxford or Cambridge was all that a clergyman needed and bishops began to require a specialized training in a theological college as well. To meet this need no less than 8 theological colleges were founded between 1836 and 1876. More than this, if the clergyman was to be used as a curate, or was to serve a new parish without ancient endowment or an old one with too minute an endowment, further funds must be found to support him, for in the church building figures no money had been allowed for endowment at all. In the middle of the century in all probability the problem was a peculiarly difficult one, since the clergyman in a poor parish was not now normally able to supplement his income by serving as a schoolmaster in a grammar school or taking service in a neighbouring parish. It was important to reduce the extent to which the clergy must depend upon pew rents, and the incumbents of certain city churches had lost what had been a fairly considerable source of revenue in burial fees by reason of the closing of their churchyards for sanitary reasons. Much of the money to supply these needs had to be raised by public subscription, and though in one way or another the sums raised were very large, it must be feared that some of the clergy made but a poor living of it.[1]

---

[1] Stanley Leighton, M.P., speaking in the Church Congress at Manchester claimed that between 1860 and 1885 the Church of England had collected in voluntary contributions for various purposes 80½ million pounds, distributed as follows (in round figures):

(1) building, restoring and endowing Churches	. . .	£35,000,000
(2) home missions		7,000,000
(3) foreign missions		10,000,000
(4) elementary schools and training colleges .	. .	21,000,000
(5) Church institutions (Literary) . . .	. .	1,000,000
(6) Church institutions (Charitable) . . .	. .	4,000,000
(7) Clergy charities	.	2,000,000
(8) Theological schools	. .	500,000

£80,500,000

See *Official Report of the Church Congress* (London 1888) p. 544. I owe this reference to Dr Best

This is an impressive record, it shows how much of the energy and money of mid-nineteenth-century England was being poured into the recovery of the Church, and there are other things which might be added to it, as for instance the creation of two new Bishoprics, Manchester and Ripon. But there is no reason to believe that it is any more impressive than the record of the Nonconformists. In fact, they were apt to claim with some vehemence that their record was the more impressive. It was pointed out that already according to the census of 1851 the Church of England supplied only 52 per cent. of the places available for those who wished to attend service, the situation being peculiarly serious in Lancashire, in Yorkshire and in Wales, and that the Dissenting position had largely been achieved since 1800, since when it was calculated that the Anglicans had added 2,698 places of worship with 1,028,032 sittings while those who were not Anglicans had produced 16,689 new places of worship with 4,013,408 sittings.[1] Since the Anglicans' problems were very different from those of the Nonconformists, and in any case they had to occupy themselves so much with making better use of existing accommodation, these comparisons on which so much temper was expended at the time are not probably very significant. What is much more important is the very remarkable advance which the Protestant Dissenters had made since 1800; perhaps particularly significant were the figures of the Congregationalists or Independents who increased the number of their chapels from 914 in 1801 to 3,244 in 1851 and their sittings from 299,792 to 1,067,760, of the Baptists who had increased their chapels from 652 in 1801 to 2,789 in 1851 and their sittings from 176,692 to 752,343, and above all of Methodists of the old connection, that is the parent body from which other dissident Wesleyan Methodist bodies broke off in the eighteenth and nineteenth centuries, who had increased their chapels from 825 in 1801 to 11,007 in 1851 and their sittings from 165,000 to 2,194,298.[2]

A tremendous effort had been made to supply church room

---

[1] E. Halévy *A History of the English People 1841-1852. The Age of Peel and Cobden*, trans. E. I. Watkin (London 1947), pp. 340-1, using the results of the religious census of 1851 [op. cit. p. 149] 233-4

[2] *Religious Census 1851* [op. cit. p. 149] CXLIV, Table 17. It seems likely that these figures contain considerable inaccuracies, but they probably give a reasonably satisfactory idea of the general position

for the population even before 1851, and it did not stop then. The Congregationalists set themselves with renewed vigour to chapel building and by 1857 their three chapel building societies had created 365 new chapels.[1] The Baptist chapels in the Baptist Union, which was probably considerably less than the whole number of Baptist chapels, increased from 1,929 in 1851 to 2,602 in 1871.[2] The Methodists of the old connexion were passing through particular difficulties immediately after 1850, but some of the derivative bodies were making remarkable progress, for instance the Bible Christians erected 300 new chapels in fourteen years, 1850-64,[3] while that very remarkable communion the Primitive Methodists, who did not start till 1810, had by 1850 1,555 connexional chapels and by 1871 had 3,585.[4] Meanwhile the Roman Catholics had increased from 826 priests in England and Wales and 597 churches to 1,599 clergy in 1872 and 1,005 public churches, chapels and stations, which did not include private chapels but did include about 700 churches which were registered for marriages.[5]

These figures should be considered together as making up the sum of a very remarkable achievement on the part of the nation in the middle of the nineteenth century, an achievement the remains and memories of which exist on all sides today. Today these remains often appear as dingy buildings in rather deplorable Gothic whose general air of desolation may well suggest a dwindling and ageing congregation, or which have in fact been alienated to secular uses, and it is easy to forget the faith and hope and indeed the initiative and money which they represented when they were erected. Yet they are the results of an effort which probably commanded more of the disinterested enthusiasm of Victorian Englishmen in all districts and

---

[1] A. Peel, M.A., Litt.D., B.Litt. *These Hundred Years. A History of the Congregational Union of England and Wales 1831-1931* (London 1931) p. 215

[2] E. A. Payne *The Baptist Union, a short history* (London 1959) p. 267 (Appendix IV). Care should be taken in dealing with Baptist figures to discriminate between new churches and churches already in existence but joining the Union for the first time

[3] *A New History of Methodism*, edited by W. J. Townsend, D.D., H. B. Workman, M.A., D.Litt., George Eayrs, F. R. Hist. Soc. (London 1909) Vol I, p. 543

[4] J. Petty *The History of the Primitive Methodist Connexion from its origin to the conference of 1860* (London ed. 1864) pp. 542-3. Statistics of the connexion from 1850-1860 and *Primitive Methodist Magazine* (August 1871) Vol IX (New Series) p. 503.

[5] *The Catholic Directory*, 1851, pp. 106-8. *The Catholic Directory*, 1872, p. 298. Unfortunately there seems to have been some uncertainty as to what to enumerate as Roman Catholic churches

classes than any other of the achievements of the reign. As was inevitable, what was done by the different Churches were used for polemical comparisons. Such a comparison to the disadvantage of the Church of England, and to do them justice of themselves, seems to have been at least part of the object of a very interesting calculation produced by the Congregationalists in their year book of 1881. This showed the proportionate increase in the accommodation provided by the various leading denominations in certain towns in Lancashire between 1851 and 1880, and established the fact that the Church of England had increased the accommodation it offered by a smaller proportion than had any other denomination. The criticism is not in fact very damaging. The return also showed that the Church of England also at the beginning of the period already provided more accommodation than any other religious body, and that in the period in question it had been able to make the largest absolute increase in the accommodation it offered. Indeed, the real lesson of the return would seem to be that in this third quarter of the century the Church of England was at the least holding its own.[1] This seems to be confirmed by other reports, and in the provision of schools it had easily outstripped its rivals.

The general lines of the history of the Church of England's educational activities can perhaps be best followed in the history of the National Society, though that in fact does not cover all the Church Education that was being given. The history of the National Society before the Education Act of 1870 falls naturally into three periods. In the first 22 years from its foundation in 1811 to 1833 there was as yet no public grant for education, in that period the Society established 6,000 to 7,000 schools with half a million children in them. Between 1833 and

---

[1] *Congregational Year Book*, 1881, p. 157. The information came from Manchester, Salford, Liverpool, Bolton, Rochdale, Oldham, Warrington and St Helens. The figures given for the Church of England are that it provided 133,351 in 1851 and in 1880 185,630 sittings, an increase of 39 per cent. The nearest figures in point of size are those of the Wesleyans, who provided 34,851 sittings in these towns in 1851 as compared to 64,488 in 1880, an increase of 85 per cent. The largest proportionate increase is that of the Baptists, 14,108 sittings in 1851 to 29,080, an increase of 106 per cent.; the next largest is that of the Roman Catholics, 25,860 sittings in 1851 to 48,798 in 1880, an increase of 90 per cent. There is of course, nothing to show in any case how often the sittings were occupied. It is interesting to compare the information given in this return with the general picture in Wickham [op. cit. p. 167]

1846 a grant towards the building of schools could be earned, but not for maintenance, and in that period the Society was educating one million day scholars in 17,000 day schools. In the third period which starts in 1846 and ends in 1870 the Government supplied grants towards building and towards maintenance, in that period there was a slowing down in the increase of the number of schools and of the children educated though there was probably an improvement in the education provided, as well there might be. Nevertheless, in 1867 on the eve of the Education Act of 1870 the Church day schools had about a million and a half children on their books with, in addition, 4,000 night schools containing 150,000 scholars.[1]

It is true that even in the last period the education provided was probably not very good. It should perhaps be remembered that probably the Commission of 1858 to 1861 on education, from whose report many accounts of the standard of mid-nineteenth century derive immediately or remotely was probably steered by men in some ways hostile to the system, and its conclusions were sharply attacked by the man who had best reason to know what was happening.[2] Still there is enough evidence to show that standards were unsatisfactory. It is also true that the gross number of children attending was unsatisfactory and that attendance was often very irregular for education was not yet compulsory. Nor was the education provided free. In the assisted schools one-quarter of the annual cost came from the Government grants, from a quarter to a third from endowments and subscriptions, the rest being derived from the fees of the children, which could be greatly reduced in the case of poverty.[3] It is also true that owing to the activities of Archdeacon Denison, and the weakness of the committee of the National Society, a most unfortunately rigid attitude was adopted about the exemption of the children of Dissenters from denominational teaching. Yet when all this has been taken into

[1] H. J. Burgess *Enterprise in Education: the Story of the work of the Established Church in the Education of the people prior to 1870* (London 1958) pp. 210 ff.

[2] Report of the Commissioners appointed to enquire into the state of popular education in England, *Parl. Papers 1861*, Vol XXI ff. Evidence. A useful summary of many of the findings of the Commission is in A. Lawrence Lowell *The Government of England* (London 1908) Vol II, pp. 300-1. For criticism of the report see Sir James Kay-Shuttleworth *Four Periods of Public Education* (London 1862) pp. 555-638

[3] Lowell [op. cit. p. 174] Vol II, p. 301, citing *Report of Commissioners 1861* [op. cit. p. 174] Pt I, pp. 68, 71, 73, 77-8

account it is as well to remember that what had been provided had been provided as the result of very considerable voluntary effort, particularly on the part of the parish clergy, who supplied a very large part of the revenue and a great deal of the work involved in maintaining the schools. They often exercised a general oversight over the schools and sometimes taught in them themselves with the help of their wives and daughters.[1]

What the Church of England had done for education was greater than anything accomplished by the Dissenters. The Commission of 1858 to 1861 found that at the time of their report the Church of England possessed about nine-tenths of the elementary schools in the country with three-quarters of the children, the Roman Catholics about $5\frac{1}{2}$ per cent., the Wesleyans 4 per cent. and the Congregationalists 2 per cent.[2] This difference is sometimes explained by the fact that the Church of England contained the wealthiest classes and, so it is said, its members were in a better position to subscribe money to earn grants which were available to all. There is probably some truth in this, but it is unlikely to be the whole truth. No doubt the classes which were well represented in the Church of England still controlled a large share of its wealth, but by 1858 the Industrial Revolution had been going on for some time and so had the increase in the numbers of Dissenters, an increase which had by no means only been among the poorest in the land. Certainly by the middle of the century a good many Dissenters were clearly comfortably off while some Dissenters had made very considerable fortunes, and if this difference in achievement had only been the result of differences in wealth, then there was no reason why it should have been so wide. Moreover, in fact, a great deal of the money which had been used to build and staff elementary schools had not come from the superfluity of landowners but from the pockets of the clergy often at the cost of severe self-sacrifice. It would be difficult to deny that a good many dissenting shopkeepers and manufacturers could have subscribed the same amounts more easily.

The explanation, however, probably lay in a difference of

[1] *Report of Commissioners 1861* [op. cit. p. 174] Pt II, pp. 72-5
[2] Lowell [op. cit. p. 174] II, p. 300, quoting *Report of Commissioners 1861* [op. cit. p. 174] Pt I, pp. 55 and 80. For the situation on the eve of the Education Act see *Report of the Committee of Council on Education 1869-70, Parl. Papers 1870*, XXII (c. 165) appendix

values and principles rather than one of wealth. Many Dissenters retained into the third quarter of the nineteenth century a conscientious scruple against accepting money from the Government for education, since they believed, for good reasons, that education was one of those things which Government should not control.[1] For this reason many of them devoted such money as they gave to education to schools which did not apply for a Government grant, though it would seem that even among those schools that had received no grant the Church of England also had a marked preponderance.[2] What, however, does seem to be likely is that the exuberant energy of the Dissenters, which is not really in question, went into other activities than the provision of day schools, activities such as chapel building, the development of Sunday Schools, Home Missions and Adult Education. It is also not to be forgotten that probably the most effective adult education a young intelligent man of the working or lower class could receive was to become a member of, and possibly a lay preacher in, a Dissenting congregation.

V

These polemical comparisons are, however, as I have suggested, little more than an historical nuisance; since they normally can only be made by omitting on either side considerations which are germane to the case they are seldom of much significance and they are apt to divert attention from more important matters. In this case surely the most important point is the immensity of the effort made in the middle of the century by religious Englishmen from every Church, Dissenting Protestant, Roman Catholic and Church of England, to evangelize and civilize those who seemed to have been deprived of the Christian message by the growth of the population, by the results of the wandering of the people or the failures of the previous centuries.

But there is another issue to be considered. Much of this work was without doubt done under the impulse of a strong

---

[1] See G. Kitson Clark *The English Inheritance* (London 1950) pp. 117-19 and pp. 135-7

[2] See speech of Lord Robert Montagu in House of Commons 17th February 1870, *Hansard* Vol CXCIX (3rd Series) 471

sense, of social responsibility and at the promptings of an unquiet conscience, and the sequel was to show that neither of these agents by itself sufficed to do anything significant. It proved to be only too easy to build churches in crowded districts to which no one came for priests to live devoted lives among indifferent masses, for schools to be founded to which the children would not or could not come, or where they learnt little except to dislike the institution by which the school had been founded. In fact, something had to be added to the conscientious virtues; and what was needed was fire, fire which would not only burn in those who despatched the mission, or in the missionary, but would cross the gap and blaze among those to whom the mission was sent. And in many cases fire was granted.

Where it came from is probably too difficult and too profound a question to be more than touched upon here. I have mentioned before the existence of a common ground between romanticism and the revival in religion. It would not be very easy to say what that common ground was. It would indeed be a profoundly difficult task to diagnose what were the forces which disposed many men in the late eighteenth and early nineteenth century to believe in those truths which were taught by imagination or intuition instead of confining themselves to what seemed to be authenticated by the limited process of calculation which men had called 'reason', to be impressed by the validity and significance of what addressed itself to the passions, and to be attracted by the appeal to history from the dullness and materialism of their contemporary scene, or rather by the appeal to a dream of history, very often a dream of the Middle Ages. But whatever the source of these tendencies it is clear that they could easily be converted into religious terms. The belief in the significance of intuition has its obvious parallel in the substitution of inner conviction as the foundation for Christian belief in the place of such intellectual calculations as the argument from design; the sense of the significance of the emotions in secular matters has its natural counterpart in the desire for a vital religion as against the cold practice of morality, and the attraction of the Middle Ages could be very easily converted to a desire to express Christian feeling through the architecture, the ritual and in some cases the institutions of what were held to have been the ages of faith.

The tendencies of the times seem to have predisposed the minds of men in this direction, and the fashions of the times provided instruments by which those tendencies could be exploited. This was particularly true of the techniques they provided to give force to the appeal to emotion. To understand how broad the effect of this was it is necessary to realize that as well as the great romantic artists and writers there was a multitude which no man could number of lesser romantic poets, lesser romantic musicians, playwrights and novelists. Few trouble about them today, but when they wrote they could move the hearts of men, particularly of simple relatively uncritical men. Indeed, they were the better able to deploy all their powers for this task since they were often not much hampered by the trammels of good taste or of common sense. This popular romanticism had its counterpart in the world of religion. The furious rhetoric which the romantic playwright produced and in which the romantic actor indulged had its counterpart in the new style of preaching which developed in the train of the Evangelical revival. The innumerable poets whose work filled the bookshops, and with a still more terrible fecundity the columns of the magazines, had their counterpart in the writers of hymns whose name was legion; it was calculated in 1880 that in the previous fifty years the Church of England alone had produced above an average of one hymnal a year,[1] but that number is probably a gross underestimate. In fact many of the lesser romantic poets of the first half of the century wrote hymns also, hymns were often their best work since their hymns often had behind them a depth of feeling and a reality of experience which their secular work did not often possess. At the same time contemporary musical developments, particularly in Germany, inspired composers and Church musicians to fit tunes and accompaniments to the hymns which, whatever we may think of their taste today, commended them in the nineteenth century straight to the hearts of men and women.[2]

These tendencies and fashions naturally extended far beyond the bounds of what can with any exactness be called the

---

[1] W. K. Lowther Clarke *A Hundred Years of Hymns Ancient and Modern* (London 1960) p. 18 (quotation from the *Literary Churchman*)

[2] I have tried to develop these ideas in an article called 'The Romantic Element —1830 to 1850' in *Studies in Social History*, ed. J. H. Plumb (London 1955) pp. 211-239

Evangelical revival. Indeed, the variety of the people who were inspired by them can be best realized by studying the great variety of contributors to that very remarkable nineteenth-century instrument of worship, 'Hymns Ancient and Modern', published for the first time in 1860.[1] The work of most of the nineteenth-century writers and translators does in fact reveal marked similarities, so marked that different religious groups could with ease, though not always with due acknowledgements, use each other's hymns. But the sources of inspiration of the various writers are very different. In some cases it was simply what may be called direct evangelical experience, in others the inspiration was at least in part historical and sprang from a desire to make available the treasures of Latin, and rather less often Greek, hymnology to contemporary Englishmen. These two apparently contrasting sources have their counterpart in the two great revivals of the nineteenth century, the Evangelical and the Catholic, which helped the recovery of the Roman Catholic Church and also was apparent in the activities of the ritualists in the Church of England; both were agents of power in moulding Victorian England.

If he is to realize the significance of such evidence as this an historian must first accomplish for himself two difficult tasks; he must silence the promptings of good taste or at least of our contemporary taste. Much that men relished in the middle of the nineteenth century will seem to him to be tasteless, often mawkish, sometimes meaningless, normally absurd, but this must not lead him to believe that it was unimportant if it meant something that was of vital significance to contemporary men and women. His other task is to discriminate between what was the mere adaptation of a fashion or the copying of a useful practice and what was the use of a form which had very profound implications for those who had originated it or were employing it. For instance in the middle of the nineteenth century, most unfortunately, the builders of Dissenting chapels started to build in the Gothic manner. What prompted them to do this was probably a general instinct that this was the right style for ecclesiastical buildings, but it must have been

[1] See *Hymns Ancient and Modern: Historical Edition*, London, 1909, pp. 805-43 and introduction, and also Lowther Clarke, passim, [op. cit. p. 178] and Louis E. Benson *The English Hymn its Development and Use* (New York 1915) Chaps VII, IX and X

very largely an architect's or contractor's fashion and cannot have carried the deep significance which the adoption of Gothic had for Pugin and indeed for some of the Anglican builders.[1] Conversely, it seems probable that many of those who used Evangelical hymns neither had shared the experience, nor would have accepted the doctrine of their authors. For instance, it may be questioned whether the very large number of people who have gained solace from 'Rock of Ages' have all of them accepted the uncompromising Calvinism which the words enforce; and there was a very favourite hymn, 'Nearer My God to Thee', which was written by a Unitarian and which was actually altered by some of those who used it so as to bear a more definitely Christological meaning.

What was borrowed without much reference to the beliefs of its originator did not necessarily lack meaning or life for the borrower. On the whole it seems probable that what did most to reform the ordinary service in the Church of England was the influence, at one remove, of movements which many of the clergy wished to keep at arm's length. At the beginning of the nineteenth century such reform was certainly necessary. Before 1820 it was doubtful whether in fact it was legal to use any hymns that had no direct scriptural basis, and what was normally employed in the service were the rather grotesque 'singing psalms', sometimes sung in a very odd way indeed. At the beginning of the century the sermons delivered in the Church of England seem normally to have been read, too often inaudibly, often with no other movement or gesture than was necessary to turn over the pages except apparently that sometimes the hand was raised, waved and then allowed to fall back on to the edge of the pulpit.[2] The practice continued into the nineteenth century, Blomfield who was Bishop of London till 1856 was said to have never, save on one memorable occasion, preached an unwritten sermon, which was the more strange because he was known to be a ready debater in the House of Lords.[3] The introduction of hymns, the introduction of a freer more energetic style of preaching must have made a very considerable difference to the life and warmth of the services

[1] On this see Martin S. Briggs *Puritan Architecture* (London 1946)
[2] Sandford [op. cit. p. 150] note 64, pp. 292-4
[3] R. T. Davidson *Life of Archibald Campbell Tait* (London 1891) Vol I, p. 251

of the Church of England; and it seems probable that the example of the Methodist revival was responsible for both. On the other hand there was much sometimes rather surreptitious borrowing from the other side. A large majority of the clergy rejected the practices of the ritualists; nevertheless, all through the second half of the nineteenth century there appears to have been a fairly continuous adoption in Churches of all schools of a more seemly, indeed a more elaborate, ceremonial than what had been normal. Probably something was lost in this in the sacrifice of the old raucous village orchestras and choirs, who definitely produced the music of the people, in favour of an organ and a certain number of boys and men in surplices which had a dangerous tendency towards gentility. But most of those who have felt this loss most sharply did in fact never hear the old choirs and orchestras, and if the general descriptions of dreariness and slovenliness of the services of the Church of England at the beginning of the century bear any relation to truth then the general improvement effected must have been very great indeed.

Nevertheless, what was going to move the people, what was going to penetrate to the savagery and ignorance of the neglected and indifferent, was not likely to be what could be discreetly borrowed in a modified form by men who did not fully share the enthusiasms of its originators. The mass of the people would in all probability only be moved by men imbued with strong missionary zeal who would act in ways that were profoundly shocking to men not equally inspired. This fact was evident in the history of the Methodists in the eighteenth century. The issue between the early Methodists and the main body of the Church of England partly turned on the not unimportant point of the discipline of the parochial system which the Methodists tended to disregard, it was partly inflamed by the ancient quarrel between the zealous and the indolent and the worldly, but it was also partly caused by a not unreasonable dislike of Methodist techniques and the hysteria which resulted from them, sometimes accompanied by violent physical symptoms. Yet it is difficult to see that the Methodists could have done what they did unless they had used the power which those techniques produced. In its eighteenth-century phase, however, the Evangelical movement was to a large extent kept under control by the native common sense and moderation of John Wesley, who disliked the physical symptoms and did not encourage them, and by the educated good taste which is evident in the hymns that he and his brother produced. Yet there is evidence enough from the record of John Wesley's own meetings to show how powerful were the forces that he was using.

But the missionary impetus which the Wesleys and Whitefield had given to Protestant Christianity did not cease with their deaths, and as men became accustomed to religious excitement and revivals they began to systematize the lessons of their experience, so that there developed what might be called a science of revivalism with a literature of its own. This was most effectively developed in the United States, and it was from the United States that from time to time a new impulse towards revivalism, or new revivalists, emerged to quicken the pace in England and to add new skills to those already at work there. For instance Hugh Bourne, one of the two founders of the Primitive Methodists, seems to have drawn on the experience of the American evangelist Lorenzo Dow in the development of the first 'Camp Meeting' in England on top of Mow Cop in Staffordshire in May 1807.[1] Much later the impulse which started the great revivals in 1859 came from the revivals which had taken place in America in 1857 and 1858.[2] In 1867 an American evangelist Payson Hammond developed in England a special type of mission to children and from this sprang the Children's Special Services and the Seaside Services at watering places which, largely in the hands of the Evangelicals in the Church of England, had curiously effective results. But the most remarkable direct incursion was in the 'seventies. In 1873 Dwight L. Moody and Ira D. Sankey, both from the United States, paid their first visit to England.[3] Their success is the more noticeable because they do not seem to have much used the fear of hell, which had been an important part of the stock in trade of earlier evangelists, and the components which they used seem to have been comparatively simple, not very elaborate oratory on the part of Moody and simple tunes sung

[1] See W. J. Townsend, D.D., etc. *A New History of Methodism* [op. cit. p. 172] Vol I, pp. 423-4

[2] J. Edwin Orr, M.A., Th.D., D.Phil. *The Second Evangelical Awakening in Britain* (London 1949) pp. 13-37

[3] G. B. Balleine [op. cit. p. 162], pp. 248 ff.

to an harmonium by Sankey. It is, however, clear from the accounts of their meetings that the skill that they had developed, particularly the skill they had developed in combining singing and speaking, was of a very high order.[1]

All this was palpably sincere and palpably single minded in inspiration; but there was always the possibility of tension between the advanced revivalists and those who did not like their methods. It developed among the Methodists over the Camp Meeting on Mow Cop in 1807. The Methodists of the old connexion were not prepared to permit another Camp Meeting, and therefore in 1810 and 1811 those who wished to use such methods split off and became another body called the Primitive Methodists. This split is extremely significant because the leaders of the Primitive Methodists were working men and their Church became to a large extent a working-class Church. It is indeed possible that the occasion of the split was significant, that in fact it was natural for working-class leaders to feel that for the people they wished to evangelize an exuberant evangelistic technique was necessary and that more educated or at least more respectable members of the middle class should shrink from departures from decorum, particularly if they were people whose first evangelistic enthusiasm had worn off. There is something of the same upper-class shrinking from the Salvation Army later in the century. If so, the difference between the more violent revivalists and the rest might turn into a class difference. But the matter should not be pressed too far. There was plenty of evangelistic exuberance in the middle class. Indeed, when a revival was at its height no one cared much for class or for respectability.

In fact, it is unsafe to parcel out the various denominations too exactly between the middle and the working class. In not a few districts at various periods the line between those two classes was probably very difficult to draw, and, where class distinctions had become more marked and more certain, different congregations of the same denomination might vary widely both in feeling and in the class which predominated. A missionary congregation or a slum parish might present very

[1] On the whole problem of religious revivalism in the nineteenth century I have received much help from the Rev. J. H. S. Kent, now of Hartley Victoria College, who will I hope write a book on the subject

marked contrasts with those attending a more respectable church or parish in another district. Indeed, it is possible that these contrasts grew greater as the third quarter of the nineteenth century went forward. Certainly religious leaders begin to complain that as the prosperous tended to live more and more in suburbs they left the city churches and tended to go to new churches remote from the dwellings of the poor, and at the same time the missionary spirit pressed further into districts where there was no one who could conceivably be called middle class.[1]

That missionary spirit was, however, probably never lacking in any of the major denominations from the beginning of the nineteenth century. Certainly it would be wrong to assume that because the Primitive Methodists had seceded from the old connexion the whole of the parent body was now complacently middle class, nor for that matter that it had lost its evangelistic fire. Indeed, the facts are not compatible with any such conclusion. The Methodists of the old connexion were very tightly disciplined and there was a considerable undercurrent of discontent among them at the Tory politics of those who governed them, and they suffered several serious recessions and exclusions; yet for all this the church membership of the old connexion increased, 90,619 in 1800 to 358,277 in 1850, which must be evidence of considerable missionary activity.[2] It is certainly true that the missionary activities of the Primitive Methodists in the first half of the nineteenth century were very notable, and it was stated in the *British Weekly* in 1909 that 'apart from Primitive Methodism there was little revivalism for some years before 1859'.[3] If this refers to the specialized technique of revivalism, this may be true, otherwise it is misleading. There is evidence that by about the beginning of the century the fire of the Evangelical revival had communicated itself to the older denominations, the Congregationalists and the Baptists.[4] It is sometimes suggested that the Congregationalists conceived that

---

[1] e.g. on suburban churches, see *Minutes of several conversations between the Methodists in the connexion established by the late Rev. John Wesley, A.M. at their Hundred and Thirtieth Annual Conference begun in Newcastle-upon-Tyne on Wednesday July 30, 1873*, pp. 278-9

[2] For figures for 1800 see *Minutes of Methodist Conference*, Vol 2, p. 55, and for 1850 *Minutes of Methodist Conference*, Vol 2, p. 421, on the political issue see E. R. Taylor *Methodism and Politics 1791-1851* (Cambridge 1935)

[3] Quoted in H. B. Kendall, B.A. [op. cit. p. 159] 89

[4] R. W. Dale, LL.D. *History of English Congregationalism* (completed and edited A. W. W. Dale) (London 1907) pp. 580-605

their mission was only to the middle class, but this is the result of the use of a truncated quotation. In 1848 the Rev. Thomas Binney told the assembled Congregationalists that they had 'a special call in *addition*' to the Evangelical mission which they had in the world in common with every branch of the Church. 'Our special mission is neither to the very rich nor to the very poor'.[1] In their circumstances it may well be that the Congregationalists took this special mission seriously, but that presents no reason to believe that they did not take their Evangelical mission seriously too; indeed, as has been seen, in that very year they engaged in anxious debate to try to see why it was that they were failing to attract the working class, a failure which they obviously profoundly deplored.

The success of the evangelical activities of the Congregationalists and the Baptists can be seen from the considerable numbers who attended their chapels on census Sunday in 1851.[2] By that time, however, it is clear that the Methodists of the old connexion and the various shoots of Methodism, the Primitive Methodists, the Calvinistic Methodists, the Methodists of the new Connexion and so on contained after the Church of England the largest section of the population, and it seems probable that the evangelical spirit worked more successfully and possibly more indiscriminately in the Methodist bodies than elsewhere. It was not, of course, inactive in the Church of England where indeed it originated, but in the Church it worked under a particular restriction. What had been a main point separating the Evangelicals who had remained part of the Church of England from those who had gradually diverged was the fact that in the Church they accepted the discipline of

[1] *Congregational Year Book*, 1848 (op. cit. p. 163] 9 ff. From facts communicated by Mr Beckwith of the Commercial Street Library, Leeds, it is perfectly clear that the Baptists in Leeds were an active missionary Church in the 'thirties; in 1836 they enlarged the South Parade Baptist Chapel to accommodate 1,400 people and in the late 'thirties there was great activity in setting up preaching stations in the poorer districts. I have no doubt it was the same elsewhere

[2] Independents 793,142; Baptists 587,978. *Religious Census 1851* [op. cit. p. 149] p. CLVI, Table 23. It should be noted that these are estimated figures reached after allowance has been made for those who attended twice, and also that they are attendance figures and should not be compared with figures given elsewhere for the Church members of the various denominations, since it seems that a good many adults attended service who were not Church members, nor were any children under 15 likely to be Church members though they attended service; the church attendance figures of the Wesleyan Methodists given in the census is 1,385,382

Church Order, and this meant that, though they took a leading part in the nation-wide agitation against slavery, in religious matters they were inclined to work through the parochial clergy rather than by means of roving missionaries who might disregard parish boundaries. It was to stabilize this process of evangelization by parishes that Simeon initiated his policy of purchasing advowsons so that the work of an evangelical incumbent might not be lost when a parish changed hands.[1] None of this of course meant that the missionary spirit had been abandoned, on the contrary very considerable use was made of the pulpit, and of that instrument of propaganda so much favoured in the nineteenth century, the tract; but possibly as a result some of the missionary practices which had been used in the earlier years of the Evangelical revival were for a period dropped, such as preaching out of doors.

In the second quarter of the nineteenth century, as was the case with so many others, the Evangelical party in the Church of England became increasingly troubled with the spiritual condition of the large urban masses who were as sheep with only very nominal shepherds, and to help the clergy deal with the situation the Church Pastoral Aid Society was formed in 1836. Its methods of proceedings excited violent controversy, and in 1837 the Additional Curates Society was founded by those who disliked it;[2] but fortunately bitter controversy never stopped the progress of the Church of England, if it had done so nothing would have ever been done in the nineteenth century when the wrangling was continuous. The parochial work of the Evangelicals went forward, for instance in 1837 there began one of the great slum pastorates of the nineteenth century, that of W. W. Champneys, the Evangelical Rector of St Mary's, Whitechapel. He succeeded a vicar who apparently contented himself by reading the Sunday service to the clerk and the charity children though he was supposed to be responsible for 36,000 souls. In twenty-three years Champneys altered all that, he built new churches, established schools and promoted social reforms, in fact he created a completely different situation from the one he had found.[3] This was the shape of things to come in

[1] C. H. Smyth *Simeon and Church Order* (Cambridge 1940) *passim*

[2] Balleine [op. cit. p. 162] 176-9

[3] William Weldon Champneys, see D.N.B. (London 1908) Vol 4, p 36. Balleine [op. cit. p. 162] 237-8

not a few urban parishes where an active Evangelical took over, and about the middle of the century the pace seems to have quickened. It was J. C. Miller, Rector of Birmingham from 1846 to 1860, who seems to have revived the practice of preaching in the open air; he was followed by others, and in 1855 Lord Shaftesbury managed to modify the law which had prohibited the meeting for religious worship of more than 20 people in any building except a church or a licensed Dissenting chapel. This opened the way for mass services in Exeter Hall in 1856. These were tumultuously attended, but though his diocesan was taking part they were inhibited by the vicar whose parish nominally included Exeter Hall. The Anglicans had therefore to go elsewhere and services were held in 'seven low theatres rented in the poorest parts of London',[1] to which very large crowds came.

It seems possible that in the middle of the century the progress of Protestant Dissent slowed down or even went into reverse. Such was the opinion of Halévy, and another historian has been so much impressed by the evidence on this point as to come to the conclusion that the great development of Dissent was really concentrated before 1850.[2] It is difficult to accept so general a statement with the period of the great revivals only just ahead, nor does it seem to be compatible with such figures as I have been able to inspect; nevertheless, it seems clear that round about 1850 was a difficult time for several religious bodies. The worst hit were the Methodists of the old connexion whose Church membership was reduced from 358,277 in 1850 to 260,858 in 1855.[3] This was, however, mainly caused by the culmination in a very serious crisis of the difficulties which had troubled them throughout the century. They were domestic difficulties which were not likely to have had much significance for other dissenting bodies, but in the early 'fifties other Churches seem to have suffered troubles of more general relevance. In the years 1853, 1854 and 1855 the Primitive Methodists suffered decreases which are variously attributed to the emigration of members overseas, the dearness of provisions owing to the Crimean War and a reflection of the

[1] Balleine [op. cit. p. 162] 245-8
[2] Halévy *Peel and Cobden* [op. cit. p. 171] 327-46. E. J. Hobsbawm *Primitive Rebels* [op. cit. p. 165] 129-30
[3] *Minutes of Methodist Conference*, Vol 11, p. 421, and Vol 13, p. 81

troubles of the old connexion.[1] The Baptists seem also to have had their troubles at this time, and were possibly affected by divisions over the Crimean War.[2] It is all a little mysterious and would bear further investigation, particularly perhaps an investigation into the results of the impact of the Crimean War not only on the history of the Nonconformist bodies but on local working class and liberal politics generally.[3]

However, whatever may have been the cause of the decline one thing is clear, it was limited in time and probably in extent. It seems probable that the loss from the Methodists of the old connexion was taken up at the time by the Baptists and other Methodist bodies.[4] In 1856 the tide began to turn for the old connexion, for the campaign for Home Missions was put on a new footing and began to produce results, and in consequence, or for more general reasons, the numbers of Church members began again to increase.[5] Two years before, in 1854, C. H. Spurgeon started his ministry in London, an event of the greatest importance in the history of Nonconformity. Then in 1859 the revivals began, first in Northern Ireland, then travelling by slightly different routes to Wales, to different parts of England and to Scotland. The revivals were dramatic events, they were apparently started by the example of the revivals in 1857 and 1858 in the United States and they added considerable numbers to the religious bodies that took part in them, but they should not be separated too sharply from the general religious history of their time.[6] They do not seem in most cases to have been sudden unexpected explosions: in most cases there seem to have been already people in the district hoping and praying for a revival; in some cases these were people who had had experience of other religious revivals if on a smaller scale, and in Staffordshire the revival had apparently

---

[1] Townsend, etc. [op. cit. p. 172] Vol 1, p. 592

[2] E. A. Payne *Baptist Union* [op. cit. p. 172] 73

[3] On this see F. E. Gillespie *Labor and Politics in England 1850-1867* (Duke University Press, North Carolina, 1927) pp. 75-76 and 106-110

[4] See *The Story of the United Methodist Church*, edited by H. Smith, John E. Swallow and William Treffry (London 1932). For statistics of United Methodist Free Church, Methodist New Connexion and Bible Christians from 1860 see p. 224 ff.

[5] *Minutes of Methodist Conference*, Vol 13, pp. 81, 276 and 483. On Home Missions see Townsend, etc. [op. cit. p. 172] Vol 1, p. 449

[6] On the course of the revivals and their probable results in additions to Church membership in various bodies see Orr [op. cit. p. 182] *passim*

already started in 1857, if not before, stimulated by the local Anglican clergy.[1] In fact, they seem to take their place in the general evangelical thrust that was going on, to be associated with the mission and immediate success of Spurgeon, with the services in Exeter Hall and in the theatres, and with the new development of Home Missions by the Methodists.

And if it is wrong to think of the revivals starting at a flash from nothing it would be as wrong to think of them dying suddenly into darkness again. There is, significantly, some doubt as to when the revival period came to an end. The date is sometimes given as 1865, but the Baptists apparently accounted the ten years between 1860 and 1870 as the 'revival decade', when it was claimed that more Baptist Churches were founded in London than in any period before or since.[2] But it would be hard to make a break at 1870 when it was in 1873 that Sankey and Moody first came to England to reach their climax in 1875, and it was after 1875 the Salvation Army began to take on its final form. Indeed it is to be noted that the evangelistic career of its founder William Booth and of his equally remarkable wife Catharine runs from before the period of the revivals till after 1880.[3]

The Salvation Army is perhaps the most significant and notable product of this exciting period, for it used with great success all the elements of applied romanticism—the rhetoric, the melodrama, the music, the evocative ritual and symbolism, but in this case it was not the ritual of medievalism but of war, which had possibly gained much associative emotional force in the third quarter of the nineteenth century because of the popularity of heroic stories of the Mutiny and the Crimea and because of the vividness with which contemporary journalism had described military events. However, the exploitation of this rather unexpected association enforces the fact that the Evangelical movement, of which it was in some way the climax, was only one side of the religious revival that swept through Victorian England. There was another form of applied romanticism inspired by the Catholic revival, in which the evocative appeal of medievalism was used to the full. There must have

[1] Orr [op. cit. p. 182] 133
[2] E. A. Payne [op. cit. p. 172] 79
[3] St John Ervine *God's Soldier: General William Booth* (London 1934) Vol I *passim*

been extensive missionary work going forward in the Roman Catholic Church itself. It would be very interesting to know more about it, starting possibly with those heroic figures the Passionists, Father Dominic Barbieri and Father Ignatius Spencer and the Rosminian Father Luigi Gentile, for it must have an important bearing on the history of a considerable section of the British working class.[1] Outside the Roman Catholics there were the ritualists of the Church of England who brought life and colour to slum parishes and fought a lively battle on three fronts against the forces of evil and animalism which all had to confront, against a Protestant mob and against the authorities of their Church.

But this account cannot be comprehensive in any direction or else the catalogue would be too long. It may, however, be as well to take one more instance to show what the needs and tendencies of the time can do to one who was not noticeably either in the Evangelical or Catholic tradition. A. C. Tait, later Archbishop of Canterbury, became Bishop of London in 1856 in succession to Blomfield. Blomfield had been a great bishop. He had consecrated some two hundred new churches, giving from his own resources at least £25,000, but he had not always been able to give life. Tait saw what was lacking, as he subsequently showed in the objects he prescribed for his Bishop's Fund, but at the beginning of his episcopate he symbolized his policy in a more picturesque way by preaching out of doors. He preached to the emigrants in the docks, to the omnibus drivers at Islington, to the costermongers in Covent Garden Market, to railway porters from the platform of a locomotive and to gypsies upon the common at Shepherd's Bush. He supported Lord Shaftesbury and his friends in their services at Exeter Hall. It is true that he had his troubles with the Anglo-Catholics about those tiresome points of ritual over which men in the middle of the nineteenth century expended so much time; but he recognized their value as men and priests and in the terrible year of 1866 he responded at once to Lowder's call to the East End to come together with his ritualistic clergy and the Anglican Sisters of Mercy on the entirely honourable common

[1] In the list of Labour members in 1929 there are 18 Roman Catholics, Hobsbawm [op. cit. p. 165] 141-2. I owe much help here to Mgr A. N. Gilbey, Catholic chaplain to the University of Cambridge; it seems clear that research is badly needed on this subject

ground of the workhouse cholera wards and the Wapping Cholera Hospital.[1]

VI

A Bishop of London preaching to the gypsies is perhaps a sign of how far things had travelled since the century started. Indeed it might perhaps be grouped with other pictures of a later date: Manning already a Catholic Archbishop administering the pledge among the drunkards on Clerkenwell Green in 1872, or the Salvation Army marching into action in Carlisle and Sheffield, bloodstained and battered from the assaults of hooligans, but gay and triumphant; for these things are all emblems of the power that had been at work in Victorian England. The agents of that power were inspired by widely different historic traditions, so much so that often enough they saw each other as the enemy quite as much as were the forces of Belial and 'mere animalism'. But it does not seem to be extravagant to see them in the light of history as one movement; the response of Christians to the challenge of the conditions of the nineteenth century. If so, it does not seem to be unfair to put to them one comprehensive question. What had they done? Treasure had been poured out, lives had been consecrated, fire had been granted: what had been the result?

It is not an easy question to answer. No doubt for innumerable individuals the results were of incalculable importance. No doubt it also meant much in nineteenth-century England that civilizing agencies had been pushed out into those urban areas where things were worst, much for the inhabitants of those areas and much also for those who were drawn into them to see what the worst was like; and it has to be remembered that the lessons of the intelligent philanthropy of the nineteenth century were often the basis of the social legislation of the twentieth. But there was one thing which had not been done, and that was what most of those engaged in this effort had worked and prayed and hoped to effect, though no doubt they conceived it in very different ways. They had not achieved the

[1] C. F. Lowder [op. cit. p. 150] 214-215. Davidson *Tait* [op. cit. p. 180] Vol 1, pp. 470-1

conversion of England, in any possible meaning of those words.

If in 1851 England was no longer a Christian country she had not become one again by 1880. There were still large areas of spiritual and social dereliction, there was still gross drunkenness, brutality and vice. The accounts of the conditions against which the Salvation Army matched itself in the 'eighties seem as bad as those which the slum priests found in the 'fifties and do not differ widely from the conditions described in the books of C. F. Masterman in the first ten years of the twentieth century. The vast size of the urban masses, the fluidity of their way of life and the weight of adverse economic circumstances presented problems greater than the most devoted personal service, the most reckless generosity on the part of private individuals, could hope to resolve. The resources of those who committed themselves to this struggle were necessarily limited and their effect was too often restricted to the boundaries of their personal influence; beyond that they might change nothing, and even where they had done most there might be little to show not long after they had gone away, or died. The tide of men flowed over the place as it flowed everywhere, and it was a tide still at the flood. The population was still increasing in such a way as at least to appear to outstrip the most exhausting endeavours. It was as if the spirit of history had said to the Churches, what the Red Queen said to Alice: 'It takes all the running *you* can do to keep in the same place.'

This was no new consideration. It was noted in the religious census of 1851 that though since 1801 the Church of England had increased the accommodation it offered by 24 per cent. the population had in fact increased in the same period by 101·6 per cent., so whereas the Church had once provided accommodation for nearly half the people in 1851 it provided for less than a third.[1] Possibly in the next quarter of a century the Churches contrived not to lose so much ground even in the most heavily populated districts, but they were not gaining. As has been recorded, the Congregationalists in 1881 made a careful enquiry into the increase since 1851 in the accommodation offered by the various religious denominations in certain Lancashire towns. The proportionate increases are remarkable, but at the end they came to the conclusion that

[1] *Religious Census 1851* [op. cit. p. 149] cxl

whereas accommodation for religious worship had been provided by all the Churches in that area for 32·8 per cent. of the population in 1851, in 1880 it was only provided for 32·3 per cent.[1] Yet between 1840 and 1876 the Church of England alone had expended in the diocese of Manchester £1,513,446 largely for the erection of new churches.[2] In 1881 the Congregationalists also made enquiry into the problem in London and they came to the conclusion that though they were in fact providing new chapels at the rate of about two a year if they were to keep up with the increase of population they ought each year to provide about six new chapels.[3] Probably things were better in the country districts and in the wealthier, less densely, populated urban districts. But in the areas where the people swarmed most it seems probable that the battle was being, if anything, lost. It was possibly the same in education. If it had proved to be impossible to provide a place in church or chapel in which everyone might worship, so it had proved to be impossible to provide a place in school in which every child might be educated. It was calculated in 1870 that there were 3,936,513 children of school age in the classes for which the schools to which a Government grant was given were intended but that there was in those schools only accommodation for 1,824,306 children, and that they had in fact only 1,569,139 children on their books. The significance of this was challenged, but it seems that this deficiency could only be cancelled by including schools where the education was probably unsatisfactory even according to the low standards set for popular education at that time, and there was no power in the land which sufficed to make all the children attend school or attend it at all regularly.[4]

The significance of this requires careful consideration. The English tradition had been one of liberty and of suspicion of the power of the State, and that suspicion had naturally particularly attached to any attempt by the State to gain control of the minds of the children. As Joseph Priestley had said: 'Education is a branch of civil liberty which ought by no

[1] *Congregational Year Book*, 1881 [op. cit. p. 173] 157

[2] *House of Commons Return 1876*, Vol LVIII [op. cit. p. 169] 643

[3] *Congregational Year Book*, 1881 [op. cit. p. 173] 153 ff.

[4] See Report from Committee of Council on Education 1870, XXII [op. cit. p. 175] XIV and XV. The challenge in the House of Commons was by Lord Robert Montagu on 17th February 1870 [op. cit. p. 176] Hansard 3rd Series, CXCIX, 470 ff.

means to be surrendered into the hands of the magistrate.'[1] That principle had been retained by many Dissenters and even by some Anglicans up till the Commission of 1858-61; however, in the years that followed even those who had objected to State education seem to have been in most cases no longer able to escape two conclusions, first that it was urgently necessary that all the children in the country should receive some education and second that that education would not be provided by voluntary effort.[2] The result was a striking reversal of opinion, for it was mainly Dissenters who in the 'sixties formed the Education League which demanded a comprehensive system of State education that should be free and compulsory if also undenominational, that is not representing the peculiar opinions of any particular body within the State.

But if this change must take place over education why not over other matters as well? In the middle of the nineteenth century it was still the hope and belief of many Englishmen that the private efforts of individuals would meet those needs which abroad were supplied by the coercive action of the centralized State. To Taine on his visit to England in 1862 this spirit was typified by the Volunteers whom he went to see reviewed in Hyde Park;[3] it was also reflected in a great deal of the charitable work of that time, as also in much legislation with its preference for local initiative and local administrative control. It was an admirable spirit and was of great value to the country; but it was not powerful or comprehensive enough to grapple with the problems of the complex ever-growing society which inhabited England in the nineteenth century, or with the dangerous forces which nineteenth-century civilization had produced. A voluntary system could not educate the children of England. If the whole of England was to become healthy, the local authorities in question had to learn from the Act of 1866 'the novel virtue' of the imperative mood, and it may be doubted whether the regular Army and the Volunteers would have made much head if they had had to face either of the great professional conscript armies that fought it out in Europe in 1870.

The only forces that could bring under control the whole of

[1] Joseph Priestley *Works*, Vol XXII (ed. J. T. Rutt 1823) p. 54, and see Kitson Clark [op. cit. p. 176] 119
[2] Arthur Miall *Life of Edward Miall* (London 1884) pp. 230-7
[3] Taine [op. cit. p. 148] 175-8

society and perform the tasks which both the conscience and the necessities of the nineteenth century increasingly demanded, were forces which had behind them not only the resources of the State but its powers of compulsion; the work of civilization, which no doubt the activities of the Churches furthered, needed also the assistance of such powerful allies as the school attendance officer, the sanitary inspector, the temperance legislator and above all the police.

But in actual fact did these religious activities further the work of civilization at all in any higher sense, at least of secular civilization? If the State was to be the civilizing power must it not, so far from working with the Churches, tend to displace them? What had happened so far had extended the reign of Nonconformity both over the middle class and an increasing section of the working class, and you do not have to read very far in Matthew Arnold's various tracts for the times to know what may have been wrong with Nonconformists. He does not spare their provincialism and ignorance, their immeasurable self-satisfaction and their lack of any critical standard, their relish for bathos, and the fact that they had seemingly locked themselves into the narrow room of 'Puritanism' and showed no desire to get out. Had, then, the extension of this power meant in any sense at all the extension of civilization in this world, in whatever way it may have been preparing men's souls for the next?

The indictment is heavy, and if the tone and the tendency to nag irritates it is as well to remember that Arnold had met the men he is writing about and we have not. Yet it may be questioned whether in fact he is really blaming the right thing. That the people about whom he wrote were as he described them is probable, the question to be asked is whether, Nonconformity apart, they had had much chance of being anything else. A rapidly expanding society, where the opportunities of education were often negligible, leisure at a discount and the needs of commerce and industry ever insistent, was not likely to encourage the values Arnold admired, whether it was dominated by Nonconformity or no. It may, in fact, be questioned whether the faults of Nonconformity were what they were because the society in which it developed was what it was, or the society was what it was because of the nature of Nonconformity. It is true that their self-righteousness may have been an unlovely trait, but self-righteousness is natural to men who have never had the chance of a generous education but have made something of life. It is true that to be locked in by Puritanism has undeniably a restrictive effect on the human spirit, but, as has been said earlier, Puritanism should always be measured by whatever it is guarding itself against; when you lock a door you may not only be thinking about what you are keeping in but what you are keeping out. In this case they were not only keeping out the angels of sweetness and light, if they did keep them out, but also such forces as rather more palpably stalked the streets of the mid-nineteenth-century town—in fact the forces of 'mere animalism', particularly drink.

In fact, it seems probable that the revival in all its forms—Anglican, Roman Catholic and Protestant Nonconformist—gave shape and meaning to many lives which otherwise would have had none. It was unfortunate that the nature and comprehensiveness of that meaning was too often limited by the comprehension and education of the men who gave it, and that those limitations were too often rendered opaque by a natural but irremovable self-satisfaction. Certainly the utterances of the best Nonconformist leaders such as Dale of Birmingham show a wider and more cultured point of view, but unfortunately the writings and speeches of lesser Nonconformists rather confirm Arnold's strictures. Even so, the appropriate question seems to be, What was the alternative? From what other source could they have gained what they gained from the chapel? And what did they gain from the chapel? This is a question which has been answered by a man who knew in his own person what Methodism could mean to a working man. 'The chapel gave them', said he, 'their first music, their first literature and philosophy to meet the harsh life and cruel impact of the crude materialistic age.'[1] It is not contended that in every case the chapel gave nearly so much as in this, nor that in every case its adherents would have had so poor a birthright without it as a Durham miner; but if it did anything like this for many of the people who were being carried swiftly along by the tide of that world it seems possible that the debt of the country to it is very great.

[1] J. J. Lawson *A Man's Life* (London, new edition, 1944) p. 69

This raises a contingent question of some importance. What had been the effect of this religious consolidation, as far as it had gone, on the shape of secular politics? It is not an easy question to answer because there is the danger of exaggeration, and because possibly both at the time, and afterwards, some religious people have been tempted to claim too much. Certainly the classes who gained self-expression and self-consciousness were also those who were likely to take the lead either in the struggle for popular radicalism or in the politics of the class struggle. The fluid mass that escaped the evangelist in all probability escaped the politician also, and, at least until the new unionism, of the Trade Union organizer. It is also true that the religion of the chapel was all important as a starting-point for working-class leaders. An able young man in very poor circumstances was more likely to develop his latent powers, to learn to speak, to learn to lead and to organize through his chapel than in any other way. His denomination might even give a potential minister or preacher the possibility of some sort of advanced education, and this might be taken, by an ambitious young man, without any very serious religious intention as was possibly the case with Victor Grayson at a rather later period. In most cases, however, the religious intention was obviously perfectly sincere, and indeed very often in many ways coloured the rest of the leader's life, even if that were passed in economic organization or secular politics, as was the case with Arthur Henderson or Ernest Bevin. Nevertheless, it must always be remembered that the Churches and Chapels were religious organizations and not organized for secular purposes; they might be powerful auxiliaries, but it was through secular organisations such as Trade Unions and political parties that the most important developments were to come.

The point is of considerable importance in relation to the development of popular radicalism. It will be remembered that after 1835 the forces of Protestant Nonconformity conquered the towns but that they failed to invade effectively national politics at Westminster. The reason for this failure was the fact that as the country was then organized a very large number of the constituencies were under the control of the gentry and the nobility. Through the Anti-Corn Law League an attempt was made partly to cancel this constituency control by hook and indeed by crook, and also, following the precedent of the Anti-Slavery Campaign, to by-pass it by developing a nation-wide agitation which should transcend constituency politics and put direct pressure on Parliament. The importance of the Anti-Corn Law League disappeared with the repeal of the Corn Laws, but the habit of these semi-moral, semi-political agitations remained. For instance, many of those who had been involved in Anti-Corn Law agitation became involved in the Peace Society. The appeal of this movement, however, was probably bound to be limited, and it drew its exponents into trouble during the Crimean War. Indeed, for some reason the political activities of organized Dissent in general seem to have been in the doldrums till after the election of 1857.

It was in the twenty years between 1860 and 1880 that the political structure of the country began to change in such a way as to give a new significance and new possibilities to the kind of agitations in which Dissenters engaged. A major cause of the change was no doubt the effect of the social developments of the middle years of the century. In a large number of con-stituencies the classes who had been content to accept the leadership of a local oligarchy in electoral matters had become sufficiently wealthy and sufficiently independent not to be con-tent with a subordinate position any longer. This was a change within the constituency, yet what normally made it effective was that some centralized body from outside the constituency intruded into it, put aside the old patrons and appealed to the discontented classes in the constituency by encouraging institu-tions which appeared to be under popular control. The result of this development was in fact not so much the creation of a number of more truly autonomous constituency organizations but the growth in power of the centrally organized party in the third quarter of the century and the decline of the indepen-dence of the individual member of the House of Commons.

It might have been thought that the Protestant Dissenters were in a peculiarly suitable position to take advantage of this situation; not only were the discontented classes in a number of constituencies Protestant Dissenters chafing at Whig indifference to the continuance of their grievances, but the nation-wide agitations which the Dissenters supported were often very ready to intrude into as many constituencies as possible to give force and direction to the actions of the discontented. Two movements in particular had survived from the period of the Corn Laws and had equipped themselves with societies something on the model of the Anti-Corn Law League, which might very well do what was desired; one was the Temperance Movement which developed that formidable body the United Kingdom Alliance in 1853, and the other was the movement for the disestablishment of the Church of England which was furthered by the Liberation Society also founded in 1853, in succession to Miall's Anti-State Church Society.[1]

The Temperance Movement was not in fact necessarily either a sectarian or a party agitation. There were important temperance advocates in the Church of England, there was indeed a Church of England Temperance Society and there were for a time Conservative members of the United Kingdom Alliance. There were also brewers in both parties. In the 'sixties, therefore, the Alliance took up a position outside the traditional parties and concentrated on demanding pledges from the candidates at elections. Very significantly it overplayed its hand. The pledge it demanded as a condition of support for a candidate or of refraining from opposing him was indeed a stringent one, he had to support the particular measure advocated by the Alliance and no other. This turned out to be more likely to hurt their friends than their foes, for a moderate temperance reformer might boggle at giving their pledge and therefore lose the support of the Alliance while a man who had no interest in temperance reform at all would not be troubled by it since he could never have hoped to gain support from any people whom they influenced. The other weakness which the policy of the Alliance demonstrated shows the basic weakness of the actions of all pressure groups. To ask a voter to make his vote turn entirely on whether a candidate gives a satisfactory pledge on a particular subject is to ask the voter to throw away his vote except in so far as that subject is concerned, and unless he is fanatically interested in that subject, or has no interest in any other, he will not do this. As a consequence of their electoral

[1] H. Carter *The English Temperance Movement: A Study in Objectives* (London 1933). On the Liberation Society see Arthur Miall [op. cit. p. 194]; but on this whole problem it is very important to read Hanham [op. cit. p. 55] 119-24

experience the Alliance had learnt by 1874 the lesson that to get what they wanted they must identify themselves with, and give general support to, one political party. For them the chosen party was of course the Liberal party.[1]

The case of the Liberation Society is more difficult. Their attempt to influence constituencies was made with much greater intelligence and subtlety, and their apparent success was greater and more important. Those who were anxious for disestablishment of the Church of England had long been profoundly dissatisfied with the Parliamentary position. The census of 1851 seemed to have shown that the Church attracted the support of little more than half the people in the country and yet in the House of Commons motions for the cancellation of Dissenters' grievances were apt to be thrown out by reasonably large majorities. This was held to be peculiarly outrageous with regard to Wales. Wales was at this time sharply and bitterly divided between an English-speaking gentry and aristocracy and Welsh-speaking farmers and working class. The established Church was identified with the gentry and the English tradition, and the Dissenters, mainly Calvinistic Methodists and Congregationalists, were closely identified with the renaissance of Welsh language and culture. It was claimed that 79 per cent. of those who had attended worship on the Sunday of the census had attended services other than those of the Established Church, yet a majority of Welsh members of Parliament, even of nominally liberal Welsh members, normally voted against the removal of Nonconformist disabilities.[2]

1862 was the bicentenary of the ejection of Puritan ministers from the livings of the Church and at the public meetings held in connection with this a movement was launched to secure a better representation of Wales from the Nonconformist point of view.[3] Apparently a little later a flexible policy was adopted by the Liberation Society in England. An estimate was made of the strength the society could hope to command in any particular constituency and in accordance with that calculation it was determined how much could be asked of the Liberal candidate at the time when he was adopted; at the same time

---

[1] Hanham [op. cit. p. 55] 122-3
[2] C. S. Miall *Henry Richard, M.P.*, (London 1889) pp. 120-1
[3] C. S. Miall [op. cit. p. 200] 119-26

conferences were held in various populous cities to explain the objects which were being sought.[1] It was claimed that this policy began to produce results at the general election of 1865 when its effect was 'to consolidate the Liberal Party', though it led perforce to the non-adoption of certain candidates who would not take the pledges the Liberationists demanded. But the real success of the scheme could not be realized till after the Reform Bill of 1867, with its large enfranchisement of working-class voters in certain constituencies. Then it was claimed that against 10 Conservatives Wales now returned 23 Liberals, among whom were 3 Nonconformists, and in the whole Parliament there were 95 members opposed to the Established Church, of whom 63 were Protestant Nonconformists.[2]

It was no doubt a great change, but when it is viewed closely the achievement is not quite as impressive as it has been made to appear and the direct control of Nonconformity over politics was less than might perhaps be thought. In fact, the Welsh revolt had not as yet been pressed very far,[3] and in England the Liberationists were still not so much a political party, or even the dominant element of a political party, as a pressure group. It seems probable that in most constituencies the most important organization among radicals and working men was not the Liberation Society but the Reform League, a directly political body which was partly secularist since it included Bradlaugh; while even after 1868 a majority of the House of Commons still favoured the Church of England. This was indeed proved for the Nonconformists in the most painful way. This House of Commons was indeed prepared to disestablish and disendow the Established Church in Ireland, but the Education Act which the Government passed in 1870 permitted the survival of the Church of England schools, to the intense anger of the Nonconformists, and Gladstone himself opposed Miall's motion for the disestablishment of the Church of England. The Nonconformists' attempts to counter-attack were partly ineffective and partly disastrous. To press their views on education they formed another pressure group the 'Education League'. This was another attempt to copy the Anti-Corn Law

[1] A. Miall [op. cit. p. 194] 251-2
[2] A. Miall [op. cit. p. 194] 263-4
[3] Hanham [op. cit. p. 55] 172-6

League, but it seems to have done very little in the by-elections in which it interfered. When the time came for the next general election in 1874 the Nonconformists refrained from supporting the Liberals with the result that the Conservatives came in with a large majority, which was not at all what they had wanted. So the Liberationists also realized that they also must not try to be a separate power, but must work from within the Liberal Party.[1]

It would seem therefore that even after the great missionary effort in the middle of the century these religious groups were not strong enough to play an independent part. Nevertheless, their importance as a component in national life can hardly be exaggerated, and it is absurd to try and write the history of politics without referring to this as the sequel to the troubled events of Mr Gladstone's first ministry shows.

The future of Radicalism was not to lie with the Reform League; as with so many extreme radical and semi-working-class bodies, it was afflicted with financial difficulties and its leaders accepted money from Glyn, Gladstone's whip, on what were in effect compromising conditions. This exaggerated the fissiparous tendencies in its ranks and it did not long survive the general election of 1868.[2] The future of the working-class movement was to lie with the Trade Unions which were more stable, more financially durable, than any advanced political society; and the future of Radicalism was to spring from the ruins of the Education League. One of the ablest of the men who had been attracted into that agitation had been a young Unitarian screw manufacturer of Birmingham called Joseph Chamberlain. Before the disaster of 1874 he had decided that there was not enough 'force in the Education question to make it the sole fighting issue for our friends. From the commencement it has failed to evoke any great popular enthusiasm.'[3] He turned energetically into general secular politics and to the practical social reform of remodelling his own city. Indeed he did more. From the organization of the Education League he evolved the machinery of the National Liberal Federation which was effectively to challenge in the name not of religion

[1] Hanham [op. cit. p. 55] 123 and 124

[2] See Hanham [op. cit. p. 55] 323-43

J. Chamberlain to J. Morley, 19th August 1873. J. L. Garvin *Life of Joseph Chamberlain* (London 1932) Vol 1, p. 146

but of democracy the oligarchies which controlled the constituencies.[1] It is a notable fact that on the other side the
Conservative party which was to match itself against this new
Liberal party traced its descent partly from the activities of the
innumerable Church Defence Associations and of Henry Cecil
Raikes; but it also became in its turn a party generally engaged
in ordinary secular politics.

These developments are significant. They have a wider
reference than to the general question of party organization.
Religious motives, the enthusiasms of religious-minded people,
the strife between religious bodies were not powerful enough to
control to the exclusion of other interests a large enough section
of the national life to predominate in politics or in anything else.
They had to work with more secular factors if they were to
effect anything which was to have comprehensive results for the
whole country. Nevertheless, a very great deal of the thought
of the country was impregnated with the beliefs and ideas and
evocative phrases that derived from Christianity. For many
people some form of Christianity was the first force to give shape
and meaning to their lives, and for many some Christian
organization had the first, or at least the earliest, claim on their
loyalty; but for these feelings to be generally effective they had
to be expressed through general political parties not through
denominational pressure groups.

But the fact that before 1874 the Nonconformists had mistaken their power, and that they had had to learn the bitter
lesson that they could not by themselves impose their will on
the nation, by no means meant that their political importance
was over. In alliance with others, as one of the most important
components of the Liberal party, they were to be formidable.
They rallied to Gladstone in 1876 and shared his electoral
victory in 1880. From that time onwards their part in Liberal
fortunes seems to have increased until in the election of 1906,
the last great Liberal triumph, they seem to have secured the
return of a larger number of Nonconformists to the House of
Commons than ever before.

That was their apogee, after that their power declined. There
were probably several reasons for this. For one thing the classes,
which had been united by a common Nonconformity and a

[1] Garvin [op. cit. p. 202] Vol I, p. 256 ff.

common Liberalism, began to go their different ways. Towards the end of the nineteenth century many of the richer Dissenters had been seduced by the lure of the older Universities and, what was worse, by the public schools to entrust their sons to such places; consequently the new generation that came to the fore after 1906 had been insensibly drawn away from the old loyalties and the old ways of thought towards the patterns of Anglicanism and the upper class. At the other end of the scale men who had been brought up in Dissent were turning to the Labour party. The career of Arthur Henderson, a Wesleyan lay preacher whose 'life began with his conversion', who was from 1895 to 1902 a Liberal agent but thereafter was to rise to one of the most eminent positions in the Labour party, is probably symbolic of the road followed by a large number of less eminent men. However, more important than this political disintegration was the secularization of spirit, which spread over life and politics in the early twentieth century.

In the twentieth century the old vision of Christianity which had meant so much in so many different ways to Englishmen in the nineteenth century began to fade. New interests, new hopes, new animosities and new ways of thought took its place. and though all Churches suffered alike it seems probable that the Protestant Dissenters were most vulnerable. Most Protestant dissenting bodies did not have behind them a strong historic organization which could weather a decline in contemporary popularity, and, probably more than other religious bodies, they had drawn their strength from ways of thought and expression which were native to the nineteenth century and were now becoming obsolete. So the Dissenters became in politics a shadow of what once they had been, though there remained force enough in the Nonconformist conscience to give a direction to the minds of people to whom the Nonconformist religion was a matter of so remote a past that they did not know what was affecting them. But at the beginning of the third quarter of the nineteenth century this decline was a matter for the unexpected future. After 1876 reunited again behind their great and mysterious leader, in full co-operation once more with the Liberal party, terrible as an army with banners, they swept down once more on the enemy. It was still the old enemy, the forces of the old régime which had possibly been shaken but certainly not dispossessed after 1868, and had rallied in 1874. Now perhaps the time had come to close with them finally; but since the forces of the old régime were also among the makers of Victorian England it is to the aristocracy and gentry that I will turn in the next chapter.

CHAPTER VII

The Nobility and Gentry—
Old Style

In what I have said so far I have tried to describe Victorian England as a community in which powerful forces, both creative and dissolvent, were at work. In 1850 not all of them had penetrated very far; in fact, the England of 1850 resembles the cruder, pre-industrial, pre-democratic, resolutely unreformed England of the eighteenth century more closely than we have been pleased to imagine, and on the surface it seemed to stay that way during the long golden hours of the Victorian interlude. But in fact, as I have tried to show, under the surface these powerful forces, the increase of population, the Industrial Revolution, the revival of religion and possibly the increase of literacy and personal self-consciousness, never ceased to do their work. That was so with the mass of the people; the question now to be faced is what happened to the people at the top.

Certainly the eighteenth century lingered at the top of society as obstinately and as self-confidently as it did anywhere in the social pattern of Victorian England. A wanderer from the 1750s would have found much to wonder at and not a little to fear in the England of the 1850s, the machines, the factories and their masters, the busy crowds, the newspapers, the subjects which all men earnestly debated, all these things he might well find strange and disturbing. But when he reached those who might be considered to be at the head of society he might feel himself to be reasonably at home. Many of them would be the grandchildren of men he had known, nor would many of their thoughts and habits be altogether strange to him.

Of course, they were living in a different world, a world in which it was clear that new and very powerful forces had come into existence which might threaten the position of these people, or with which they might have to make their peace. That fact might be obscured to men and women whose minds were intent on the pleasures of high life or the joys of the hunting field; but to anyone who read more than the fashionable intelligence in his morning paper, or took the slightest interest in politics—and a large proportion of the English aristocracy were politically minded—the facts of the case were open and palpable. New men had come on to the stage endowed with new forms of wealth, the teeming cities, the busy industrial districts had produced new and very ugly problems, and a man had only to listen to the debates in the House of Commons, or for that matter to look along its benches, to be aware of these facts.

Partly as a result of these social developments, but also as a result of political changes which had been going on from reasonably far back into the eighteenth century, the shape of politics was certainly different from what it had been in the age of Walpole and the Pelhams. Then the Government had been in a very real sense the King's Government and as such had relied upon the votes of a body of placemen and professional politicians with, in the background, a mass of country gentlemen who considered it to be their duty to give it their support unless things were going very wrong. Party meant very little, except perhaps in the form of the relatively small groups often based on family or personal connexions which in government or in opposition were the mobile units in eighteenth-century politics. Much of this had disappeared, or apparently disappeared, by the middle of the nineteenth century. The groups had disappeared, the placemen in the House of Commons had been reformed away, or most of them had gone. The personal power of the monarch which George III had exercised, and with which George IV had played, had evaporated. A real party system had come into existence. A country gentleman both at his election or in the House of Commons adopted a party name, though he very often boasted of his relative independence; and the supporters of the Government normally supported it, when they did support it, not because it was the King's Government, but because of its party label or political affinities.

All this was no doubt very important, because the development of the party system was, as is well known, an essential factor in British political and constitutional development. It was necessary in order to secure that politics should mean something, that they should present in intelligible form the conflicts of thought and interest that divide the country and that Government should draw its power from organized opinion which has contrived to convince a majority of the people. But, if this is so, it has to be confessed that with 1852 the development of the party had reached an unfortunate phase, for after 1852 it is not very easy to read any intelligible meaning into the party system at all.

The Conservative party after 1852 was in reality a survival from an earlier and more violent phase when Parliamentary reform looked as if it might broaden into revolution and the nation was rocked by the struggle over the Corn Laws and the other social and political troubles of the 'forties. But those days were over, the worst threats had been left behind and peace or at least a truce had been made with the other side. Under the dexterous leadership of Disraeli the Conservative party had in fact abandoned agricultural protection and was to make itself responsible for Parliamentary reform. In other matters, in most matters, it would not be easy to see what, save the personal leadership of Derby and Disraeli, separated the Conservative party from Lord Palmerston and those who thought like him. If party represents organized opinion it would not be very easy to say what specific opinions were uniquely organized in the middle of the century by the Conservative party. In fact, it was a very remarkable achievement on the part of Derby and Disraeli to keep it together at all, and the fact that they did so was very important for the future; but for the moment its survival was rather a *tour de force* than anything more immediately significant.

If on the Conservative side politics lacked meaning, on the other side they lacked coherent organization. For more than twenty years after 1846 the Conservatives were unable to command a majority and the Government was normally Whig or Liberal, though its nature was varied from time to time by the intricate personal manœuvres of a select group of statesmen and a curious *pas de deux* danced by Lord John Russell and Lord Palmerston. Behind the Government was the usual apparatus of Whips and the like who organized, or tried to organize, the Government majority and who tended to work for a particular man rather than for a party conceived in more general terms. Normally a sufficient number of members were prepared to support a Whig Government or a coalition in which Whigs predominated; but there were relatively independent groups such as the Peelites and the Manchester men whose political support could by no means be predicted, and clearly there were enough members of Parliament who sat so lightly to their allegiance as to make it always possible that the Government's legislation or even its existence would be at the mercy of a debate in the House of Commons.

The result was the confused party politics of the 'fifties. If it is the function of parties to give force and meaning to Parliamentary government, then this party system was a failure; if it is the function of a party system to represent accurately the realities of national life, it largely failed in that also. The forces which were remodelling Britain had not yet forced an effective entry. They might be represented and considered in politics, but they did not share the control of them, nor had they an apparent chance of gaining control. The control was in hands which had not won it, but received it by prescription and inheritance. As Bagehot said of the British electoral system in 1859, 'Too little weight is given to the growing parts of the country, too much to the stationary'.[1] He was thinking of the distribution of Parliamentary constituencies and he spoke with reason, for London and the manufacturing districts were badly under-represented, but he might have applied what he said to the general distribution of political power. Too little went to those who were making the future, too much to those who had inherited from the past, and that meant in the mid-nineteenth century too little to industry and commerce and too much to those who represented agriculture. As Bagehot complained, Parliament had 'an undue bias towards the sentiments and views of the landed interest'.[2] The landed gentry, so he noted, not only claimed to monopolize the representation of the counties, they also sat for the boroughs as well, and they filled the Cabinet. As he said, 'the series of Cabinet Ministers presents a nearly unbroken rank of persons who either are themselves large landowners, or are connected closely by birth or inter-

---

[1] W. Bagehot *Essays on Parliamentary Reform* (London 1883), p. 12
[2] Bagehot [op. cit. p. 209] 8

marriage with large landowners'.[1] He might also have said that they were normally either themselves titled personages, or were connected closely by birth or intermarriage with titled personages. In fact, it might have been more revealing to have done so, for what he was thinking of was not just one economic interest, agriculture, to be measured against other economic interests such as industry or commerce. It was something more significant than that, it was a caste, an order of society, which might, and indeed in the matter of the settled estates did, value what held it together as a caste more than what would serve it best as an economic interest. It was in fact the old governing class of the country, still in control twenty-seven years after the Reform Bill.

One of the reasons for this survival was of course the deficiency of that Act, not only the inequitable distribution of seats but also the limitations of the franchise and the ways in which it could be manipulated. But another reason was the fact that within the framework of the nineteenth-century party politics and under the skin of nineteenth-century life many eighteenth-century or near eighteenth-century practices and relationships were still effective. Possibly the section of political life to which the simplest and most naïve of the old controls could be applied was shrinking. The number of boroughs in which a patron or a family could simply nominate a member was getting smaller. Professor Gash calculates that in the House of Commons in 1847 such boroughs could be said to have produced rather more than 80 members; Dr Hanham has calculated that after 1868 this figure should be reduced to rather more than 40.[2] This was partly the result of the Act of 1867, but not wholly so. As towns had got larger and more wealthy, the power of the ground landlords seems to have diminished and the landlords seem to have become less confident about using it. Probably it would be true to say that after the middle of the century there were no undiluted Treasury Boroughs. The trouble which Augustus Stafford stirred up in 1852 when he tried to claim such boroughs for the Derby Government, and the situation which the subsequent debates revealed, showed that the times had passed or were passing when in a place like Devonport a candidate could rely on dockyard votes simply because he was a Government

[1] Bagehot [op. cit. p. 209] 11   [2] Hanham [op. cit. p. 55] 45

candidate; indeed, regulations had been issued to decrease the direct political control of dockyard appointments. But where direct control had been relinquished it had by no means always been replaced by what we would consider a democratic appeal to opinion. In not a few cases the rights of a patron of a borough had only been challenged by the profuse use of bribery on the other side. In some cases boroughs had sunk up to the ears in corruption never to emerge till the borough was disenfranchised or the constituency was changed. And in most counties and boroughs except perhaps the very largest boroughs the influence of employers, local notabilities and landlords provided the important factors in deciding elections.

The conception of 'influence' which pervaded mid-nineteenth century politics in Britain had a very long history. It existed in various forms. It might be the power exercised by a local magnate, very often a peer, over his neighbours, secured often by suitable hospitality at the right moment, affability to the right women or by more concrete local services. Or it might be the power of an employer to influence the votes of his men, or a town landlord those who lived in his houses. But the best known form of influence was that of the rural landlord over the votes of his farming tenants; indeed, so well known is this relationship that historians have sometimes talked as if this was the only form of influence and as if influence was only exercised on one side in politics, which is very far from being true.

Contemporaries were inclined to distinguish between 'legitimate influence', based on a natural relationship and mutual respect and 'illegitimate influence' based upon intimidation, but in fact it is not easy to draw a very clear line here. It is true that the sanction behind intimidation, the actual dismissal of those who voted for the wrong candidate or their eviction from their holdings, commonly called the 'squeeze', was relatively rare in England, though there were notorious political evictions in Wales and in Scotland. But this was a matter in which feelings varied insensibly from the defensible to the indefensible. Certainly the hold of influence on a workman or a farmer might spring from gratitude, loyalty or a genuine belief that the landlord or master would know best what was in the interests of both, or it might be, and seemingly very often was, simply the result of unthinking custom, or it might derive from

plain fear or a desire to curry favour; and many of those involved would have been very hard put to it to say which of these
habits of mind were the operative ones.

What is undoubtedly true is that influence was a dominant
reality in mid-nineteenth-century politics particularly in the
counties. Indeed, in the counties it was probably stronger after
1852 than before. Earlier in the century the farmers had been
frightened, and not always sure that their landlords were
protecting their interests. This was particularly so when the
landlords used their influence to support a party led by Robert
Peel, but the feeling lingered on even after the landlords had
broken with Peel in 1846 and led for instance to the election of
Mr Ball, an independent protectionist farmer for Cambridgeshire, in 1852. After 1852 the farmers seem to have cared less;
influence unimpaired and unchallenged resumed her sway so
that the landlords could play their old game of Whigs and
Tories without being troubled by real issues. But influence was
strong in the towns as in the counties, possibly where it was
exercised through industry it was based less on blind habit, but
even so it existed, and in such circumstances a large part of the
work of those who organized a political party was the fitting
together of a jigsaw puzzle of a great many personal influences
in county and borough. Indeed, it is a significant fact that the
man who normally managed a constituency for a candidate
was not a party agent who would represent a general political
cause, but a solicitor the natural representative of a private
individual or private property. To a large extent the organization of the best organized party, the Conservative party, was a
curious network or web of solicitors representing the appropriate people in the constituencies and linked up with a firm of
solicitors in London—Baxter, Rose and Norton—which produced first Philip Rose and then Markham Spofforth to be
agents for the Conservative party.

Theoretically anyone on any side of politics could acquire
influence, and certainly anyone who had the money and could
still his conscience could bribe people. The system was in its
way an open system, and in fact a good many strange characters
managed to get into the House for strange and not always very
defensible reasons. The House, and society in general, would
have been sweeter if some of these people had not been Members,

but it was a fact of considerable importance that the House of Commons had never been completely monopolized by a closed caste and was of course still less so now that the manufacturing districts and Ireland and Scotland were more effectively represented. Nevertheless, there is little doubt that most of the power which these ancient techniques yielded went to the nobility and gentry. They had inherited or acquired much more electoral 'influence' than anyone else, and not a few disputed elections disclosed the fact that the respectability or gentility of a candidate did not in fact prevent bribery from being used on his behalf. The well-connected were used to playing the game of politics and these practices were a legitimate hazard of that game; a gentleman might not perhaps use them directly, but gentlemen were normally prepared to employ others who would certainly use them on their behalf. And clearly many people were satisfied to leave the game of politics in the hands of the gentlemen and the lords who usually played it. England had, as Bagehot said in his English Constitution, a 'deferential electorate', and for some reason constituencies liked being represented by a scion of the nobility.

It is important not to overestimate the importance of this. Some of the best connected members seem to have been singularly silent and undistinguished. It would indeed be extremely interesting some time to make an analysis of the number of times some members made a contribution to debate, or even possibly appeared at a division, and then perhaps to speculate why they had ever gone to the trouble to get themselves elected; possibly in certain cases it was no more than the result of a dim but persistent feeling that it was the right thing for a member of their family to do at a particular stage in life. Such people no doubt made little impact on politics, and on a general impression after reading Parliamentary debates and contemporary newspapers it would seem that members representing radical or manufacturing constituencies and members who were not of the aristocratic families made in general a much bigger shewing in debate and before the public than the general run of those of good family. It must be confessed that this is only a general impression and based on no sort of accurate analysis, but if it is correct the fact is important in a polity in which so much turned on public discussion. More than this, the fact that many of those who were reasonably well-connected also claimed that they were Liberal clearly had its effect on the policy of the country. But it might well be that a man's social origin limited the scope of his Liberalism and the extent of his sympathies; indeed, this might be true not only of those born into the upper class but of those who by habit of life or inclination were drawn into association with them. As a result there could be two kinds of Liberal, and, for instance, Dissenters sometimes complained that even when represented in Parliament by nominal Liberals they only got very torpid support for the removal of their disabilities. Indeed, it would seem that though in general the policy of the country was Liberal and the governments were in their way Liberal, in the 'fifties and 'sixties the prejudices, ways of thought and limitations of the old proprietary classes still lay heavy on politics, as it seems also to have been normally members of those classes whose hands still held most of the winning cards.

II

In the middle of the nineteenth century, then, the political system was still to a remarkable extent the plaything of the nobility and gentry, and in particular of the hereditary owners of the great estates. These classes were not numerous. The sides of the social pyramid sloped inward sharply, and the numbers in the upper classes were clearly much smaller and of an altogether different order of figure than the numbers in the groups below what can be called the line of gentility. Since the holding of land was concentrated into a very few hands the number of landed proprietors who were in a way the nucleus of this system was very small. A very rough count of the English landowners in Burke's *Peerage* and *Landed Gentry* in the 'fifties seems to yield about 3,000 names, or to use a more accurately calculated figure, an enquiry into the holding of land in England in 1871 revealed the fact that about a quarter of the land in England was owned by 1,200 persons and that about a half was owned by 7,400 people. Among these landowners were some with very great estates indeed. In the *Complete Peerage* there is a list of 28 noblemen who in 1883 each possessed estates of more than 100,000 acres in the United Kingdom.[1]

These were no doubt the richest men in the kingdom, and it seems likely that there were not many fortunes in the country large enough to rival the accumulations even of the slightly less overwhelmingly endowed landed proprietors. This did not mean that considerable fortunes had not been made in commerce and industry, but in many cases the owners of them had consolidated their position economically and socially by buying estates, so that as the century went forward among the landed proprietors could be found the Peels, the Arkwrights, the Barings, the Strutts and other families who had made their fortunes before they bought their land, many of whom became assimilated, or partially assimilated, into the old social system. It is probably true that in due course the progress of the Industrial Revolution threw up certain unassimilable fragments, men who had made fortunes but who showed that they remained rigorously outside the old system, largely by continuing to be Dissenters in religion and spirit, men like Sir Morton Peto, Sir Titus Salt or Samuel Morley. Even so, the attractive power of the old system was curiously great and the powers of its digestion remarkably strong. It is interesting to note that Samuel Morley, in his heyday a keen Dissenter a strong Temperance Reformer and a Radical who gave money to the Reform League, ended his days with an estate in the country, being polite to his local vicar, having sent his sons to Trinity College, Cambridge.[2]

There would no doubt come a time when even in the upper half of society the income derived from agricultural land would necessarily be less than the income derived from other sources. This change, however, would not necessarily reduce the predominance of the great estates for many of them commanded very considerable, and increasingly important, non-agricultural sources of revenue—the royalties from coal-mines, the income derived from urban house property or ground rents, or from the development of a watering place or a port. It is also probably true that from early in the century the gentry as well

[1] *Complete Peerage*, Vol VI (London 1926) p. 713 (Appendix H) taken from Bateman's *Great Landowners*. Clapham [op. cit. p. 115] 252-3
[2] Edwin Hodder *The Life of Samuel Morley*, 3rd ed. (London 1887) pp. 377-85

as the nobility were developing non-agricultural sources of income, so that it is not at any point easy to be sure that the incomes of any considerable group were wholly dependent upon what could be derived from the land.[1] The effect of this was probably very important; it probably militated against the social and political conflicts of nineteenth-century Britain conforming too closely to the conflict of one form of wealth with another form of wealth. Even when the owners of commercial and industrial wealth had been drawn into the old system they probably retained some feeling for the world in which their fortunes had been made. It was no doubt of importance that members of a family like the Barings should be high in the councils of the aristocracy, and it is significant that it was a Peel, the child of industrial wealth but the owner of an agricultural estate and a keen experimental farmer, who performed the great act of reconciliation in the repeal of the Corn Laws. It was also probably of great importance, both at that moment and later, that the interests neither of the aristocracy nor of the gentry were wholly identified with the fortunes of agriculture; and it probably made a very great difference to the social history of the country that when the fortunes of agriculture collapsed many of the great estates had other reasonably solid supports.

But it seems likely that this line of argument should not be pressed too hard in considering the crisis of the repeal of the Corn Laws, nor the history of the decade or so that followed it. It seems probable that in the middle of the century what came from agriculture remained a more important part of the income of most great estates than what derived from other sources.[2] If, as seems to be true, the position of the nobility and gentry was better established immediately after 1850 than it had been earlier in the century it was probably so because the condition of agriculture was better, not because of the development of non-agricultural resources.

[1] It is to be hoped that the sources of income of the great estates will be revealed in the forthcoming book by Professor David Spring of Johns Hopkins University, Baltimore. The problem of the gentry presents peculiar difficulties because it is not easy to define the class to be analysed or the kind of business interest to be analysed, but since the matter seemed to be both interesting and important I asked my friend Professor W. O. Aydelotte of Iowa State University to try to make a calculation based on the incomes of members of Parliament between 1841 and 1847. This he very kindly did and I print the results in an Appendix

[2] This apparently is the opinion of Professor David Spring, particularly after analysing the history of the estates of the Earl Fitzwilliam

This was not only the result of more satisfactory prices, but also of the working of the great improvements in agricultural technique which had been developed in the 'thirties and 'forties, and also of better estate management which had an important contingent cause. One of the greatest dangers to an estate was that it should be inherited by a spendthrift, as for instance by a man who would waste its resources by building a vast palace in the English countryside, or who would become involved in one or two of the more outrageous county elections, or who would throw too much away on the race-course or on the gaming table. In the middle of the century those dangers still existed. Fashionable debauchery did not cease when the Marquis of Hertford went to his own place in 1842, and the influence of folly was even more persistent. By 1847 the 2nd Duke of Buckingham and Chandos had ruined himself, and it is still difficult to see how even so silly a man had contrived to waste so magnificent an inheritance.[1] The 4th and last Marquis of Hastings, 'The King of Punters', went speedily and effectively to his ruin and death after the Derby of 1867, and the man whose fiancée he had stolen, Henry Chaplin, dissipated much of his estate by reckless expenditure on the race-course. Other possibilities of traditional extravagancies continued. Some very expensive country houses were still being built, unfortunately normally in the Tudor or Gothic style, so that folly did not even earn the compensation of notable aesthetic achievement.[2] But these cases were increasingly rare. Evangelical Christianity had made its inroads into the nobility to be followed a little later by the Oxford Movement and the Catholic revival, and even when its members were not definitely infected by some particular religious movement the general tone of people in high society in the middle of the century seems to have become much more responsible, more moral and more sober than it had been at the beginning. Whatever the results for their souls, the change had very beneficial effects on their finances.

In fact, it would seem that in the middle of the century many of the great estates were being run very effectively. The amounts set aside from the income of the estate for its improve-

[1] David and Eileen Spring *The Huntington Library Quarterly*, 'The Fall of the Grenvilles, 1844-1848', Vol XIX (February 1956) No. 2
[2] See Ralph Dutton *The Victorian Home* (London 1954) pp. 101-3

ment, either for definite agricultural improvement or for the provision of cottages and schools, were often exemplary, and it seems clear that those in charge were paying close attention to the best agricultural knowledge of the day. The records of the Royal Agricultural Society seem to suggest that often enough this interest in agricultural development came from the noble owner himself, but even where that was not the case it seems probable that they were very well advised, either by land agents or by those solicitors who had acquired a very remarkable knowledge of how great estates should be run.

Nevertheless, even though the agriculture to which the great estates contributed was in many ways efficient and scientific it would be a misunderstanding of the part it played in the making of Victorian England to think of it primarily as an industry organized like any other industry—primarily for the purposes of efficient production. It was, as has been said, rather organized to secure the survival intact of a caste. The proprietors of the great estates were not just very rich men whose capital happened to be invested in the land, they were rather the life tenants of very considerable positions which it was their first duty to leave intact to their successors. In a way it was the estate that mattered and not the holder of the estate, and the law went to very considerable lengths to prevent the holder from alienating or wasting the capital. This had not always proved to be effective against the unscrupulous and the extravagant, but it had the most unfortunate result that it made it very difficult or impossible to mortgage or sell land to gain capital that was needed for agricultural improvement, though money could possibly be borrowed for agricultural drainage under the Act which Peel had passed at the same time as the repeal of the Corn Laws.[1] It was also difficult to grant leases which would run for longer than the life of the existing owner. On the other hand, the land might become burdened with the results of the accidents arising from hereditary ownership, the estate might become overweighted by the jointures paid out to several dowagers, or it might be held during a minority in the chilling hands of very cautious trustees.

The laws which maintained these conditions were probably most hotly resented before the Corn Laws were repealed, when

[1] 9 and 10 Vict., c. 101

it was felt that the bread of the people was kept at a high price in order to support this system. But even after the repeal many continued to dislike them as unequal obsolete laws unduly favouring one section of the community against the rights of others who worked the land, and of the community itself, which had a general interest in the land. However, this system had another result which provided more direct and immediate offence to others who were not members of the aristocratic caste. It presupposed the rules of primogeniture. On the owner's death, in order that the estate might be kept intact it must not be divided among the other children, it must pass to the eldest son. For other children support must be found elsewhere. They might particularly, if they were girls, be furnished with an endowment raised on the security of the estate, thus burdening it with debt; or, if they were boys, they might enter the Church or the Army or the public service. If they did so, or wanted to do so, the whole force of aristocratic influence was turned on to find billets for them or to secure their promotion: indeed, at times it seemed as if the main object of politics was to enable a man to manœuvre himself into a position from which he could successfully ask for places for his younger sons, for the husbands of his daughters, for their children and for his other dependants.

In the past many, probably most, people had not been shocked by these practices; they had seemed to be no more than a very proper attention to natural ties. Where the general contents of the post-bag of a mid-nineteenth-century minister have been preserved they seem normally to demonstrate amply that it was not only members of the aristocracy who expended a great deal of their working life trying to turn up a job for themselves, or for those near and dear to them. Nevertheless, opinion in the nineteenth century progressively hardened against the whole system of patronage and its concomitants, fortified no doubt by the fact that there was an increasing number of articulate people who had no hope of participating in its benefits. Men began to object to pluralities in the Church, or to the presentation to all the fattest livings of clergymen with no obvious qualification for the duties and no very evident intention to perform them, if it was at all inconvenient to do so. They began to object to the purchase by aristocrats of commissions in the Army and of the promotion of inexperienced men over the heads of veteran officers who lacked sufficient money or influential connexions to get their deserts. They objected to the survival of offices with quaint medieval titles which enabled gentlemen of good birth to charge fees for performing services significant no doubt in the remote past, but which the passage of time had deprived of any imaginable purpose, or any intelligible meaning. Most of all they objected to the idea that the proper way to recruit the Civil Service was to permit aristocrats and politicians to nominate whom they would to be its members.

In 1854 the Northcote-Trevelyan report proposed to modify this system, but the political classes were not yet prepared to give it up at least as far as the Home Civil Service was concerned. The system remained apparently unchangeable and to those not profiting from it came to seem to be patently intolerable. In the winter of 1854-55 British administration contrived through sheer incompetence to let a magnificent army freeze and rot to death in the trenches before Sebastopol only nine miles from its base, and in 1856 in *Little Dorrit* Dickens wrote his bitter and brilliant chapter on the Circumlocution Office and the great family of the Tite Barnacles. Dickens was not being quite just, he only knew the office from the outside. It was not the aristocratic principle alone that had raised the Circumlocution Office in all its deadly perversity, it was partly the stringency of the rules of accounting imposed by the House of Commons for economy, and the general tendency of any large administrative system to strangle itself; indeed, the most charming and gracious of all the representatives of the aristocratic system, Sidney Herbert, burnt himself out trying to correct it, to be bitterly abused on his deathbed by Florence Nightingale, another member of the aristocratic caste, for not having done more. Nevertheless, the responsibility of the aristocracy was heavy. On the military side there was a heavy case against officers like the Earl of Cardigan who had purchased important positions which they were incompetent to fill; and there was something peculiarly indecent in the efforts made by the Horse Guards to silence the critics, efforts which are alluded to in the preface to *Little Dorrit*. And even if Parliamentary meanness rather than aristocratic jobbery was responsible for much that happened in that terrible Crimean winter, the administrative system that permitted these things had been built up by the old political classes. It had existed for their benefit. If Dickens' attack was not sufficiently discriminating it would be difficult to say that his anger was not well deserved.

This question of desert did not as it turned out matter very much. However reasonable or unreasonable were the administrative reformers, in 1856 the most significant fact about them was that they failed, even with the Crimean revelations to help them. Lord Palmerston in the end triumphed with insolent ease over them in the House of Commons. The lives of heroes had been vilely cast away, but the Tite Barnacles remained in comfortable possession; and behind the Tite Barnacles there still prospered the objects of John Bright's enmity 'the Lords and Great Proprietors of the soil'. In national politics they still held the power which he grudged to them, and in the countryside they were dominant.

III

Very much of that mid-nineteenth-century countryside was beautiful. Much of it was prosperous, supporting the most advanced farming in the world, much of it had been effectively drained and cleared of scrub and yet it suffered from very much fewer unsuitable urban and modern intrusions than it does today. The cottages were picturesque if often insanitary, and the scene was often diversified by ancient manor houses and noble palaces normally in full occupation. The countryside was indeed a curious mixture of the modern and the very old. You went to it by railway, but through the windows of the railway carriage or from the trap that carried you from the station might be seen homes and fields where lives were passed in the terms of conditions and relationships that had been developed long before the age of steam.

Presiding over that life were the country gentry, in the first half of the century in many districts the main source of governmental power. The correspondence of Graham, the Home Secretary with Peel as Prime Minister and the Duke of Wellington during the troubles of 1842 and 1843 shows how much the

Government at that moment felt that they depended on the vigour and staunchness of the local magistrates and how important it seemed to them that the country gentry should interest themselves in the work of the Bench and Quarter Sessions and so retain their 'natural influence' in the counties. After 1850 times were quieter, and possibly the successive Governments did not need the co-operation of the gentry so urgently. Various counties developed rural police forces; indeed after 1856 they were universal. As new administrative needs were developed for the rural areas they were handed over to elective *ad hoc* bodies and not entrusted to magistrates in Quarter Sessions. But the fact that the cumbrous network of separate districts for different services was developed was possibly partly caused by an unwillingness completely to dispossess the old government of the county in favour of a general elective body; while as far as the rural police were concerned, it seems that at times the gentry who were magistrates found it difficult to remember that they were not also their servants.

And whatever his legal duties, the moral responsibilities of a country landowner were still considerable. He had direct duties to his tenants: indeed few relationships were supposed to have more complicated historic and emotional overtones than that of a landlord with his agricultural tenants, particularly if their families had been on his land for several generations. Sir William Heathcote would have no Dissenters among his tenants even at the risk of pecuniary loss, so that there should be no difference in religion between landowner and tenant.[1] A landowner also had a duty to his neighbours, and where his neighbours were also his tenants or men employed by his tenants possibly living in a village at his gates his obligations became very strong indeed. He might share them with the local parson and, when in the middle of the century the parson developed marked Evangelical or Puseyite tendencies or a passionate desire to restore the church or to restore it in a way that the Squire disliked, there might easily be trouble.[2] Yet whatever he thought of the parson it was the duty of the Squire to attend church on Sundays with his family and servants to

[1] F. Awdry *A Memoir of Sir William Heathcote Bart.* (London 1906) p. 1 and p. 96
[2] On relations between squire and parson see Owen Chadwick *Victorian Miniature* (London 1960) and Thomas Hughes *James Fraser Second Bishop of Manchester* (London 1887) pp. 59-66, 72, 78-81

give an example; when he was in the country the Duke Wellington always went to church with that express object. It was probably the duty of the parson and the Squire to provide a school for the village, in which the Squire's wife and daughters possibly, and the parson's womenfolk more certainly, might sporadically attempt to teach, though in either case they were more likely to teach in Sunday School than in day school. Both sets of women seem pretty often to have accepted the duty of visiting the cottagers and giving help, advice and reproof in cases of illness, destitution or folly.[1]

How far this system was realized and in how many villages in different parts of the country it would be difficult to say, or what its results were. At a guess, and it is little more than a guess, it seems possible that its standards became higher, and its operations probably more intrusive, in the third quarter of the century than in the first. It must for instance have made a considerable difference to all concerned to have a resident incumbent at the church instead of a starveling perpetual curate, or a clergyman who rode in from a neighbouring parish to do duty. In some villages there seem to be some physical traces of what was done. Where there has been a very large estate it sometimes seems clear that the same architects have been employed in a good many villages to rebuild the cottages and to build the school. Elsewhere there may be a trace here and there of model cottages, a drastically restored church and the buildings of a National School. But for the school it seems probable that a parson was more likely to have carried the burden than a squire, partly because the clergy seem to have taken that responsibility more seriously than the landowners, and partly because there seem to have been a good many villages where there was a resident clergyman but no resident gentry to help him out. And if the physical remains of these activities are often far to seek, the moral results must be very largely not discoverable. No doubt the gentry were often intolerable, intrusive, arrogant and overbearing, and no doubt their operations were often deeply, if silently, resented, if in other cases they were taken for granted. They were probably quite often beneficent; indeed, the aristocratic ideal as practised by

[1] These relationships can be seen at their best in the life and in the novels of Miss Charlotte M. Yonge

ay had certain advantages over other more exalted
s realistic, based not on books but on experience
the life of the country which is uncompromising in
tion of fact, and it depended on personal service not
on th__ __and that someone else should be paid by someone
else to do what is to be done. On the whole it seems likely that
it did not a little to promote the civilization and welfare of
those it purported to serve, and even more probable that the
rule of the squires did much for the intelligent development of
agriculture, for it is to be remembered that it was this class
that produced such men as Philip Pusey and Sir John Bennet
Lawes.

However, whatever its virtues, one point is very clear and
very important: this aristocratic system was not going to prove
to be adequate to satisfy the moral and political demands of
the England of the third and still more of the fourth quarter of
the nineteenth century. One of its most serious defects was that
it was extremely arbitrary in its incidence. Often enough people
who have been brought up in a great country house have left
on record an account of the country folk of their youth, among
whom they claim were some of their best and oldest friends.
So no doubt they were, but they were probably rather a special
selection of country folk. A child would get to know very well
the groom who taught him to ride, the gamekeeper who taught
him to shoot or the gardeners in the grounds where he played,
and he would find his way easily about the village at the park
gates, the sons and daughters of which might very likely come
into service at the hall. If the tradition of the house was a good
one, as it very often was, these people would be friendly treated
and reasonably well looked after; but their condition would
bear little resemblance to that of the families of labourers living
not so very far off and working for farmers whose own margins
might be very small indeed.

This difference was reflected by something which a good
many observers seem to have noticed in parts of the mid-
nineteenth-century countryside, the difference between the
'closed' and 'open' village. There were some villages where the
property was in the hand of one landowner, which were very
strictly regulated particularly if the village was near to his
house; who lived in the cottages there and how they behaved

would be kept under very close control. This could be rather overwhelming, but in certain ways the villagers would benefit. It was in such villages that the model cottages would be built, in such a village there would probably be a national school at the edge of the park where it could be shown to visitors, and in such villages the rates would be kept down because no paupers nor people likely to become paupers would be permitted to remain there while the numbers of cottagers living there at all would be carefully restricted. This, however, necessarily meant that much of the labour needed by the farms in or near the village would in all probability be drawn from an open village, where there was no such close control, since the property was either in the hands of several small landowners or a remote landowner who cared very little about it. In such a village, life might be freer than it would be under the shadow of a great house, but the housing might be bad, there might be no school and since the village contained those people who were most likely to become economic casualties the rates might be high. From such an open village the labourer might have a long weary walk to his work near the closed village, for it must be remembered that the bicycle which has made such a tremendous difference to the lives of country people was not yet within the bounds of possibility. A good estate like that of the Duke of Bedford or the Duke of Rutland would try to make itself responsible for all the labourers it employed, and not draw from a community for which it in return did nothing, but it seems probable that not all landowners were in a position to do this, nor that they troubled much about it.[1]

The Poor Law obligation was more equitably spread by the Union Chargeability Act (28 and 29 Vict., c. 79).[2] But the matter has a wider reference than to the poor rates. A social system whose comprehensiveness depended on the knowledge or power or activity of individual landowners was not going to satisfy indefinitely the social conscience or the growing personal self-consciousness of the nineteenth century; nor were the standards, which many landowners thought were good enough for the poor, going to suffice. It is always dangerous to talk

[1] See Sir James Caird *English Agriculture in 1850-1851* (London 1852) pp. 75-76, 197, 516
[2] Clapham [op. cit. p. 115] 508-9

about the general conscience of a class which has long passed away, and it is normally certain that in fact no generalizations in such matters are accurate. Nevertheless, there does exist a certain amount of disquieting evidence about certain land-owners. For instance, various parish priests have left on record not only the wretchedness of the conditions of life of the men and women in their flock but also how unsatisfactory they found to be the attitude of the local gentry and too often of their brother clergy.[1] This evidence can find support from elsewhere. In fact, it seems clear that there were too many people in the countryside, alike among the farmers, landowners and the clergy, who rather easily believed, if they ever thought about the matter, that very miserable conditions were good enough for the poor since they had never known anything better. The results of that conception were inevitably and rightly to cause trouble whenever the country labourer was in a position to press his case.

In mid-century that time had not yet come. In the 'fifties there was little that the labourer could do to improve his position. He was not in a position to found an effective trade union, he was out of the way of political agitation, and to indulge in incendiarism which had in the past been one way of expressing his grievance was merely to commit a brutal and useless crime. No doubt if he was active and courageous he could take his sport in the woods at night in spite of the risk of gamekeepers and of 'justices' justice' if caught; or if of more sober cast of mind he could seek the Primitive Methodists and look to a better world where God would put down the mighty from their seat and exalt, in his own good time, the humble and meek. Nevertheless, if he should ever be granted a secular opportunity the labourer would have no reason to be content with the position the farmer and landlord had decreed for him, and then in the fulness of time both farmer and landowner would have to come to terms with that uncomfortable and unaccommodating challenge.

Nor for that matter, in spite of the sentiment and long-standing loyalties, was there necessarily a community of interest

---

[1] See Lord Sidney Godolphin Osborne *The Letters of S.G.O. . . . published in 'The Times' 1844-1888*, ed. Arnold White London, 1891. E. Wingfield-Stratford [op. cit p. 103] 191-4. W. Tuckwell *Reminiscences of a Radical Parson* (London 1905)

between landlord and tenant. After all, in the last resort they were on two sides of a bargain, and in a way their interests were necessarily in opposition to one another; and it was a bargain in which the law very definitely leant to the landlord's side. In England, leases were by no means universal so that the tenant might have no security of tenure, and, whether he had a lease or no, the law did not give him when he left his holding adequate rights to compensation for any improvements he might have effected in the land or in the farm buildings during his tenure. If he had sunk capital in the land he might lose it, as he might also do, together with all his tools, if there was a distraint for rent, which it was far too easy to effect. These things were not only the potential source of grave personal hardship, they had serious results for farming. Owing to the fact that he might so easily forfeit anything that he put into the land, the tenant might be deterred from applying capital to the land, and owing to the laws governing settled estates it might be impossible for the landlord also to raise sufficient capital to put into the land by the sale or mortgage of part of his property, so that in the result neither side might be in a position to supply the capital which was needed to develop that high farming, upon which the survival of the British agriculturist must increasingly depend, if difficult times came.[1]

In addition to the state of law about settled estates and compensation for improvement there was another grievance on the part of the agricultural tenant which may not in the last resort have been so serious but which seems to have given rise to great irritation; this was the grievance of the sporting rights which were reserved for the landlord. And here again it is to be noted that the landlord's rights were not only a grievance to the tenant but an offence against good farming, for the tenant might be required to maintain coppices and thickets on his land as cover for game which might destroy his crops but which he was not allowed to shoot. He might also be required to maintain cover for foxes, but fox hunting seems in most cases to have united neighbours in the country. The

[1] In all matters concerning the relationship between landlord and tenant, and in particular on the history of the breakdown of that relationship I am much indebted to the advice and help of Mr Cresap Moore, whose forthcoming work on *The End of the Politics of Deference* will I believe throw much light on this matter. I have also had the advantage of reading his unpublished dissertation

society revealed by Surtees or by Leach's pictures, the society frequented by Jorrocks and Soapy Sponge is coarse and earthy, but it is not in any way exclusive. There is a good deal of evidence that an extraordinary diversity of social types gathered at the covert side and that in the excitement of the chase men of rank and high position could be treated with very little reverence indeed. It was otherwise with shooting, which was very largely a sport for landlords to be enjoyed to a large extent at the expense of everyone else.

It would probably be wrong to think of that beautiful mid-nineteenth-century countryside as simply a scene of selfish exploitation and working-class misery. Conditions were too varied for that, and it seems clear that even among the working classes at that time there could be contentment and happiness. It would certainly be wrong to dismiss the aristocratic ideal as hypocritical and worthless; without doubt it was responsible for much good, if its action was often too uncertain and its standards too low. It would be a mistake to think of the agricultural community as being bitterly divided all the time with class hostilities. There were strong loyalties and deep mutual affection which united men in very different classes. Yet if you look close, the situation seems full of danger and challenge. It was going to be necessary some time to meet the challenge of the state of many farm labourers, it was going to be necessary to meet the challenge of the relationship of landlord and tenant, it would probably be necessary to answer the question whether the land should be the endowment of a class and the playground of the gentry or should be used in the most effective way possible for the production of food. And it might be necessary to answer this question: What would happen if the agricultural prosperity which they enjoyed in these golden years at last disappeared?

It is difficult to remember these things if you look at the innumerable hunting pictures of the middle of the nineteenth century, the rubicund gentry jolly and confident, the heavy swells with their whiskers, the pretty girls in their beautiful riding habits and queer top-hats and the robust beef-fed farmers. It is hard not to think that here is a power so deeply rooted and growing so powerfully that no blight could cause it to decay, no tempest strike it down. Yet on reconsideration of the whole matter it may be that a disquieting question may propose itself, a question which may also be suggested by the spectacle of Lord Palmerston chaffing the Radicals in the House of Commons after the Crimean War in 1856. It is this, 'For how long can these people cheat their fate?'

CHAPTER VIII

The New Politics
and the New Gentry

It is convenient to take the year 1867 as the point at which the old régime began to break. It is, of course, to a large extent only a date of convenience. Much that took effect in the next twenty years had started before 1867. The increase and more general distribution of the wealth of the country had begun much earlier in the century. The relatively wealthy men who came forward to claim their place in the new constituency organizations had no doubt been developing their fortunes and their aspirations for some years before 1867, and the economic and social developments that seem to have given a new self-confidence and independence to many of the rank and file must have been maturing for some time. The nonconformist activities which were so important in the election of 1868 must be referred back at least to the activities of men like Miall and Richard in the early 'sixties; in fact, the way was possibly prepared for them by the revivals of the 'fifties, certainly they were rendered effective by the growth in the number of non-conformists that had been going on throughout the century.

Nor, as has already been pointed out, was the Act of 1867 an effective instrument of change. There was too little redistribution of seats to allow the newly enfranchised majorities their full power in the House of Commons. The qualifications for the franchise had now become so complicated and the problems they raised so difficult, particularly in relation to the lodger franchise and the vexed problem of compounding for rates, that it is difficult even now to know how many new voters were enfranchised in particular constituencies. In several boroughs it was probably much less than was expected, while the country was still sealed off from the town with a higher voting qualification.

Nevertheless, on two important points the Act of 1867 signified a change. First it was the practical settlement of an important controversy. If the Reform Act of 1832 with all its defects had meant the final acceptance of the principle of progressive reform to meet the changing demands of the community, probably the Act of 1867 signified the acceptance, no less final, of the principle of democracy. Non-democratic elements still remained, and rejoiced in their strength. Those who did not accept the principles of democracy continued to find the prospect very disagreeable. The Liberal realists remained. The most trenchant expression of their views was probably James Fitzjames Stephen *Liberty Equality and Fraternity*, which was published in 1873, and the tendency towards Liberal realism seems to have inspired many of the Liberal Unionists in 1886. Nevertheless, in 1867 the dice were thrown. Those who feared democracy had said their say and had not been able to halt the course of events, and there could be no return or divergence, only a choice between delay and advance in one particular direction. The principle of democracy had been adopted, with whatever limitations it was going to be applied and whatever it might really mean in the actual disposition of power.

The other result of the Reform Bill of 1867 was more practical and immediate. In a good many constituencies there had been a considerable addition to the electorate, and in many constituencies these additions had been drawn from classes which had not been enfranchised before, changes which not only seemed to make new political developments possible but also a new type of constituency organization necessary. Therefore during the preparations for the election of 1868 the Liberals began to develop expedients in a good many constituencies which gave some part in the choice of candidate to the working-class voter.

When, however, the election was over, particularly after the Reform League had started to come to pieces, there seems to have been a probably unconscious and undesired tendency for these methods to be dropped and more oligarchical organizations to be developed. It was probably a natural tendency. In the circumstances of the time it was not probable that political leadership would remain in working-class hands, and in a voluntarily organized, voluntarily financed institution power is likely to come to those who supply most of the funds.[1] If it is possible to gain the necessary resources by a very large number of small subscriptions, then power is likely to be widely diffused through the whole association, if on the other hand it is necessary to depend on a small number of large subscriptions, then power is likely to be more concentrated; and it is probably always more easy to collect fairly large sums from a few deeply committed rich men than a great number of small sums from a crowd of small men whose interest in politics may not be very great.[2]

But even if working-class participation was going to be less than had been expected, there were to be other reasons for changes in the constituency organization of the Liberals after 1870. For one thing there was the intense dislike which the Dissenters felt for the education policy of the Liberal Government and for those Liberal members who had supported it, and there were also the aspirations of wealthy and important men whose fortunes were of relatively recent growth who wished to force their way further into the party's councils than the older local leaders quite desired, while the prevailing emphasis on democracy encouraged the belief that the control of the party ought to rest with the rank and file rather than with a self-appointed oligarchy at the top. These ideas and this situation were exploited by Joseph Chamberlain and the other organizers in the foundation and development of the National Liberal Federation. The plan was to encourage the foundation of local Liberal Associations on the Birmingham model. The ultimate power in such Associations appeared to lie in ward meetings which the poorest Liberal could attend after paying only a nominal subscription, and they seemed so well suited to the democratic need of the moment that they were rather quickly developed in a variety of towns. In 1877 Chamberlain summoned a conference of these associations to Birmingham to found a federation, which should bring the representative system more effectively to bear on Liberal policy, and to be addressed by Gladstone, the rejected leader of the people, who had retired from politics after 1874 and who now mysteriously reappeared at their head inspired by profound anger at the atrocities of the Turk and the wickedness of Lord Beaconsfield.

[1] Hanham [op. cit. p. 55] 11 ff.   [2] Hanham [op. cit. p. 55] 131-3

In actual fact there was something delusive in the claims of the National Liberal Federation. As has often been pointed out the Birmingham Liberal Association was not truly representative in its government, the power did not in fact rise from the ward meetings and direct the affairs of the executive, it descended from the executive and the ward meetings did much as they were told.[1] When the Liberal Federation came into being it was in fact more successful in reducing the personal independence of members of Parliament than in putting into effect the wishes of the rank and file. In several great towns there was a change of control at this time, but it was often not so much the transference of power to the people as the replacement of one rich man by another who was not very different in economic background and social position from those he displaced; sometimes it was no more than a change of generation. Most of this, however, was probably unavoidable, it was probably inevitable that the Liberal party should be controlled by a minority and at that moment by a wealthy minority. The idea that the control of any political party can lie in the hands of the rank and file is probably a phantasy, the mass of ordinary people are probably too inchoate, too confused in mind and too intermittent in their interest to give any definite lead, and the idea of democratic initiative is often the cloak for the operations of a small minority, to whose views the majority normally gives assent. Of course, if a section of the party feels that it is kept at arm's length, or new potentially leading personalities are misunderstood or opposed, there will be trouble. This was indeed to happen, for in due course the Liberal party was to pay heavily for its failure to give working men a larger part in the control of its constituency organizations, a failure which can be studied in the mismanagement of Keir Hardie at the beginning of his career. But at that moment the natural leaders of the Liberals were probably wealthy industrialists, men like Chamberlain, Mundella and Sir James Kitson, who were prepared to promote a Radical policy. It was appropriate that power should rest with them, and at the moment, whatever its hidden defects, the National Liberal Federation was justified

[1] For an analysis of the constitution of the Birmingham Liberal Association and the way in which it worked see Lowell [op. cit. p. 174] Vol I, pp. 483 ff. On the development of the caucus see Hanham [op. cit. p. 55] 125-54

by success, for it participated on a very large scale in the great Liberal victory at the general election of 1880.

That was indeed a spectacular victory. At that moment it might well have seemed that Disraeli's Reform Bill had given the Liberals a permanent lease of power. The Liberals had won a decisive victory in 1868. It is true that they had been badly defeated in 1874, but there had been special reasons for that which were no longer valid. In 1874 the Dissenters had been at issue with the party, by 1880 they had been integrated into it. In 1874 many of the counties were still under an obsolete domination, in 1880 this seemed to be breaking up. In 1880, with their great leader at their head and with in many towns a new constituency organization presenting so it seemed the most advanced features of democracy, they swept into power. In 1884 they triumphantly reformed the electorate a third time and destroyed those anomalous pocket boroughs on which so much of the power of their adversaries had rested, at the same time they enfranchised the working man in the counties to complete the good work. In 1885 they were rewarded with another great victory, and at that moment there might have seemed to be every excuse to prophesy that even if the Liberals did not retain power permanently at least the Tories would never regain it.

In fact, the future was to be surprisingly and significantly different. The reasons for this are important. The simplest of them is that, as so often, political success produced its own antidote. When the party was being realigned on a new axis after 1865 and while it was being fused into a single whole by the volcanic powers of Gladstone's personality, it was natural that certain indigestible and recalcitrant fragments should resist this process and slip over to the other side. The movement started in the 'sixties when Palmerstonians such as W. H. Smith began to go over to the Conservatives, it reached its culmination in 1886 when large numbers of Liberal Unionists seceded at the time of Gladstone's first attempt to grant Home Rule for Ireland. This secession was the more drastic because the deserters included not only large numbers of the Whig nobility, and of the academic Liberals at Oxford and Cambridge, but also Joseph Chamberlain himself.

Even more important than this, there were areas of the

country in which Conservatism was naturally strong, not because it was imposed by any dictatorial political control but because it was favoured by the people. There were also areas where by the natural process of events it was going to become strong. Conservatism seems to have had considerable natural strength in parts of Lancashire, partly deriving from feelings which dated from the time when the Tories had supported and the Liberals opposed factory legislation, and partly no doubt based upon the strong Protestant feelings which flourished wherever there had been a numerous invasion of the Roman Catholic Irish. This Lancashire Conservatism had its roots in past history; elsewhere Conservatism was being brought into existence by social changes in the country which had only recently become pronounced, in fact the same changes which in this period were altering the structure of the Liberal party. The basic cause was the greater diffusion of wealth. This had created a relatively prosperous and stable section of the working classes which at the moment, except in Lancashire, probably normally voted Liberal. It had improved the position of large sections of the lower middle class, who, at least if they were Dissenters, almost universally voted Liberal. No doubt such people were anxious for at least the appearance of greater political importance in party control than they had had in the past, and a policy which more nearly suited their susceptibilities than that of the Government which came into existence in 1868. The same process had also produced rich men who were anxious to play a leading rôle in the party and were attracted by a radical attack on the landed nobility. But this same diffusion of wealth had also inevitably produced a number of people who had reached an economic and social position which a radical policy on the part of the Liberal party might seriously threaten, or at best would not improve.

The extent of this social tendency has yet to be fully explored.[1] It is not yet clear how far down the social pyramid it penetrated. Certainly in the upper ranges there had developed a group who had managed to develop to a greater or less extent what might be called the apparatus of a gentleman such as additional servants, a trap or carriage, special education for their child-

---

[1] Mr J. P. Cornford of Trinity College, Cambridge, is working on this, and I owe much to his suggestions

ren.[1] In a good many cases the margin seems not to have been great, while the expense of maintenance increased continuously. They had therefore reason to fear the pressure of other classes; moreover they had become separated from the sympathies and class loyalties which their parents had entertained, and, as the third quarter of the century went forward, to an increasing extent they came to live in places remote from other classes and from the surroundings in which their parents had grown up. For as the cities grew and public transport improved, more and more of those who could afford it went to live in suburbs increasingly far from the centre of the town and the large masses of the working-class population.

This migration had very important social consequences. As has been said, in 1873 the Methodists drew attention to the serious implications of this tendency. They complained that it caused Wesleyans to desert the old chapels in the centres of the cities which numbered poor people in their congregation and said they, 'not a few, moreover, have been lost to us altogether by this modern custom'.[2] But if lost to the Wesleyans, it seems not impossible that these might have been found on Sundays in the Anglican churches which were springing up in the outer suburbs, and if so the change might symbolize their adoption of the habits and feelings of the new single class communities which were coming into existence on the edge of the great towns, and which might well present to the Conservatives constituencies where their chances of success were very good indeed.

Amid the disappointments and disasters of the general election of 1868 there were here and there signs that these possibilities did exist for the Conservatives. There were successes in Lancashire, whither Gladstone had gone unmuzzled in 1865 and whence he now retired. W. H. Smith beat John Stuart Mill in Westminster and possibly, most significant of all, Lord George Hamilton defeated Labouchere in Middlesex, a district which, as apparently the party managers did not yet realize, had recently become suburban.[3] But this was a harvest which

[1] On this see J. A. Banks *Prosperity and Parenthood* (London 1954) pp. 48-112, 170-196 and *passim*

[2] *Minutes of Wesleyan Conference 1873* (loc. cit. p. 184] 178-9

[3] Lord George Hamilton *Parliamentary Reminiscences and Reflections 1868-1885* (London 1917) pp. 1-12

could not be gathered by the old methods. It would not be possible to organize these new Conservative voters by relying on the influence of a local landowner and by the old-fashioned method of simple bribery. As with the Liberals, it would be necessary to create representative, or apparently representative, constituency organizations to replace, or apparently to replace, the old self-appointed oligarchical controls; and the old oligarchies might not much relish the process.

Now, local Conservative constituency clubs had existed in the days when the party had been first organized in the 'thirties. There had been registration societies, Conservative Operative Societies and Constitutional Clubs, but they had been very definitely political auxiliaries. Their main duty was to keep an eye on the register and they seem to have had nothing at all to do with the choice of a candidate, which is the most important function of a constituency organization.[1] In any case most of them seem to have disappeared in the course of the century, but as the pace quickened in the 'sixties other associations came into existence to take their place. As the militant Nonconformists became more obstreperous, Church defence societies sprang up over the country; there seem to have been a good many of these and they would bear more investigation than they have as yet received, and in 1867 a Union for the whole country came into existence at first primarily to counter the assaults of the Nonconformist pressure groups, which however became a general political organization for the whole party and turned in due course into the National Union of Conservative Associations. At least one of the Conservative Operative Associations had survived in Lancashire and other Conservative working-class clubs seem to have come into existence there. W. H. Smith developed and largely subsidized a club in Westminster, and clubs were developed elsewhere very often for Conservative working men.[2]

All this was a beginning of what had to be done, but it was inchoate and in some ways unsatisfactory. It was particularly undesirable to segregate working men into separate political organizations, as Disraeli seems to have realized, and the

---

[1] On these clubs R. L. Hill *Toryism and the People, 1832-46* (London 1929) and N. Gash *Politics in the Age of Peel* (London 1953)

[2] Hanham [op. cit. p. 55] 105-9

effective reorganization of the party started when the old party agent Spofforth, fit representative of the old régime, was replaced by John Gorst, a man of a different class, a barrister who had himself sat in Parliament and was to sit there again. Gorst consolidated the party organizations, endeavoured to put down the use of bribery and to promote the formation of real representative constituency bodies. He probably succeeded in a good many urban constituencies, though it is a little difficult to be quite sure how far his claims were justified; he certainly regarded himself as one of the architects of victory in 1874. One thing is however clear, he met with a good deal of opposition. Part of this probably came from the people who disliked the new type of party organization, particularly when it by-passed the magnates of a constituency who had up till now held the keys of power in their hands. Part was certainly due to the character of Gorst himself, for though he was a man of ability and integrity he was a difficult man, disappointed with the rewards he had received and capable of saying and doing unwise things. The result was that he was forced to resign in 1876. After that things went from bad to worse. Gorst had retired, Disraeli as Prime Minister was interested in other things and indeed soon went to the House of Lords, and those in charge were incompetent and not sensitive to new conditions. Consequently the organization fell off, corruption crept back again, and it was possibly partially as a result of these failures that the Conservatives suffered their severe defeat in 1880.[1]

The immediate sequel was an attempt to reorganize the party and the return of Gorst to office, but the old difficulties re-appeared and he left his job again in 1882. This time, however, he found a very brilliant ally; Lord Randolph Churchill, the son of the Duke of Marlborough, was already waging a lively campaign both against Gladstone, his natural target, and against the leader of his own party in the House of Commons, Sir Stafford Northcote. It is probable that Gorst with his know-ledge of the constituencies and of the party organization gave force and direction to Lord Randolph's attack on the official leadership, certainly Lord Randolph realized part of the situation very clearly indeed. He realized that if the Conservative party was to regain power it must attract new classes and

[1] Hanham [op. cit. p. 55] 114-17 and 356-68

that it must break away from the old oligarchical methods to enable new men to have their part in the management. He therefore developed the creed of Tory Democracy and for a season endeavoured to turn the Council of the National Union into an effective representative body, while he helped to create a new popular Conservative organization in the Primrose League. But brilliant and swiftly successful though he was, he may not have fully realized what hand he ought to play. For if it was true that the most likely recruits for the Conservative party were men who had achieved wealth, then an advanced social policy which competed with Chamberlain for the support of the working classes was not likely to attract them.

He also may not have realized the full realities of his own personal situation, or the power of those he was playing against. He was confronted in fact by a much more formidable figure than the amiable and ineffective Stafford Northcote, for the real leader of the party was the leader in the House of Lords, that formidable bearded figure the Marquis of Salisbury, and it is also possible that Lord Randolph did not recognize the full danger, brilliance and ruthlessness of one very close to him, who had indeed been one of his allies, but was Lord Salisbury's nephew, A. J. Balfour. In play with such men he needed all the resources at his disposal, but he was wilful, intoxicated by his own brilliance, and probably did not realize the importance for his game of Gorst with his knowledge of the constituencies, certainly he seems to have come to terms with Lord Salisbury in 1884 behind Gorst's back, to Gorst's annoyance. But at the moment all seemed to go well and in 1886 he reached his apogee as Chancellor of the Exchequer and leader of the House of Commons, and then, as is well known, he completely collapsed. He proved himself to be an impossible colleague, he tried to force his views on the budget by resigning, but it was found possible to supply his place and, since he was not supported by the party in general, the whole of his magnificent position was forfeit.[1]

---

[1] On Lord Randolph Churchill the standard work is Winston Spencer Churchill *Lord-Randolph Churchill* 2 vols. (London 1906); to this must now be added R. V. R. James *Lord Randolph Churchill* (London 1959). Neither author is, however, primarily interested in the problems of party organization still less in the social changes which lie behind the development of parties; on all such problems further work must be done

The tragic and significant fact about the Lucifer dive of Lord Randolph Churchill is that apparently it had no effect whatsoever on the course of events. The Conservative party went forward conquering and to conquer. 1886 seems to be one of the decisive turning-points in political history. Between 1868 and 1885 the Conservative party and the forces it represented in the country appear to be in irremediable decline while the Liberal party is in the ascendant. After 1886 the Conservatives enjoyed power till 1905, with the exception of the years 1892-95. In 1906 the Conservatives suffered a very severe electoral defeat, it is true, but they virtually returned to power in 1918 and have continued to hold it ever since with three short intervals, 1923-24, 1929-31 and 1945-51. No doubt these results can be interpreted in different ways, but however interpreted the contrast with the period before 1886 is remarkable, and it is heightened by the fact that the great Liberal party went into decline after 1918, a decline ironically much assisted by the working of the system of single member constituencies introduced by the Reform Act of 1884.

Of course, adventitious factors had much to do with this revolution of fortune. For instance, the ruin of the Liberal party was much assisted by the daemonic power of two Liberal statesmen of genius. The way that Gladstone handled the Home Rule issue between 1885 and 1886, and the way in which he handled Joseph Chamberlain probably made the rent at that date worse than it need have been; and the energy with which Lloyd George tore the party in two between 1916 and 1918 no doubt contributed a deadly blow at a moment of great political peril. But it seems probable that the misadventures of political history cancel out one against the other; there were certainly mismanagements and misfortunes on the Conservative side, and a terrifying electoral disaster in 1906, but their results were not so fatal. It also seems unlikely that one issue, like the issue of Irish Home Rule, really controlled the course of political history for more than a relatively brief period, in so far as it did control it over the whole electoral field at any time.

What probably in the long run determines the shape of politics are the social movements, the groupings and regroupings in the mass of the community, which are beyond the reach of politicians; and what happened at this moment has already been suggested. In the second and third quarter of the nine-teenth century a mass of industrial and commercial wealth had come together at a central point in the social pyramid. It extended from the great manufacturers and merchants down-wards through the shopkeepers and clerks to the upper ranges or the working class, the skilled workmen and craftsmen. The people in this section often differed widely in their ideas, their religion, their way of life and their politics. But enough of them resembled each other closely enough to supply the foundations of the great Liberal party which was the most important poli-tical fact in the country between 1865 and 1885. However, as is normally the case with the situations which such forces produce, at the very moment when one social pattern had become marked a close inspection could have shewn that the currents of change were preparing a new social pattern that would succeed it, and that in its turn would at least partially define the politics of the country for the next twenty years and probably for longer.

Speaking in very general terms, two processes seem to have been at work. At one point the increase in wealth, the increase in self-consciousness and confidence in a section of the working class had gradually created a new social group whose centre of gravity so to speak was at a lower point in the economic and social pyramid than in the group on which the Liberals had depended. More people in this group would have more markedly different interests from those who were the natural leaders of the old group than had been the case in the past, and they would want different things. Whether in fact this must necessarily have led to the replacement of the Liberal party by a Labour party it would be impossible to say, but it seems likely that if it had not done so an effective Liberal party in the second quarter of the twentieth century would have been very different in structure and in policy from the one which Gladstone led, or Chamberlain aspired to lead. However, while this was happening at one point in the scale, at another point the currents of social change were depositing another group which was to form the foundation of a new Conservative party.

II

The effect of this second process became evident before the first process became in any way decisive. It appears in the unexpected renewal of Conservatism at the end of the century; but it was a renewal, not a return. There could be no return to the political conditions that had been normal before 1865. The aristocratic society which had been so firmly planted in rural England could not survive unchanged till the end of time, or even, without any change, till the end of the nineteenth century. Rural England itself was changing and contracting, contracting physically so that the actual acreage in which rural conditions can be said to have existed or to have existed without the intrusion of some urban element had become progressively less, contracting morally so that it became of much less importance to the country.

The town had invaded the countryside in a variety of ways. The growth of industrial cities and towns had meant that areas that had quite recently been farmland had sometimes become covered with densely packed working-class houses, or sometimes had been more loosely and extensively penetrated by suburbs of varying social standing or further out still by the houses of wealthy men whose centre of gravity was the town. Sometimes industry had pushed its fingers directly through the countryside, sometimes creating new towns or sometimes only industrialized villages. This is what had happened with the development of coalfields in Durham or South Wales, or with the railways which introduced alternative employment into districts where previously the background had been completely agricultural and called into existence new urban centres like Swindon and Crewe.[1] Or in some cases there might be the development of small pockets of industry, a brick-field, a brewery, a tannery. But whatever was the process of urbanization it was a threat to the coherence of the countryside. In some cases there might be a flow into the area of people like the Irish

---

[1] E.g. on the growth of Swindon see *Studies in the History of Swindon* by L. V. Grinsell, F.S.A., H. B. Wells, M.A., H. S. Tallamy, M.A., A.L.A., and John Betjeman (Swindon 1950)

who were strangers to past traditions and not by nature amenable. In some cases many of the young men would be diverted into a new form of labour which meant a new way of life, while men of wealth and importance would emerge who would not be subject to the ordinary influences of the country but rather hostile to them.

The first two Reform Bills had in some sort protected the lords of the countryside from the results of this process. The first enfranchised, as boroughs in their own right, the industrial towns whose inhabitants would otherwise have voted in the counties and possibly liberalized a number of them, but because it increased the numbers of county constituencies and retained a large number of country pocket boroughs it did not allow the industrial towns so enfranchised to preponderate in the new electorate. The second emphasized the separation of the county and borough electorate and also permitted the survival of a number of small country constituencies which offset the members of the great centres of population. None of this could, however, reverse the fact that the urban population was in the second half of the nineteenth century continually gaining in size over the rural population and that urban conditions were intruding into the countryside; while the authors of the third Reform Bill of 1884 had no desire at all to protect the country from the influence of the town. The country voter was given a vote on the same terms as the borough voter, there was a drastic redistribution of seats, many of the small pocket boroughs were finally disenfranchised and it was believed that the Liberals intended so to rearrange the constituencies that rural voters would normally be grouped with a majority of urban ones by whom they would be submerged. It was for this reason that the House of Lords demanded to see the heads of the Bill for redistributing seats before they passed the Bill for enfranchising new voters. It seems doubtful whether they did themselves much good by this procedure.

But the Reform Act of 1884 was only the last stage in the process by which the Conservatives in large part lost the battle of the counties. There were two factors in this process. In the first place the agricultural prosperity upon which so much depended first became unstable and then disappeared. As Lord Ernle wrote of this period, 'Since 1862 the tide of agricultural prosperity had ceased to flow; after 1874 it turned and rapidly ebbed.'[1] But at the same time there were signs of increasing independence on the part of farmer and labourer, and growing tension between tenant and landowner.

There seem to have been a variety of domestic reasons for this, and, especially after 1868 there was the disturbing example of Ireland. In Ireland it was clear that the main centre of trouble was the power of the landlords, and from 1869 onwards the Liberals started to legislate first timidly then drastically to reduce the power of the landlords and transfer the real control over the land to their tenants. Conditions in England were widely different from those in Ireland and the English landlord could make a case for himself which the Irish landlord could not normally do. Nevertheless, there were uncomfortable analogies, and land reform was in the air. Consequently it is not surprising that the minds of English Radicals turned with ever greater insistence to the position of English landlords and to the law which favoured them so notably. It might not be at all likely that at that moment the matter would be effectively pressed at once as far as the Liberals were prepared to go in Ireland, or as many Radicals desired for England. But the tendencies of the time meant that proposals would be made on such matters as the form of the law affecting compensation for tenants' improvements or of the laws affecting Settled Estates, matters on which many tenants not necessarily Radical urgently desired changes which the Conservatives were reluctant to concede.

In addition to the legal question, there were other sources of tension in these years. As early as 1862 there were signs of trouble between landlord and tenant over the proposals in a Game Preservation Act which many farmers very much disliked. In 1864 an old agricultural grievance emerged again which had on earlier occasions been inconvenient for the Conservatives, the grievance of the Malt Tax. This was a tax for which the farmers had a very great dislike, an exaggerated dislike as it turned out, for when in the end it was repealed they did not gain nearly as much relief as they had hoped for; it was, however, a tax which had for long been considered to be necessary

[1] Lord Ernle *English Farming Past and Present*, 5th Ed. (London 1936) p. 377 and ff.

for the country's finances and the Conservative leaders could not risk a promise that they would be able to do without it if they got into power. Unfortunately for them, Gladstone as Chancellor of the Exchequer held the financial initiative in this matter. In any year he might decide that it was now possible for him to modify or abolish the tax, things which the Conservative leaders could not possibly pledge themselves to do in undisclosed circumstances in the future. In 1864, just before the election of 1865, Gladstone modified the tax, which tempted many farmers to try to get the whole tax abolished. At the general election of 1865 two independent farming candidates took the field to agitate for the repeal of the tax. They were not Anti-Conservative, the men they attacked were Whigs, and one of them, C. S. Read, was prepared to take office for a short time in Disraeli's Government. But their appearance was a serious portent for the Conservatives; they had not been sponsored by the usual landowning influence and the policy they advocated was one which the Conservative leaders could not possibly support.

It might have been possible to counteract these tendencies if the Conservatives could have found a policy which would unite both landlord and tenant in the face of common dangers. But they could not do so. Earlier in the century when the Corn Laws had not yet been repealed tenant and landlord had been united on the common policy of the protection, but even then the Conservative leaders were unable to retain the Corn Laws. Towards the end of the third quarter to have declared for the re-imposition of the Corn Laws would have been to sacrifice all hope of ever gaining a majority in Parliament again. The only moment during these years when circumstances suggested a policy on which landlord and tenant could agree was during the cattle plague of 1865 and 1866. The policy which the agricultural community desired to be adopted to deal with the plague was that of the compensated slaughter of infected animals and the prohibition of suspect imports from abroad. The Government did not wish to adopt this policy, since it appeared to be a kind of protection, but in 1866 the county members united to force the hand of the Government, and were successful. But this was a very narrow bond of union at a time when other matters, sporting rights, compensation for tenants' improvements, the laws concerning settled estates, the wishes of the landowners and the tenants, were splitting the countryside.

Then in the early 'seventies a new source of danger appeared, the formation of Trade Unions by the farm labourers. This was the cause of more disagreement between the tenants and the landlords, for the landowners seem to have to some extent sympathized with the Unions, or at least not to have wished to antagonize men who it now seemed clear would at some time or other have the Parliamentary vote. Therefore the landlords intervened in various instances to prevent the farmers from destroying the Unions, and the farmers on their part took steps to secure that those landowners who were too favourable to the Unions did not stand in the general election of 1874. In spite of this, it was not likely that the labourers would favour the landlords. They had little reason to love the order of the countryside in which the landlords had taken their pleasure. Their leaders were apt to be Primitive Methodists and therefore to include the disestablishment of the Church of England in their programme. Altogether it was not going to be difficult to persuade them that their real enemy was the landowner, that if his influence was removed and the legal trammels which hampered the farmer were destroyed the lot of the labourer would be better.

Nor were there lacking those who were anxious to enlist the farm labourers into a general radical movement, and when the labourers came to form their Unions they gained a very formidable ally. These Unions developed in 1871 and 1872 in various counties, but the beginning of the National Movement is always held to have been the meeting at Wellesbourne in February 1872 which was addressed by Joseph Arch. Wellesbourne is in Warwickshire, the same county as Birmingham, and twelve days later Joseph Chamberlain made a passionate speech there calling attention to the wrongs which the agricultural labourer had suffered and proclaiming his right to have a share in governing the shires in which he lived. Chamberlain's close friend Jesse Collings also became trustee for the National Agricultural Labourers Union of which for a time Joseph Arch was organizing secretary.

The situation therefore in the early 'seventies was full of dangers for landowning interest, but the full extent of them was

concealed. At the time of the Franco-Prussian Wa
recovery of prices, if also an increase of rents. T
political position in the counties seemed to be very
The landlords still retained their leadership in cou...,
as the history of the chambers of agriculture seems to show, a...
except in very rare cases held the elections to Parliament in
their hands. In a description of Gorst's work in developing
Conservative Constituency Associations before 1874 Gorst's son
said that: 'In the counties these associations always remained
aristocratic in character and chiefly consisted of country gentlemen and the superior class of farmers.'[1] This was a contrast
to the more popular associations which were being developed
elsewhere, but the policy seemed to be justified by its results.
In the general election of 1874 the Conservatives won 143 of the
seats for the English counties, excluding Monmouth, as against
only 27 county seats won by Radicals and Whigs.[2]

It was a fatal victory. The years 1874 to 1879 proved to be
disastrous for the English corn-grower. There were a series of
very bad harvests culminating in the terrible year 1879, but
prices did not rise because of the importation of foreign corn
and rents did not fall, or at least did not fall fast enough. In
previous years when things had gone wrong with agriculture the
Conservatives had been able to blame the Government, which
was normally Liberal or Whig; now the Government was itself
Conservative and did, indeed situated as it was politically was
probably able to do, singularly little for the farmers.

At the outset the Conservative Chancellor for the Exchequer
was able to make an important concession to the county rate-
payer, transferring certain expenses from the rates to the central
government and providing increased grants for others.[3] But he
was not able to abolish the Malt Tax. With the legal grievances
of the farmers the Government dealt ineffectively, making what
seemed to be half-hearted efforts which did not get to the roots
of the problem. In 1875 they produced an Act to give the tenant
compensation for improvement which was held to be ineffective
and derisory.[4] In 1877 they produced the Settled Estates Act,
which was largely a consolidating Act but allowed tenants for

---

[1] Quoted in Hanham [op. cit. p. 55] 114-15
[2] Hanham [op. cit. p. 55] 25, note 1
[3] 37 and 38 Vict., c. 54. Hanham [op. cit. p. 55] 38
[4] 38 and 39 Vict., c. 92

to apply to the Chancery Division of the High Court for leave to sell the land or to grant leases binding on their successors, though it allowed in certain conditions the granting of leases up to 21 years.[1] This was much less than what was needed. What was needed was to give to the tenant of an estate for life liberty to grant leases or to sell land without referring to a court at all. In 1880 the Tory Government, hard hit by the disasters to agriculture, apparently determined to yield this and a new Bill, the Settled Land Act, was brought forward, but the sands had run out, Parliament was dissolved without anything effective having been done. The snapping-point had come.[2]

During the period of the Conservative ministry discontent among the farmers had been growing. In 1875 there had been indignation at the miserable nature of the Conservative Act for compensation, and C. S. Read, one of the independent farmers' candidates of 1865, retired from the Government. In 1879 a farmers' alliance had been formed by a certain James Howard, with apparently the assistance of O'Donnell, an Irish Home Ruler who was interested in the landlord question in Ireland. In 1880 the farmers' alliance played a part in the contests for the counties at the general election, as did also the National Liberal Federation. Two land reformers were returned, Howard for Bedfordshire and Duckham for Herefordshire, but it is not altogether easy to form an estimate of the influence of either body, since it is difficult to abstract what they did from the results of other factors operating in this election and it is not satisfactory to trust too completely to their own accounts of the matter. Certainly the results of the election were not only damaging to the Conservatives, at that moment they were menacing for the future. The Conservative English county members were reduced from 143 to 116, and it seems probable that the results might quite easily have been worse for the Conservatives. *The Annual Register* for 1880 says that this election

[1] 40 and 41 Vict., c. 18

[2] For the Government's intentions in 1880 and indeed for a masterly account of the legal position see Lord Cairn's speech on 23rd February, *Hansard* Vol CCL (3rd Series) 1644 ff., on the Settled Estates Act and the Settled Land Act see R. E. Megarry and H. W. R. Wade *The Law of Real Property* (2nd ed. London 1959) 274 ff., and Sir A. Underhill *Select Essays in Anglo-American Legal History*. (Cambridge 1908) Vol III, pp. 679 ff. I owe much in this matter to the help of Dr H. W. R. Wade. I ought to add that any mistakes in this account of the law are undoubtedly my own

was remarkable for the number of seats contested, particularly of county seats, which looks as if the Liberals saw signs that in a good many places the old monopoly was breaking up; but even so it seems that they did not recognize the greatness of their opportunity, for the *Register* adds: 'How slow Liberals were to believe in the possibility of gaining any victories in the counties, may be judged from the fact that in one county, North Lincolnshire, the candidate, Mr Laycock retired from his canvass, came forward again a quarter of an hour before the nomination took place, and was returned at the top of the poll.'[1]

Thereafter new blows were rained in a savage succession on the unfortunate landowning interest; for the Liberals did all those things the Conservatives had been unable to do, and some things they can have only envisaged in nightmares. In 1880 the Ground Game Act was passed which gave the occupier an inalienable right to destroy hares and rabbits on his land.[2] In 1880 the Malt Tax was converted into a beer duty. In 1882 the Settled Land Act was passed two years too late.[3] In 1883 an Act was passed giving a tenant adequate rights to compensation for improvement, in 1883, also, the Corrupt Practices Act was passed which, even more than the Ballot Act of 1872, made old methods of electioneering impossible.[4] In 1884 the farm labourer was enfranchised, the whole country was cut up into equal electoral districts and the small patronage boroughs disappeared. In 1885 another general election was held under the terms of the new Reform Act, during which a concerted attack was made on the landowners and Joseph Chamberlain raged horribly over the whole scene breathing fire from his mouth against the landowning Whigs as much as against the landowning Tories. The result was a curious reversal in politics, for though the Liberals were not nearly as successful as they had hoped to be in the towns, they were saved by the votes in the county constituencies, and so secured in the end 335 votes to the Conservatives' 249.[5] Indeed, in the counties men from

---

[1] *The Annual Register*, 1880, New Series (London 1881) Pt I, pp. 50-1
[2] 43 and 44 Vict., c 47
[3] 45 and 46 Vict., c. 38
[4] Tenants Improvements 46 and 47 Vict., c. 61. Corrupt Practices 46 and 47 Vict., c. 51
[5] Garvin [op. cit. p. 202] Vol II, p. 124

completely outside the old landowning caste won seats, such as a townsman like George Newnes the Wesleyan publisher, who was elected for Cambridgeshire, or a labourer like Joseph Arch, who was elected for North-West Norfolk.

Things do not end simply or quickly in England, but this looks like the end of a very long chapter. In many places the old form of political influence had been destroyed, and old political methods seemed to have become obsolete. The agriculture which had seemed so important socially and politically had received a shattering blow, to be followed by others, for the misfortunes of the corn-growing districts were followed after an interval by the threat to British livestock that came from cold storage. The balance of the country had changed, and the agricultural community were now heavily outweighed by the town-bred people who must be provided with food from whatever source it could come most abundantly and cheaply, and that source was not the farmer at home. Commercial and industrial wealth now bulked larger in the country's capital and income than did the landowner's agricultural wealth and the income which was derived from it; and very soon the mechanism of representative government was to be introduced into the administration of the shire itself. In 1888 the County Councils Act took nearly all of their administrative powers from the justices of the peace and gave them to the new elective county councils, and one of the greatest of all historians realized the significance of the occasion. It was the passing of the Act of 1888 that led F. W. Maitland to write his very brilliant paper 'The Shallows and Silences of History' to mark the disappearance of a form of government of very long standing and of great historical significance.

Indeed, to a man with historical imagination the moment might well seem to be a notable one. Those old elements in English society—the landed interest the gentry the nobility—had played a very long and very important part in English history. Even if the hereditary connexions were not always so long dated or so continuous as some of their number liked to pretend, as orders of society the body of the nobility and gentry had come confidently out of the mists of time, and now perhaps in the bustling industrial Liberal England of the nineteenth century there was no longer room for them. At length, now that

the fourth quarter of that century was well under
bright day was done and they were for the dark.

III

But were they for the dark? If you had taken your stand in
Hyde Park on a fine afternoon during the season of some year
towards the end of the century and watched the carriages go by
it is possible you might have been tempted to believe that
several of them had not got very far in that direction. Of course,
there was much new wealth in London, but I think it would be
found that a good many of the well-dressed people you saw
were the bearers of ancient names. That would be certainly true
if you went into the House of Commons, and if you penetrated
the countryside you would still find many ancient halls and
noble palaces in full occupation, if some of the vicarages and
rectories were beginning to look a little threadbare, and some
of the halls and country houses were let for the summer to rich
townspeople.

In fact, much of the life in the countryside might seem in
appearance to be the same. Much of the agricultural prosperity
had gone, and many of the young men had gone also, which
may be part of the reason why agricultural radicalism had not
been pressed as far as at one moment seemed probable. But
many of the old relationships seemed to have survived, and in
many constituencies the habits of the politics of deference seem
to have continued but thinly disguised by the forms of a more
representative system.

What lay behind many of these survivals was no doubt the
fact that so many of the great estates had been able to draw
their income largely from non-agricultural resources. As a
result some of the great noblemen were still among the richest
men in the country; the will of the 3rd Marquis of Bute which
was proved in May 1901 shewed an estate valued at £1,864,310[1]
and that of Earl Fitzwilliam in June 1902 one valued at
£2,950,000[2] and there were some other very large noble
fortunes at that time. How far this wealth on the old scale

---

[1] *Complete Peerage*, Vol II (London 1912) p. 445
[2] *Complete Peerage*, Vol V (London 1926) p. 525

 continued to be enjoyed by all the nobility or still more by the gentry it would be impossible to say without a good deal of research; no doubt an estate which depended too completely on agricultural rents was very hard hit. But even with the gentry there must have been a fair number with non-agricultural resources and investments, and not a few who had married into non-agricultural fortunes. More than this, to judge by very haphazard impressions, there seem to have been a good many places where a substitution had happened, where the old family had sold out and disappeared and a new family whose wealth had been made elsewhere occupied the big house and kept it up —house, gardens, stables and as much of the rest as they cared to take. This was of course an old process, but it seems possible, at a guess, that as the value of non-agricultural investment increased such new families would put a smaller proportion of their wealth into the land and in fact live to a larger and larger extent on money drawn from other sources of revenue; while in the early twentieth century the advent of the motor car must have made it much easier to live in the country and retain roots in the town.[1] As a result of all this it would seem that a change came over certain areas of the English countryside. They partly ceased to be districts where most of the inhabitants lived on what could be earned from the production and sale of food for the general market and came to depend more largely on the fact that rich men found it pleasant to live in them, or at least to take their sport there.

On the other hand, if men from the town came to live in the country, men from the county families had for long taken up their abode in the town. Possibly there had always been branches of noble families and still more of the families of gentlefolk who had not drawn their livelihood from the land but from the law or Government service, or a sinecure, or some other form of revenue. As a result there was a section of the community who maintained their claim to be gentlefolk but who were not directly connected with any agricultural estate, and probably lived in London. The existence of this section was extremely convenient to others whose origins were more equivocal. As has been said, as wealth became more diffused

[1] For an example of the effects of the motor car see Rudyard Kipling *Something of Myself* [op. cit. p. 140 179]

there were many people who began to assume the trappings of gentility, but for many of the more wealthy the trappings would not be enough; they would want the name, and if they were careful they could gain the name simply by assuming it. They would suddenly emerge like Mr Veneering in *Our Mutual Friend* with a mansion, a coat of arms, Parliamentary ambitions and, as a guest at his dinners, a scion of the real aristocracy who would discover to his bewilderment that he was one of Mr Veneering's oldest friends.

The existence of such aspirations, and the uncertainty of social definition, led however to an agonizing problem which possibly in the nineteenth century caused more trouble and heartburning in well-nourished bosoms than any other secular problem: Who were gentlefolk and who were not? In more antique times this problem may have been a relatively simple one, a gentleman was a man who sprang from an appropriate family, or who had had a grant of arms, or owned an appropriate estate. But in the eighteenth, and still more in the nineteenth century, these relatively simple tests seem to have become ever more difficult to apply. Society was becoming increasingly complex and changing rapidly. Men and women became less certain of the sufficiency of the simple ideas of a hierarchy of birth and began to supplement and confuse the conception of a gentleman with the attribution of mental and moral qualities. A gentleman would naturally have received the education of a gentleman, his manners and his conduct ought to shew a refinement which was one of the attributes of gentility.

This conception, however, produced complications which are investigated with great subtlety by Jane Austen in her novel *Pride and Prejudice*, which was probably mainly written in the eighteenth century. In that book the Bennet family are by most tests below the line. Their connexions are low and unfortunate and the coarseness of the behaviour of Mrs Bennet and her younger daughters, indeed the over slippered ease of Mr Bennet himself, all serve to emphasize the position. This Miss Bingley is keen to point out to Mr Darcy, and Mr Darcy cannot help mentioning in his first proposal of marriage to Elizabeth Bennet herself. But the sharper eye of Elizabeth, as certainly that of her creator, has disclosed another set of values. Elizabeth finds little to admire in the arrogance of Mr Darcy's aunt Lady Catherine de Bourgh, though she was unquestionably highly placed in society, nor for that matter in the behaviour of Mr Darcy himself. Therefore she is at pains to tell him that he has spared her the concern which she might have felt in refusing him had he behaved 'in a more gentlemanlike manner'. This statement seems to have caused Mr Darcy an unexpected shock, he apparently winced, physically, when she said it. In the novel the matter is then papered over. Mr Darcy explains away part of his behaviour and goes on to reveal a more agreeable character most improbably concealed behind his pride, and the matter ends in a fairy-tale marriage between Darcy and Elizabeth. It is difficult to avoid the belief that what really happened was that Darcy returned to sulk in Derbyshire and that Elizabeth married Mr Wickham to learn at leisure that an agreeable manner is not necessarily evidence of the possession of more sterling qualities.

The end, however, does not signify; it is the moral of this and of other novels by Jane Austen which seems to be important, for the moral seems to be that, whereas the qualities which might reasonably be attributed to ladies and gentlemen, refinement in manners delicacy of sentiment and propriety in conduct, were of great value, they were not the monopoly of, they were not indeed always possessed by, those to whom the world conceded distinguished social positions. To make this point was not to stake a claim for general social equality or for the merits of honest worth wherever it might be found, it was not in effect to deny the values of gentility, but it was a reappropriation of them. The desire to do this was perhaps typical of an age when society was changing, when the old social values no longer completely satisfied, but when people were unwilling to abandon them altogether.

However, few people were likely to judge the matter with the penetration of Jane Austen, nor to share the austerity and firmness of her principles. There existed generally a vague idea that the conception of a gentleman ought to include moral attributes, it was indeed an idea which hovered through much nineteenth-century thought and was not without its influence on social values, but as a conception it was unlikely to be precise enough or powerful enough to be the ruling principle in determining social position. People were not going to test a man's gentility solely by the touchstone of his morals or his behaviour, the results of an attempt to do this would be too revolutionary and inconvenient; but some tests were needed which would extend the number of gentlemen, and which would rationalize and moralize the conception of a gentleman for a generation which the old naïve touchstones of blood, or heraldry, or landownership would by no means suffice.

One obvious test that came to be of increasing importance was the test of education. If to be a gentleman implied a certain refinement of motive, a certain liberality of spirit which took a larger view of human affairs than the meanness of motive and narrowness of view which were the probable results of experience confined by the walls of the counting house or the factory, then it was right and desirable that the natural instincts of a born gentleman should have been fostered by an appropriately liberal education. Therefore it came to be increasingly assumed that a gentleman would have had the education of a gentleman, a proposition which in time might carry the convenient converse that someone who had had the education of a gentleman was likely to be a gentleman. It was a conception that was going to be of very great importance in the nineteenth century and its development and consolidation was much assisted by the fact that an increasing number of people were receiving what could be considered the education of a gentleman, that it came to be increasingly clear where that education could be received and that there constantly developed more and more facilities for it. In fact, the conception hardened into a belief that the education of a gentleman was likely to have been received at a certain type of school and at one of the older universities.

This is probably reflected in the history of the older universities. One of the most remarkable developments in the early years of the nineteenth century is the increase in the size of Oxford and Cambridge. The admissions at both had fallen to a very low ebb in the eighteenth century, Cambridge had indeed fallen to a lower point than Oxford and had reached its nadir later, that is between 1760 and 1765. After 1800 the numbers at both started to climb. At this point Oxford increased more slowly than Cambridge; Cambridge developed a steady rise in matriculations after 1807 and became larger than Oxford in 1817.

Cambridge in fact remained ahead of Oxford till 1870, when Oxford drew ahead to be passed again quite soon, but in fact both Universities remained curiously close together shewing in the line of their development the same major fluctuations. This suggests that what was taking place was under the control of general social considerations and was only to a minor extent influenced by the particular characteristics or standing of either body. In both the rise at the beginning of the century continued till about 1826 when the annual admissions to either ranged between about 300 and 400 men. After that there was a period of fluctuation at about that level which lasted roughly till about 1860, then both Universities started to climb swiftly, the numbers of freshmen for instance admitted each year at Cambridge increasing from 400 in the 'fifties to 800 in 1880.[1]

The numbers, of course, are very small when compared with the numbers of other groups and classes in the country. But this group is an important one, its nature was going to have far-reaching effects on society; it is therefore very desirable, though not very easy, to try to see what factors were causing this growth, and what were likely to be the results of what was happening on the nature and characteristics of Oxford and Cambridge. No doubt in this as in other matters the basic factor in both periods of growth was the increase in the population of the country and the increase in its wealth. Probably the first period of growth was also facilitated by the beginnings of University reform. In both Oxford and Cambridge gross scandals, odd and not very defensible personalities and some very queer institutions and customs persisted till well on into the nineteenth century. But from the beginning of the century an increasing number of University teachers had an eye to their duties and in certain colleges both the teaching and discipline were good. In fact, particular colleges developed characteristics and attracted particular groups. Christchurch became a school for Tory statesmen, first Oriel and then Balliol attracted intellectual men, Trinity College, Cambridge, attracted the sons of

[1] J. A. Venn *Oxford and Cambridge Matriculations in 1544-1906 with a graphic chart illustrating the varying fortunes of the two Universities* Heffer (Cambridge 1908). The figures for Cambridge from 1550 to 1850 are reproduced in one of the volumes published by the Royal Commission on Historical Monuments in the *City of Cambridge* Part I facing page lxxxiii of the introduction. In 1908 Dr Venn also published with Heffer a chart showing the admissions to the various Cambridge Colleges

Whig noblemen, gradually displacing its neighbour St John's in that service, first Magdalene, Cambridge, and then Queens', Cambridge, attracted Evangelicals, and so on and so forth.

But all this would only appeal to certain particular sections of the community. Even when it was reasonably taught, the curriculum in both Oxford and Cambridge was exceedingly narrow; if a good University education had been the main object of a student he would in fact have been better advised to go to Glasgow or Edinburgh as many Englishmen did. Moreover, the whole atmosphere of both Oxford and Cambridge was aggressively Anglican; indeed, Dissenters from the Church of England could not take a degree at Cambridge till 1856 and could not matriculate at Oxford till 1854, while the various posts and distinctions in either University were not generally thrown open to them till 1871. Therefore, though no doubt the first period of growth in Cambridge and Oxford was a response to a growth in wealth and numbers it was likely to be at that time mainly a response to the growth in numbers and wealth in certain classes with certain special social values and aspirations, and not in others. To many of the people who were making money and shaping the future of the country Oxford and Cambridge would be as yet forbidden and very foreign ground; places which supplied an education which many of them probably did not as yet much desire.

It is, for this reason, not surprising to find that those who have made analyses of the social structure of Oxford and Cambridge in the nineteenth century have revealed the fact that the classes who were traditionally associated with Oxford and Cambridge, the landowners and the clergy, were still predominant.[1] The increase so far had largely been in the term of the increase of particular groups and not reflecting the nature of the increase of wealth in the whole country, still less of the increase of numbers in the whole population. This did not mean that there had not been a good deal of infiltration

[1] Hester Jenkins and D. Caradog Jones *The British Journal of Sociology*, Vol I, pp. 93-116. Arnold Anderson and Miriam Schnaper *School and Society in England: social Backgrounds of Oxford and Cambridge students. Annals of American Research* (Washington 1952). The work of Anderson and Schnaper suggests that the social origins of those going to Cambridge were more mixed than those going to Oxford and the general result more plebeian, which would account for the fact that Cambridge increased more quickly than Oxford. I am not however entirely satisfied with their analysis

from outside by men whose family traditions had been remote from the Universities, but who desired to share the social values of those who normally went there. There are indeed obvious and very eminent examples of men whose parents had made fortunes in commerce or industry and who passed through Oxford or Cambridge in the first half of the nineteenth century. Many of them entered into the life of the aristocracy, indeed two of their number, Peel and Gladstone, rose to the highest place in the land.

How far such infiltration took place through the Universities it would be hard to say until more extensive research has taken place, nor how effectively in the first half of the century the mere possession of a University degree placed a man above the salt. It must be remembered that social origins at both Oxford and Cambridge were at this time mixed, possibly more mixed in the early years of the century when the locally restricted scholarships and locally restricted fellowships still existed than in the second half in the century when these had been reformed away, as the social origins of the clergy of the Church of England, for whose benefit Oxford and Cambridge so largely existed, were also very mixed. At this point, however, the matter becomes involved in an important question which is slightly different from the question of education as a social test, though related to it. Could it be that a clergyman of the Church of England must be presumed to be a gentleman not only on account of his education but also on account of his profession? The problem is important because it raises the whole question of the claim to gentility by reason of a profession, and therefore the whole problem of the gentility of the professional classes in general.

Certainly not all the clergy had been in the past automatically gentlemen ·Everyone is familiar with Macaulay's drastic picture of the country clergy in the reign of Charles II in the third chapter of his history. It is probably oversimplified, as such vivid historical pictures are apt to be, but modern research has suggested that it is substantially true. If so, it would be hard to call many of these people gentlemen, whether you use the ancient test of blood, or the more modern test of refinement of manners. They were a separate caste, narrow and professional in their outlook in life, bucolic in their habits, barbarous in their manners and often plebeian in their origins and associations. In the eighteenth century, however, a gradual change seems to have taken place. Probably country livings had become more valuable and a larger number of well-connected men had condescended to take them. More country clergy came to hold a high position in the countryside and to mix on equal terms with the gentry. More of them became magistrates. Their learning often became more secular and more liberal, they were more often antiquarians rather than theologians, and if refinement of manners was to be the test such refinement was perhaps often more likely to be found in the vicarage than the Hall. Jane Austen was of course a clergyman's daughter and her standards were learnt in the parsonage; but a certain type of early nineteenth-century country clergyman of whom she approves—educated, reasonably well endowed with high principles, if to our mind with a strangely secular outlook—seems to present a good model of what many people in the nineteenth century thought a gentleman probably ought to be like.[1]

Of course, there were obvious exceptions. There seem to have lasted well into the century a reasonable number of clerical grotesques, and apart from them there were always clergymen with very lowly beginnings and clergymen in very poor, even sordid, circumstances. There were also clergymen who were possibly too much in earnest to be quite gentlemen, indeed some people sometimes talked as if in spite of Simeon and the Venn family it was unlikely that an evangelical would be a gentleman, but theirs was perhaps a form of Churchmanship which did in fact attract clergymen of humble or as one man put it of 'disgusting' social origin, as it also seemed to be half-way to Dissent. Nevertheless, as the century went forward the presumption developed that a clergyman of the Church of England was likely to be a gentleman. It is the presumption behind the great saying of Archdeacon Grantly in Trollope's novel the *Last Chronicle of Barset* published in 1867. When the Archdeacon confronted in his library the battered perpetual Curate of Hogglestock, a graduate of Oxford it is true, but a man bearing

---

[1] Possibly the best account of the development in the eighteenth century is in the unpublished thesis in Trinity College Library by P. A. Bezodis *The English Parish Clergy and their Place in Society 1660–1800* (2 vols.)

in his mind and body, and in his clothes and boots, the scars of the harshest poverty, he still would not agree that their positions were unequal. 'We stand', said he, 'on the only perfect level on which such men can meet each other. We are both gentlemen.'

It was the consolidation of a caste. To those who were traditionally gentlemen had been added men who were gentlemen by education and profession. It was a caste which would obviously include members of another ancient profession, also largely fed from the older Universities, the profession of a barrister. But the matter was to go further. The later eighteenth and the early nineteenth centuries saw the beginning of the development of other organized professions in their modern form. In many walks of life—in medicine, in the army and the navy, in architecture and in engineering—it came to be realized that an increasingly higher standard of technical capacity would be required by anyone who wished to do their work successfully, and at the same time in many of these professions the rewards became greater, and it seemed at least for many of those who practised them that they had a claim to a more assured and distinguished social position than their predecessors might have had in the past. To make good this claim, however, in many cases it was necessary to organize the profession, in order to make sure that its members maintained its standards and that their ranks were not invaded by the unsuitable and the untrained. Something could be done to further these ends by organizing professional societies if the profession as a whole could be made to accept their authority, but in the end if the organization was to be really effective it was in many cases necessary to go to Parliament to gain powers to keep out of practice men who were not properly qualified and to impose a code of behaviour on all those who had been admitted to practice, as a protection both for other professionals and for the public whom they served.

The road to full recognition and effective professional organization was long and arduous, and not all professions in the nineteenth century achieved the full position of an officially ogranised profession with the sanction of the State to enforce the discipline of its professional institutions. But in the eighteenth century there are a good many signs of what was to come.

Several important professions developed a consciousness of their identity in the course of the eighteenth century and produced professional organizations fairly early in the nineteenth. For instance, it was in the late eighteenth century that the architects began fully to realize themselves as a profession, and in 1834-35 the Institute of British Architects was founded; it was Smeaton, who died in 1792, who seems to have conceived the profession of Civil Engineer, and in 1818 the Institution was created to be incorporated in 1828.[1] The Institution of Mechanical Engineers followed in 1847. At the same time two other respectable professions which were going to play a very important part in the making of Victorian England were being created from groups whose calling was by no means new but whose position in the community had not been well established before or in many cases rated very high. From the mass of despised pettifogging attorneys of the eighteenth century there developed the respectable profession of solicitors effectively organized by a succession of Solicitors' Acts, a profession in whose hands an immense amount of confidential business was placed; and from the very mixed and in many cases very rough crowd of surgeons, and apothecaries and physicians evolved the medical profession as we know it controlled by the Medical Act of 1858.[2]

If, however, a profession was to emerge and take shape in this way, two things had to happen. First, inside the profession active members of it had to emerge who were anxious to organize it, to improve its standards of performance and to raise its status; and secondly, members of the public outside the profession had to become prepared to accept it at a new valuation, and perhaps to concede the very considerable legal powers which were conceded to such bodies as the British Medical Council or the Law Society. The second process is very significant because it entailed a partial reconsideration of the values of society. There is reason to believe that such a

[1] On the architects see H. M. Colvin *A Biographical Dictionary of English Architects, 1660-1840*. (London 1954) p. 23. The history of the Royal Academy of Arts, founded 1768, also fits into this picture
[2] On the solicitors see R. Robson *The Attorney in Eighteenth-Century England*. (Cambridge 1959) and M. Birks *Gentlemen of the Law* (London 1960); on Medicine see C. Newman *The Evolution of Medical Education in the Nineteenth Century* (London 1957); for a general bibliographical note on the professions in the eighteenth century see Robson [op. cit. p. 261] 168-71. See also A. M. Carr Saunders and P. A. Wilson *The Professions* (Oxford 1933)

partial reconsideration was going on from the beginning of the nineteenth century. The increasing complexity of society and the complication of the services it required enhanced the value of the men who could supply the requisite techniques, while the increasing rationality with which all but the stupidest men tended to think about these matters encouraged the belief that men who were trained to perform difficult and responsible services, for which they were likely to be well paid, were at least as socially valuable as men who had done no more than inherit an ancient name with possibly not much money and not much sense to go with it.[1] It was perhaps a convenient way of thinking for those who wished to find jobs for young men who did not wish to forfeit their title to be gentlemen. Certainly there seems to be an example of the change in 1820 when Sir Walter Scott was discussing the occupation to be followed by a nephew of his. If, he said, the boy had the appropriate disposition he might become a soldier, but otherwise 'he cannot follow a better line than that of an accountant. It is highly respectable.'[2]

There is, indeed, a good deal of evidence for the existence in the second quarter of the nineteenth century of a fairly large society of professional men—barristers, civil servants, literary men and others—whose status was assured and to whom the title of gentleman would hardly be denied, except by rather old or very stupid people. There were probably the largest numbers of these people in London, and it seems possible that the foundation of certain important London clubs—the United University founded in 1827, the Athenaeum in 1824, the Oxford and Cambridge in 1830 and the Garrick in 1831—is evidence of the kind of life that they lived and the estimation which they claimed for themselves. If it was the world which Pen entered when he came down from Trinity in Thackeray's novel *Pendennis*, it had its contacts with fashionable society, if one of its exits was also into the Fleet prison. But the ethos and the method of life of professional men were often very different from those of the aristocracy, and not a few people in this stratum came to look on those who might consider themselves to be their social superiors with little interest and some contempt, believing

---

[1] This seems to be very much the sense of Jane Austen's novel *Persuasion*

[2] Saunders and Wilson [op. cit. p. 261] 209. J. G. Lockhart *Life of Scott* (Edinburgh 1837) Vol IV, p. 379

that the real aristocracy of the country was—but perhaps the phrase is late Victorian—'the educated and professional classes'. It was possibly from this group that the non-democratic liberals of the third quarter of the century were drawn.

There is, however, a potential conflict or at least contrast between two of the concepts that were enriching social values. A *professional* man was not necessarily an *educated* man. He was by definition a *trained* man, but from a nineteenth-century point of view a professional training was not necessarily an education, certainly not the education of a gentleman. The most normal form of technical education had been apprenticeship. The barrister had learnt his trade in chambers, the solicitor as an articled clerk, the medical practitioner in the surgery or the hospital, the officer with his regiment, and the clergyman, if at all, in the parish. There is much to be said for this type of training when it is carefully attended to by those in charge, certainly the training received by mechanical engineers at Maudslay's factory in London was of the greatest importance in the development of the British Engineering industry.[1] As, however, technological skill develops and comes to depend more and more on general scientific knowledge, systematic advanced training of some sort, possibly University training, becomes necessary for the technician, either in addition to the period passed as an apprentice, or as a substitute for it. This change is of the greatest importance because it links practice and practical skill with an extended view of more general knowledge in the sphere in which the practitioner is to work, and opens up to the technician the possibility of using the results of general research. It is a change which is reflected in the increasing importance of a University qualification for medical men. In the early years of the nineteenth century many medical practitioners gained their training at Edinburgh or Glasgow, and the importance of such men not simply in medicine but in all spheres of English life was very great indeed.

Such a technical University training, however, could not in the early years of the nineteenth century be obtained at Oxford or Cambridge, where for long any scientific teaching that there was was disjointed and casual; nor would such technical

[1] See C. H. Wilson and W. Reader *Men and Machines. A history of D. Napier and Son 1808-1958* (London 1958) particularly 1-10

education quite satisfy the conception of the education of a gentleman. The education of a gentleman was supposed to lift him above the narrow bounds of mere professional competence, to teach him about men and life, not to impart one skill but to discipline his mind so that he could grapple with any kind of problem. Such a knowledge of life and of men, and such a mental discipline, could, it was held, be gained most certainly from a training in the Classics possibly stiffened by intensive drill in the old-fashioned type of mathematics which formed the staple of the course at Cambridge. If, therefore, professional men were to be men of liberality of mind with the status of gentlemen, they should accept a general education before they turned to their more professional training.[1]

This order of events seems to have commended itself to men of high professional standing. In 1840 Sir Thomas Acland approached Sir Benjamin Brodie, a leading physician, to ask how his son, the future Regius Professor who in later years did so much for medical training at Oxford, could be trained as a doctor. Sir Benjamin answered. 'Send the boy to Oxford and let him pay there no attention to his future profession, but do as he would if he were going into Parliament like you. When he has taken his degree send him to me, and I will tell him what to do next.'[2] If this course seems a little strange it is only fair to remember that it was in the state of scientific knowledge of the middle of the century a perfectly practicable course. It was indeed much the same as that followed rather later in the century by another eminent physician Sir Clifford Allbutt, who became in due course Regius Professor of Physic, in this case at Cambridge. Allbutt went up to Cambridge mainly interested in literary and artistic matters and did not decide to become a doctor till 1858, which was relatively late in his University career. He only took the Natural Science Tripos in 1860, after he had taken his Bachelor's degree in 1859 and after he had started courses in St George's Hospital in London. He was the only man in the first class in the Tripos that year, but

---

[1] The most accessible presentation of the conception of a liberal education is in John Henry Cardinal Newman *The Idea of a University* (London 1935, first published 1852) especially Discourse VII 'Knowledge viewed in relation to professional skill', pp. 151-78. See also Lockhart [op. cit. p. 262] Vol V, pp. 33-35

[2] J. B. Atlay *Sir Henry Wentworth Acland, Bart, K.C.B., F.R.S., Regius Professor of Medicine in the University of Oxford. A Memoir* (London 1903) p. 33

there were only six names in the list altogether; he took his M.B. at Cambridge in 1861.[1]

A less able man would not probably have been able to move forward at this remarkable speed, and a very large number of men must have found that to go through a whole general University course before they started their professional training was not financially practicable. But the idea behind such an order of events remained in men's minds. When in 1858 the new General Medical Council drew up the regulations for the education which should lead to a medical qualification they also tried to secure that the future practitioner should have a preliminary education which should have implanted as far as possible what they considered to be the aptitudes of a gentleman.[2]

Something of the same way of thinking seems to have attended some of those who were interested in developing rules for the training of a solicitor. In 1846 Sir George Stephen told a select committee of the House of Commons that it was 'most important that the profession should be so educated as to be qualified for carrying on intercourse (i.e. with men of every class of society) as gentlemen themselves, but I apprehend that that qualification cannot be attained except by educating them as gentlemen, with much greater attention to their *general* endowments and information than is at present the case'.[3] A certain number of solicitors thought these frills unnecessary, and a probable distraction for the young from more important matters; but even in 1821 a large enough body of those interested were sufficiently convinced by such arguments as to secure that in the terms of the Act of that year graduates had only to serve three years in Articles.

In these professions the aim was to secure that the professional man had the same liberal education that a gentleman might be presumed to have had. The reformers of the public administration had something of the same object in mind. They wished to secure that those admitted to the public service had had the

---

[1] Sir Humphry Rolleston *The Right Hon. Sir Clifford Allbutt; a Memoir* (London 1929) pp. 1-12

[2] Newman [op. cit. p. 261] 194-8

[3] Sir George Stephen to the Select Committee of the House of Commons on Legal Education as quoted in Robson [op. cit. p. 261] 66; the whole matter is discussed in Robson pp. 52-67

education of a gentleman, and had profited by it and indeed were admitted to the public service by the test of the extent to which they had profited by it and, in the end, by no other test. That is for appointment by nomination by politicians and aristocrats appointment by competitive examination was to be substituted, the examination being directly geared to the courses at the older Universities. The key date in that development is 1853. In that year posts in the Civil Service in India were thrown open to competitive examination. In the same year Gladstone set in hand the famous Northcote-Trevelyan enquiry which in 1854 produced a report which established the principle of government by men who have received a liberal education. It was some time, however, before the full ideal was realized. The Civil Service Commissioners were appointed with the duty of examining candidates in 1855, but at first they could only extend their influence by subjecting nominated candidates to a qualifying examination. It was not till 1870 that Gladstone was able to secure that most posts in the Home Civil Service could be obtained by an open competitive examination. When, however, this was achieved the examination gave the greatest advantage to those who had had a liberal education.

Roughly the same course was being followed with regard to commissions in the Army. Commissions and promotions in the Army were in the middle of the century very largely obtained by purchase, and in the past, though it had been recognized that officers in the artillery and engineers needed a specialized training, the young officer in the infantry and cavalry was supposed to learn his craft with his regiment. In 1849, however, the Duke of Wellington had laid down the rule that no one should receive a commission unless he was of good average ability and had received the education of a gentleman. To enforce this an examination was developed which a man who wished to gain a commission by purchase had to pass before he took it up. Then in 1857 and 1858, partly as a result of the failure of the Crimean War, the regulations for Woolwich and Sandhurst, which up to now had really been boys' schools, were drastically altered. The age of entry was raised to between 16 and 19 and entrance was to be by competitive examination, though, in the case of Sandhurst, only from among candidates nominated by the commander in chief. Direct commissions

could still be obtained by purchase but the cand
same examination as for Sandhurst, they were a
order of merit and received their commissions ii
In 1871 purchase was abolished and in 1875 comm
cavalry and infantry were thrown open to competiti
tion. But before that the Army examinations hac ɴad their
effect on the educational system of the country, for they were
the tests of entry into a profession which was unquestionably
gentlemanly, and yet one for which other subjects than Latin
and Greek were obviously relevant.

For all this development would obviously have its effect on
the educational system of the country. It was increasingly
important to have received the education of a gentleman, there
were more openings for anyone who had received the education
of a gentleman, and there were more gentlemen in circulation,
which by a very natural process meant that there were more
gentlemen's sons to be educated, particularly if you counted
the sons of the clergy. Consequently there was an ever-increasing demand for the education of a gentleman. No doubt this
was in part responsible for the increase in the numbers of Oxford
and Cambridge after 1860, though this was possibly assisted by
the admission of Dissenters to degrees at Oxford in 1854 and at
Cambridge in 1856. But before then this demand for the
education of a gentleman had been responsible for an even more
significant development, the development of what came to be
known as the public schools.

The starting-point of this curious movement is a group of
seven ancient schools, which are normally given as the original
public schools; they are Westminster, Eton, Harrow, Winchester, Charterhouse, Rugby and Shrewsbury. They were schools
which were held to be distinguished by the fact that the nobility
and gentry had sent their sons to them; that distinction had
however been intermittent, for the fortunes of most of them had
suffered very violent fluctuations. Generally speaking, in the
eighteenth century they were rather curious places, where a
certain amount of Latin and Greek was taught with the frequent

---

[1] On admission to commissions in the army between 1850 and 1870, see Report
of the Select Committee of House of Commons on Royal Military College at
Sandhurst, *Parl. Papers 1854-5*, Vol XII, p. 311 ff. (in particular for a summary of
the situation then see the letter submitted by Sidney Herbert) and the Report of
the Royal Commission on Military Education. *Parl. Papers 1868-9*, Vol XXII

...nce of the birch but where otherwise the life of the boys as largely unsupervised and was in consequence often coarse, brutal and tumultuous to a degree which it is difficult nowadays to realize. Often enough the only virtues which the life at public schools with any certainty inculcated seem to have been those of the dark ages—courage, ability to bear pain and loyalty to immediate companions, and if there had been no reform in these places it is difficult to see how they could have survived through the relatively civilized nineteenth century, much less play the part which they did play. But they were reformed, or partly reformed, and the part they played in making Victorian England was very great.

The work of reform started in the first half of the nineteenth century in different ways at different places. Eton, Harrow and Winchester were all affected at one time or other by reforming headmasters and at Shrewsbury Butler and after him Kennedy were able to teach the Classics more effectively than ever before. But the most important reformer was of course Dr Arnold, who became Headmaster of Rugby in 1828, a post which he held till 1842. If it had not been for Rugby it may be doubted whether the public schools could have survived. Even after Arnold had done his work in Rugby the reforms in other schools had often not been pressed very far, nor were they always very secure—a slackening of control by a weak headmaster and they were apt to slip back towards their earlier state of rugged chaos. Their whole condition was minutely investigated by a Royal Commission appointed in 1861 which reported in 1864, and the repor⁺ amply demonstrates how much was left to be done.[1] There had possibly been improvements in curriculum. In every school the Classics course seems to have included some mathematics and, except at Eton, a modern language. At Rugby, where the whole curriculum seems to have been much more intelligent than elsewhere, there was teaching in both French and German, but modern languages were not studied there by those who took natural sciences. There had been minor attempts to tackle science elsewhere, but, said the Commis-

[1] *Parl. Papers 1864* XX (Vol 1), *Report of H.M. Commissioners appointed to inquire into the Revenues and management of certain Colleges and Schools and the Studies pursued and Instruction given therein.* The schools investigated were Eton, Winchester, Westminster, Charterhouse, St Paul's, Merchant Taylors, Harrow, Rugby and Shrewsbury

sioners, 'natural science, with such slight exceptions as have
been noticed above, is practically excluded from the education
of the higher classes in England'.[1] Except at Rugby the curriculum seems to have been not only narrow but often incompetently
handled, even Latin and Greek were taught in many cases by
incredibly obsolete methods, and there were bitter complaints
from University teachers about the poor preparation which
many pupils from the public schools had received in almost all
subjects. In several cases the methods of management seem to
have been questionable, the premises unsuitable and the life
still very rough indeed.

In many of these ancient schools the numbers were falling off,
or fluctuating. At Eton the numbers were large, but Eton had a
peculiar relationship with the aristocracy. From what the
Commission revealed it might have been confidently expected
that most of the other ancient foundations would in due course
have disappeared with the exception of Rugby, and that the
number of public schools would have been so small and the
examples of the survivors so unattractive that the whole idea of
public school education would have petered out. This is, however, precisely the opposite of what happened. Instead of the
numbers of public schools dwindling a very large number of
new ones were founded. Some of the most important of these
were Cheltenham in 1841, Marlborough in 1843, Rossall in
1844, Wellington in 1853, Clifton in 1862, Haileybury in 1862,
while Repton, Sherborne and Uppingham were converted from
obscure county grammar schools.

Life at many of these places was probably better than it was
at some of the ancient foundations, the curriculum was more
varied and possibly the teaching better.[2] Many of them had
developed a modern school in which the emphasis was on
modern languages or mathematics and even on scientific subjects rather than on the Classics. From the subjects taught at
Rossall it would seem that the needs of the great mercantile
community of Liverpool had some influence. But elsewhere the
most effective modernizing influence in education seems to have
been that of the Army examinations. Cheltenham was the great
pioneer in these matters, the modern school there was larger at

[1] *Public Schools Commission* [op. cit. p. 268] 32
[2] Brian Simon *Studies in the History of Education 1780-1870* (London 1960) p. 302-3

the time of the Public Schools Commission than those at Marlborough and Wellington about which the Commissioners also collected information, and the headmaster was bolder in his assertion of the advantages and desirability of maintaining a modern department; and at Cheltenham it was said that 'the reading of the higher classes is mainly guided by the Woolwich and Sandhurst examinations (which are to this Department what the University course is to a high classical school)'.[1] At Marlborough the modern department seems to have been much smaller and at Wellington the matter was obviously complicated by the strong feeling on the part of the headmaster, Benson, that even for future soldiers Classics should be the basis of education.[2] In many of these schools the influence of the example of Rugby was strong, several of them must be considered to be colonies of Rugby. In fact, Rugby must have done more than any other agent in causing the creation of new and improved models of the public schools throughout England.

It is a remarkable development when the full case is considered. The remarkable fact is not that in a country, which was so rapidly increasing in wealth, new and improved schools should come into existence for the sons of the well-to-do; it is the fact that they should be on the public school model. They were not the schools which might have been expected to develop in a growing commercial and industrial community. The study of Latin and Greek continued to dominate their curricula to the continued neglect of subjects like modern languages or science which might have been considered to be more useful. They were dominated by the clergy of England to an extent that one would have thought would have made them repugnant to Dissenters, in a period when Dissenters were increasing in importance and wealth. Their institutions and customs looked back to a past remote from the influences of industrialized society and very different in its virtues and in its failings. But it was in those anachronistic virtues that lay the attractive power. The nature of that attraction can best be judged in what the Public School Commissioners have to say in favour of the ancient public schools after they had minutely analysed what

[1] *Public Schools Commission* [op. cit. p. 268] Vol I, 548

[2] David Newsome *A History of Wellington College, 1859-1959* (London 1959) p. 134; see also Benson's own evidence before the Public Schools Commission, Vol I, p. 534

was wrong with them, and it is worth while quoting at length and in their own words for it sums up what became one of the most cherished ideals in Victorian England.

'Among the services which they have rendered is undoubtedly the maintenance of classical literature as the staple of English Education, a service which far outweighs the error of having clung to these studies too exclusively. A second, and a greater still, is the creation of a system of government and discipline for boys, the excellence of which has been universally recognized, and which is admitted to have been most important in its effects on national character and social life. It is not easy to estimate the degree in which the English people are indebted to these schools for the qualities on which they pique themselves most—for their capacity to govern others and control themselves, their aptitude for combining freedom with order, their public spirit, their vigour and manliness of character, their strong but not slavish respect for public opinion, their love of healthy sport and exercise. These schools have been the chief nurseries of our statesmen; in them, and in schools modelled after them, men of all the various classes that make up English society, destined for every profession and career, have been brought up on a footing of social equality, and have contracted the most enduring friendships, and some of the ruling habits of their lives; and they have had perhaps the largest share in moulding the character of an English Gentleman.'[1]

That was the lodestone. Its tractive force was not much affected by the problem whether there were decent opportunities at any school for learning French, or arithmetic, or science. The ideal which drew people was this ideal picture of the education of a gentleman, an ideal which had somehow flowered from the rough soil of the ancient schools and more ancient universities. It was an education based on the cultivation of classical literature, the formation of character through the prefectorial system and fortified by a love of exercise and the open air. There was much to be said against it. Its intellectual scope remained very narrow, on the part of the teachers as well as of the taught. Its failure to develop the teaching of science was going to be very serious indeed for the future of Britain, when the leaders of industry began to be drawn into its sphere.

[1] *Public Schools Commission* [op. cit. p. 268] Vol I, 56

It is true that scientific studies had been introduced into both of the older Universities, but the progress was very slow. If the list of the Natural Science Tripos contained in Sir Clifford Allbutt's year, 1860, contained only six names, it was not till 1875 that the Natural Science Tripos contained more than twenty names.[1] No doubt this had its effect on the public schools, for not only did many boys go on to Oxford and Cambridge but most masters came from them. Consequently the range of studies was restricted, and the standard of industry clearly not always very high. The taint of brutality remained even into the twentieth century in spite of the supposed responsibilities of the prefects or monitors, and the love of exercise developed into the cult of organized games which might support the silliest of false values.

Yet it may be the case that the Commissioners made was not wholly nonsense. In that materialistic England there was some value in an education which was not completely utilitarian and which produced at the lowest, particularly after Arnold had done his work, a greater sense of responsibility and a greater sense of freedom than existed in other systems. It was the legacy of the old English aristocratic class to an ever larger class, and it is only fair, when thinking of what the public schools were, to conceive what an aristocratic education based on a strictly military system as in Germany would have been like, or a middle-class education directed strictly to technological and commercial ends. At any rate, whether they deserved to do so or not the public schools exercised a powerful attractive influence over the educational system of the country. Not only were many new public schools founded but a great many boarding schools were built which more or less approximated to them.[2] Schools of other traditions, dissenting schools, Roman Catholic schools were drawn to model themselves upon the public schools and humbler boys who, alas, could not hope for more than an unsatisfactory primary education, in due course were given a fairy land remotely based on the public schools in the fifth form at St Dominick's or the adventures of Billy Bunter.

This attraction drew individuals into the social sphere of the public schools from sections of society naturally remote from it.

[1] D. A. Winstanley, *Later Victorian Cambridge* (Cambridge 1947) p. 190
[2] For a list of schools see J. A. Banks [op. cit. p. 236] 228-30

At first no doubt the public schools attracted primarily the sons of the nobility, gentry and professional classes, but at least by the fourth quarter of the century and probably earlier very many of the wealthier people in the industrial districts seem to have been sending their sons to the public schools.[1] Even so stern an opponent of the aristocracy and the old governing classes as Joseph Chamberlain sent his sons to Rugby, and the one, Austen, who was destined for a political career, to Trinity College, Cambridge, where he took his degree in 1885. The next year, 1886, Albert Kitson took his degree from the same College, the son of Sir James Kitson who took the lead in the National Liberal Federation after Chamberlain had left it.

It was the final stage of the consolidation of the caste. First there had been the broadening of the conception of a gentleman by the emphasis on the test of the education of a gentleman, a broadening of which the professional classes had made use. Then there had been the development and multiplication of the institutions which could give that education, and now the sons of the leaders of industry were drawn in also. They were very often drawn to places of education remote from the places where their parents had made or were making their money. They mixed with the sons of men of different traditions. They learnt a new way of talking and of thinking. They were trained in disciplines which often enough had no relation to the scientific side of their work. They were drawn away from the men who must continue to be the rank and file and non-commissioned officers of industry, and they became acclimatized to a life which very often drew them and their money out of industry altogether.

But even before this last stage, what had been happening had in other ways led to the separation of classes and to the denial of privileges to the sons of poor men which they had previously enjoyed. In most of the ancient schools which had been turned into public schools there had been provision in the intention of the founder, or of some other benefactor, for the education of poor children, or at least of local children. In many cases it was for such scholars that in fact the school had been founded; but as the school was developed into a public school their needs

[1] On this tendency among the manufacturers of steel see Charlotte Erickson *British Industrialists—Steel and Hosiery 1850-1950* (Cambridge 1959) pp. 30-44

were often pressed to one side for the benefit of richer strangers, and these local children were often largely eliminated. This very often caused bitter local feeling and the Public Schools Commission indulged in a good deal of special pleading to justify what had happened. But justifiable or unjustifiable, the process went forward and the division became more marked.[1] The tendency was probably reinforced by the reform of the Oxford and Cambridge scholarships, which ceased often to be attached to particular localities where poor lads had a chance of getting them and were thrown into open competition in which those trained at the public schools were very much more likely to be successful.

Without question this social consolidation had disadvantages for the country; what advantages it may have had would presumably in part depend on the values which were gained from the educational system itself, from the development of freedom, a sense of responsibility and the retention of the conception of a liberal education. These possible merits deserve a fair historical appraisal which they do not always get, and it is possible that the conception of a liberal education, not as the privilege for a few but as a necessity for all, may be an important one. Fortunately, however, such an attempted judgment would be out of place here. The object here is to discover the factors that helped to make Victorian England. One of those factors had been, from the beginning, the aristocratic power in the country. It had presented itself at first in the formidable shape of the old noble and landowning interest which for a remarkably long period dominated the political and social life of the country. The processes of history, in due course, began to shake that domination, though to the very end of what might be called Victorian England remarkably large fragments of it remained. Meanwhile, however, there had been forming in its shadow a new type of aristocracy, a new caste, more extensive, more adaptable, less open to the attacks of economic change or of discriminatory taxation, and that aristocracy certainly remained in full vigour when Victorian England, however defined, came to its end. It is indeed with us still.

[1] Simon [op. cit. p. 269] 312 ff.

CHAPTER IX

An Epilogue and a Recapitulation

The first thought that comes to mind on looking back at the society that occupied England in the age of Queen Victoria is that one knows very little about it either in detail, or for that matter as a whole, as a subject for generalization. The movement that is going on is so continuous, the variety so great that every historical comment seems fumbling and inaccurate, every generalization inconclusive and incomplete. Even were it possible, as in most contexts it is not possible, to assemble all the necessary facts, or to trace all the relevant actions of all the individuals involved in one movement or transaction, there remains the problem of understanding the motives of a large number of men and women with whom there cannot now be any sort of contact. The situation in any part of England at any moment in the period is, I think, best suggested by those clear photographs of street scenes in various towns, of which a fair number seem to have survived from the second half of the century. They are of things that really happened and of people who really lived and have not been recalled to a reconstructed existence with the help of the historian's ink-bottle; and therefore the result is something we cannot fully understand. The street is filled with people who were once without question there going about their business; but no one can ever recover who they all were, what they were doing before the photograph was taken or what they were going to do afterwards, still less what occupied their minds. Nor can anyone recover that sense of common reality, that natural understanding of the world in which they moved as the matter of everyday fact, which they all shared at that moment, and which disappeared for ever as soon as they retreated from life into history.

It is important to remember these things, since men's statements about groups and communities and ways of life which have come to an end tend to seem more precise and inclusive than it is possible for them to be; at best an historical generalization must omit much that is relevant, while even what it does propose as a positive statement is likely to be no more than a tentative hypothesis. Nevertheless, the first general statement which it seems worth while to put forward about the making of Victorian England may seem to be not open to question but rather intolerably trite. It is that the England of Queen Victoria was necessarily a continuation of the periods that immediately preceded it and that in the process of forming it the results of inheritance, in some cases inheritance from very remote periods, played a most important part. It is worth while to emphasize this fact for this reason. The society in which we live is obviously the continuation of Victorian society; there are striking differences between our society and theirs, it is true, but our dress, our political ideals, the mechanized background to our lives and our crowded towns all yield enough resemblance to any society that has existed after the invention of gaslight, railways and the electric telegraph as to lead us to forget that many matters in their society might closely resemble what existed in periods which seem to be absolutely different from our own.

In fact, this error has a more significant cause than a superficial resemblance between ourselves and the Victorians. When an important revolution has taken place it is perhaps always difficult to remember how much of the ordinary world must necessarily survive the revolution and supply part of the background of life after all is over. The nineteenth century was pre-eminently a century of revolutions, and the temptation has been to start history afresh when it begins, assuming that what went on in the centuries of the old régime must by that date have reached its natural end. This is an error that must conceal many of the elements which went to the fashioning of Victorian England. Victorian England was no doubt to a large extent the creation of the political and industrial revolutions of the nineteenth century, but the order of society, which had existed for centuries before those revolutions, lasted robustly into, and in some matters after, the third quarter of the century. Those who were at the head of that order had to make concessions and partially to accept a new system of values, for powerful social forces had come into being which were alien and in some cases hostile to them, while the principle of heredity and prescription upon which their position had been founded was condemned by the political theory that came to be the orthodoxy of the day. Nevertheless, the political power of the old ruling class survived, as did their predominance in society. It is probable that well into the second half of the nineteenth century the landed aristocracy included a large number of the richest men in the country and they certainly remained its social leaders. Till 1867 the grip of their influence on a large section of the electoral system was patent, much of it survived till 1880, some of it probably long afterwards. At least till 1868 the aristocracy normally supplied most of the Cabinet and the Prime Minister, while the paternal sway of nobleman, squire and parson overshadowed much of the countryside.

All this had important results, for it is not only necessary to reckon with this survival in order to understand Victorian England, it is necessary to retain a knowledge of it in order to understand the society that succeeded Victorian England. Not only did some of the native power of the old ruling classes survive into the twentieth century, but as the nineteenth century had gone forward and wealth had accumulated in various hands new social elements had come to amalgamate themselves with the old aristocracy, or to model themselves upon them and to lend to old habits of mind and modes of life a new power of survival, which they would not have otherwise possessed. Therefore, though much that had typified the gentry and the aristocracy had come from the remote pre-revolutionary past, they were enabled to put their trademark on much that went forward with vigour into the future.

Nor was the old order of society all that survived from earlier, and as many hoped irrelevant, centuries. There was also much of the old disorder, and, for many, much traditional degradation. There had been in the eighteenth century, probably there always had been, a cruel primitive background to society, a background of brutality and callousness, of bestiality and heavy drinking and much wretchedness and degradation, inadequately remedied or controlled by any public authority. These things did not vanish when the nineteenth century began, nor had they altogether disappeared by the time it had run half its course. Certainly the law gradually became more effective, and more humane, repressing what was savage and primitive in society, and even eliminating something of what was absurd and brutal in its own operation. Gradually society learnt more of its duty to protect those who were at the mercy of economic and social forces which were too strong for them, to ameliorate their environment and even to educate them. But these processes were often slow, the machinery that had to be used untried and suspect, and many of the lessons to be learnt extremely uncongenial.

Nor did all the forces that were making for change in the nineteenth century inevitably tend to increase the general happiness, or progress, or civilization, of mankind. Two of the most powerful of them were not directed by any conscious human intention to any clearly conceived end; they acted blindly and the evil, or the good, that they achieved were the results of chance. The rapid increase of population in England, Wales and Scotland and, till 1845, in Ireland is on any calculation one of the most important factors in the development of nineteenth-century society, and in many ways its most obvious result was an increase in human misery, particularly in the first half of the century and particularly when the immigrants from Ireland are brought into the picture. In Ireland certainly, and probably in England at least in the early years of the century, it seems to have depressed standards of life by the increase of numbers without a comparable increase in resources. It also probably greatly increased the fluid mass of men, women and children at the bottom of society for whom nothing was provided but casual and unskilled labour and an existence in miserable tenements, hovels and cellars with no necessary provisions for a decent and healthy life, and who received in most cases no intellectual or spiritual training or guidance whatsoever.

Part of this mass provided a social and spiritual problem which Victorian England was unable to solve. Its nature was partly revealed by the activities of various religious missions, by the enquiries of social scientists and by the experience gained by practical philanthropists, though it seems probable that it was only in the last twenty years of the century that men were beginning to learn its full extent and something of the true nature of its challenge. But there were others who might in the middle of the century have been included in the general undifferentiated mass of the poor who were, in due course, rescued, or partially rescued, by another blind force that was at work in nineteenth-century society. In spite of the pretensions, indeed the sincere convictions, of many of those who promoted it, it would be idle to deny that the Industrial Revolution was indeed blind. Those who launched it and furthered it most often had their eyes on the profit immediately to be made or the improvement in machinery or method immediately to be devised, and not normally on the general results their labours might have for mankind. Even when they believed that they knew what they were working for, they were probably liberating forces which in the long run they could not control. Nevertheless, whatever their ideals or their lack of ideals, they produced wealth and gainful employment and an abundance of goods, particularly in the third quarter of the century. As a result Victorian England was not only a much larger, much more dynamic, community than had ever existed before in the island, it was a much richer one, and its wealth percolated down through the various middle classes to a section of the working class who would otherwise have been poor indeed.

Greater wealth brings a man greater self-reliance, and a greater capacity to stand up for his rights, or to join with others for that purpose. The increase in wealth among the working classes led to the development of Trade Unions which were larger than the craft unions which had flourished in the first half of the century and extended to other types of labour than the craft unions had served, while the increase of wealth among the working classes and middle classes led to the developments in politics which began to become noticeable in the general election of 1868. The social, political, industrial revolutions went forward together and the whole movement seems so purposeful that it is difficult to remember how speculative it all was and what a large part chance had had to play in the matter. Even the prosperity which sustained it depended upon payment for exports which the rest of the world might, or might not, continue to take regularly from Great Britain; it depended also upon a system of credit and foreign exchange which was never under secure control. The development of mechanization was morally neutral; it might work good or it might very easily work evil. To some of those who served it it brought wealth and an improved status, to others the destruction of their handicrafts and ruin, and to others exploitation, particularly if they were women and children; while the extension of industrialism was not likely to secure that the towns where its workers lived were places which were fit for human habitation. If poverty and numbers had crowded men and women into slums, the demands of industrialism would make congestion worse and the filth and smoke it produced add to the squalor and misery of the scene.

If standards were to be maintained and improved, if the demands of humanity were to be attended to, it was not going to suffice to rely on the fortuitous development of increasing prosperity, or, for that matter, on voluntary service however devoted, or on private benevolence however munificent. Englishmen of the nineteenth century would have to learn this lesson which many of them were so extremely reluctant to learn. To master the forces which their society had engendered, to do something for the myriads who thronged their streets, to respond at all effectively to the demands of justice and humanity, they had to use increasingly the coercive power of the State and the resources that could only be made available by taxation; only so could conditions in factories be regulated and the more helpless types of labour protected, only so could the towns of England be sewered, scavenged, partially rebuilt and prevented from becoming, or remaining, mere suppurating middens, the breeding-places of misery, degradation and infectious disease, only so could schools be provided for all and all children made to attend school.

It was hard for Englishmen who believed that they had learnt from their history the importance of freedom and the dangers of the power of the State to accept the teaching of these necessities, and perhaps it was fortunate for them that they did not see the full import of what they had to learn. If the power of the community is to intervene effectively in the complicated problems of modern society, it must be guided to its task by experts and applied through regulations which experts have devised. The general public must not only surrender its freedom, but surrender it to the control of servants whose actions it cannot understand. At least from 1833 when the factory inspectors were appointed, or with the appointment of the Poor Law Commissioners, this expert administrative opinion was being developed. It was accumulated through the activities of a number of newly appointed public servants, commissioners and assistant commissioners, inspectors, servants of enlightened local authorities and men in a variety of public offices. They learnt the science of what was to be done and applied their knowledge by influencing legislation or by administrative methods. What was done by such men in the middle of the century with, at best, uncertain support from Parliaments and Ministers, and confronted by a wayward, or recalcitrant, public opinion, is in retrospect very remarkable. It is one of the truly important factors in the making of Victorian England and in this case is an example of the human intelligence definitely directing affairs towards a clearly conceived end. But it is also worth while to recognize this movement for what it was, for it was the beginning of the development of the modern State controlled by civil servants, acting by means of administrative regulations and assuming ever-increasing power. This development started in a liberal society that believed itself to be pledged to the policy of *laissez-faire*, it was largely unwanted, altogether unplanned and in many cases to a curious extent not noticed, but, and this fact seems to be significant, unless that society was to commit moral, or even literal, suicide, it was also inevitable.

Important as the independent actions of public officials were, they could have done nothing unless they had had some support from some form of public opinion, and in fact public opinion did come to their support or the furtherance of the reforms which they were implementing in a variety of ways. There could be a general popular agitation as there was for factory reform, there could be a general wave of opinion, possibly fanned by a momentary newspaper agitation, such as followed Chadwick's revelations about the health of towns, or there could be the pressure of specialized groups such as those which later in the century supported sanitary reform, or there might be the action of dedicated individuals working through local authorities, or through Parliament. The situation was obviously complex, and it is important to realize this. There is sometimes a tendency among historians to impose on the forces supporting or opposing particular social reforms rather too well-defined a pattern, ranging this or that religious group, or this or that class or party, exclusively on one side or other of particularly important issues; but such attempts should be viewed with suspicion, they are very often polemical in origin and they are very often based on impressions which have not been confirmed by what ought to have been rather elaborate and laborious research. Such facts as easily come to hand do indeed suggest that there is a great deal more to be learnt from the analysis of public opinion, particularly of local public opinion in the nineteenth century, and that when the full picture is painted it is not likely to be a simple one.

However, it seems possible now to say this. There was much opposition to proposals for which the moral case must seem to us overwhelming; men were indolent, or obdurate, or stupid, or callous when to us the call to a particular action would have seemed to be urgent and inescapable; they were, as they are now, inclined to be diverted from what was right by a preoccupation with their own interests. But throughout the reign of Queen Victoria there was in most classes in the country a general tendency towards humanitarianism and reform. It acted with different intensity with different people at different times. Where interest, or ignorance, or prejudice, intervened, it was too often sluggish, or selective, or non-existent. For some who claimed allegiance to it it was no doubt the merest lipservice to a rather loosely conceived ideal. With some it was intermittent, a capacity to be excited by particular revelations or responsive to an organized agitation but not otherwise continuously active. With some it meant absorption in some special social need or abuse, and with some it was a passion for the general welfare of humanity or a clearly conceived social programme. But in whatever form this tendency existed, it helped to give a shape to English nineteenth-century history, to secure that on the whole matters were always moving in a particular direction, if they were not always moving very fast.

It would be right to keep this general tendency very vague in conception, if the vague rather meaningless word 'progressive' is applied to it that is definition enough; indeed probably that is too precise. But there were two much more definite currents of opinion which affected men's minds right through the century and which also played a considerable part in making Victorian England what it was. One might be called the political revolution, the movement from oligarchy or aristocracy towards democracy, the other was the revival of religion. They are not to be completely separated from one another, for the revival of religion helped men who were emerging from obscurity and poverty to realize themselves, and to define their relations with society and make their claims upon it, while the political revolution gave meaning and force to the Dissenters' attack on the privileges of the Church of England. Each also in particular matters contributed to the general tendency towards humanitarianism. But it would be wrong to think of either as ancillary to anything else. Each pursued for its own sake its own well-defined objective which could occupy the most important place in a man's mind, possibly to the exclusion of everything else.

The challenge of the political revolution had become an important factor in politics in the eighteenth century. In the agitation for Parliamentary reform that started at the time of the American Revolution the claim had been made that all Englishmen ought to have a share in the government of the country because they were Englishmen or even because they were men; and at the same time men had begun to say that the object of society was the good of every man and to challenge the claims of prescriptive right to be a possible justification for the privileges of particular classes or individuals. The challenge became clearer and more insistent after the French Revolution had broken out, if the resistance to it also became more conscious and more passionate. Thereafter the issue was probably normally present in one form or other in most men's minds all through the century and it continued to affect the general shape and direction of public discussion. The social tensions of the first half of the century gave this challenge urgency and relevance, but when those tensions had relaxed and British politics were stagnant, there was no moment when there were not groups of people working for manhood suffrage, better social equality and the abolition of privilege, and probably very few moments when some people were not acutely apprehensive of the advent of democracy and the excesses associated with it. Naturally, when the pace quickened again in the 'sixties these hopes and fears became more lively and dominant, but the fact that all through the century most men had been conscious of this problem, often enough acutely conscious of this problem, is one of the most important facts about the making of Victorian England. It supplies, so to speak, the plot of the play.

But if the political revolution supplied the natural focusing point of Victorian political discussion, explicit or implicit, the Christian religion coloured what many Victorians, particularly lower- and middle-class Victorians, thought about everything. Mid-nineteenth-century England was very heavily charged with religious feeling, or religiosity. This was not to be wondered at; in the existing state of education Christianity and the Bible supplied the only comprehensive system of thought of which many people were aware. They supplied the only philosophy or ethics easily available, the only cosmology or ancient history. They intruded into all exhortation and instruction and even into what was read or seen for pleasure; the sensational novels revelled in Christian sentiment, or what passed for Christian sentiment, such sentiment was constantly invoked in stirring language on the stage, while the Bible, or Christian symbolism, or mythology, supplied subjects for many of the engravings and oleographs that men and women hung up in their houses.

Christianity was, however, at that moment not only unavoidable and all-intrusive, it was also dynamic. At the stage of cultural and emotional development which many people were passing through in the nineteenth century, the Christian religion in one form or other could present itself in such a way as to present an almost irresistible appeal to the heart. Why this should have been so raises some very difficult problems, but that it was so is clear. Thus was kindled a fire that spread through the whole country. All religious denominations engaged with ever-increasing zeal in the attempt to re-convert England, churches and chapels were built, missions despatched, revivals staged; what was spent on that work in the way of human effort and sacrifice, and for that matter of financial expenditure, is one of the really important facts of English history of the nineteenth century. Indeed, if it were possible to add up the numbers of hours spent by human beings hoping, planning and working for selected objectives in the reign of Queen Victoria, it seems possible that the re-conversion of England and the achievement of democracy and abolition of privilege would come highest on the list.

If, however, this was so, then most of the hopes which were entertained during the century were unfulfilled at the end. In 1900 all England had not been re-converted; there were still large areas of paganism and spiritual dereliction. In 1900 democracy still lagged on the road, manhood suffrage had been achieved, but the House of Lords retained its full powers, in many constituencies the old influences, thinly disguised under democratic forms, were still strong, and social equality was far to seek. This was not, in either case, what many human beings had hoped and had expected to see, but such disappointments are the commonplace of history; the record is studded with incomplete revolutions and unfulfilled missions. Men seem habitually to exaggerate the power of their ideas to control the future, as they habitually underestimate the chance that what opposes them will survive and even increase in strength as time goes on; or that the whole situation will change and their dearest wishes become irrelevant. These disappointments are therefore not surprising, and since they refer to the twentieth century, they are not really the concern of this book. But as it happens in each case the failure seems to disclose something about the progress of affairs in Victorian England.

Presumably the primary reason for the failure to convert England was the magnitude of the task. The most strenuous endeavours, the utmost devotion, could not keep pace with the increase of population and bring back into the fold, if they had ever been in the fold, the numbers of human beings which the tide of humanity had deposited in miserable physical environments, with no moral traditions and a way of life in which settled habits were difficult and the needs of the moment imperative. But the twentieth century saw something more significant than the mere fact that the Christian mission failed to keep pace with the increase of population; in the twentieth century the absolute number of observing Christians seems to have begun to fall off. Possibly the phenomenon becomes most marked with the empty churches and secularized chapels of the second quarter of that century, but such movements do not start abruptly and it seems likely that the causes of this change stretch back into the nineteenth century.

If so, it would be very interesting to know what these causes were, for they possibly throw some light on the making of Victorian England. Of course, an intellectual case against Christianity had been fairly widely current among well-educated people in the eighteenth century, and had received in the nineteenth century popularization by the positivists and the secularists. Their activities, however, do not seem to have restricted the effectiveness of the Christian mission in the mid-nineteenth century, and it is not easy to learn how many people they reached, particularly how many uneducated people. During the nineteenth century—with the activities of the geologists, or of the people who attacked the morality of such doctrines as that of eternal punishment and finally with the effective emergence between 1860 and 1870 of the doctrine of evolution—the cogency and force of the attack on Christianity as popularly received was very greatly increased, and from the record of a good many personal histories it seems to have been from the late 'sixties onwards increasingly more unlikely that a really highly educated man would be a Christian. But again the difficult question is raised: By what stages and by what dates did these opinions reach very large sections of the public? It is not indeed easy to see what evidence would satisfactorily bear on this problem. It is, of course, possible to find out the circulation of significant books, or to enumerate those who attended secularist meetings, or joined secularist societies, but those numbers seem to cover a relatively small proportion of the population, and possibly a small proportion of those affected by the drift of opinion from Christianity. Indeed, it seems possible that in a good many cases what was most likely to destroy the old beliefs was not so much the acceptance of a theory hostile to Christianity as the development of a doubt, of a general uneasy feeling that Christianity had been disproved by someone, which would combine with the increase in the number of secular interests and amusements to cause a retreat from the old habits and certainties.

All this is unfortunately extremely speculative, and it would be interesting to know more, for perhaps it would be best to take this change, and the changes immediately associated with it, as the significant end of Victorian England. It is also not very easy to trace or to understand some of these associated changes. For instance, there seems to be evidence that in the first half of the twentieth century the power of religious revivalism began to drop off. It still remained a potential weapon, but it seems to have become more difficult to use and less effective and lasting in its results when used. The cause of this might be a growing scepticism about the doctrines commended by revivalists or the importance of the issues they intended to drive home, or it might result from a change of fashion which made a certain type of emotional appeal, which had seemed moving and soul-searching to large sections of one generation, seem silly and slightly disgusting to their successors. Such changes do occur in history and they probably have a very important influence on its course, but they are not easy to isolate. Certainly in the last years of the nineteenth and the early years of the twentieth century a change of fashion was taking place and the satirical attack on the taboos, the sanctities, the sentimentalisms and the rhetoric of the Victorians was beginning. But again the same awkward problem suggests itself: By what stages did an attack which commended itself to the intellectual and fashionable spread to really large sections of the population? Probably it did so in the end with the unfortunate result that for very many people Victorian England became a period to be ridiculed and attacked but never understood, denied both the advantages of contemporary sympathy and objective historical study.

The history of the political revolution offers a contrast to all this. Here there is no reversal of intention. On the contrary, as the century ended the demand for the revolution became more urgent and more comprehensive. It was increasingly realized that political change was useless without important social reforms to accompany it, and one of the strongest counts against Victorian England was the inequalities and injustices which it had permitted to continue. It was an accusation which the facts seemed fully to authenticate. Whatever the causes, and to whatever extent it may be suggested that forces which had developed in the century had mitigated a situation which might have been much worse, the society which the twentieth century inherited was in many ways a cruel and unlovely one. There was much hopeless poverty at the base of society and for many of the working class who were in a slightly more fortunate position there were no extravagant rewards and there was great insecurity. Popular education was only gradually improving. The cities were often both degrading and ugly. There were still considerable slums, and large numbers of dreary streets which were next door to slums. There was a great deal of vulgarity. There may be a difference of opinion about the virtues of good

Victorian architecture and design, it is unlikely that there can be any about the mean results of mass production and of a hasty unthinking commercialism. Society could still be very cruel and callous in its treatment of the weak and unfortunate; whether that was the result of inherited callousness, or an inability to civilize a society which had suffered so great an increase in numbers, or to the operations of the capitalist system, may be of great interest to historians but it did not matter so much to the victims.

This all presents a sad contrast to the high hopes for humanity which had so often been entertained in the course of the century. Of course, the answer to this might be that in fact many of the best men had so often hoped for the wrong things, or for the right things to come in the wrong way. Men had hoped for instance that once liberated from the entangling power of the State and the corrupting power of the old aristocracy the forces inherent in society, particularly when reinforced by the new powers of industry and commerce, would liberate mankind from the cruelties and injustices of which it had always been the victim. The experience of the nineteenth century proved that that calculation was mistaken. But the interesting fact is that the philanthropists and the seers had not even secured the reasonably attainable things which they had earnestly desired. They had hoped for instance, for political democracy and the abolition of hereditary privilege, and by the end of the century these things had not been achieved.

Probably the main reason for these recurrent disappointments was the fact that the political revolution could not outrun the social and economic developments which were required to support it. While the titled and proprietory classes retained their social and economic predominance and before other classes had achieved sufficient wealth and independence to stand clear of them, it was idle to expect them to see their old grip on the country loosened. This was, however, not normally very easy to see at the time. Looking back at the very great power that remained in the hands of the aristocracy and gentry after the repeal of the Corn Laws in 1846, it must seem to us to be extremely unlikely that they would immediately assent to a reform of Parliament which would mean the surrender of that power; but that fact was not obvious to John Bright. The situation in 1885 must have seemed even more promising. Electoral reform was reasonably complete, the old aristocratic power seemed to be breaking up and the end of the battle probably in sight. That it was not so was no doubt due in part to the remaining strength of the old classes, which was always greater than their opponents credited and to the explosive impact of the Irish question which they could not have foreseen. But it may also have been due to a possibility which the promoters of a political revolution were not able to realize and accept. The process of social and economic development may increase the power of those elements in society which demand change, but it may also increase the power of forces to whom changes, at least those changes which are most insistently demanded, are increasingly repugnant.

If this diagnosis is true, it seems to agree with a general view of the process by which Victorian England can be said to have been made, upon which my book is in some sort based. The forces which control history are partly intellectual and conscious, and partly unconscious and blind. What happened in England in the nineteenth century was partly controlled by conscious human reason, as in this matter of the challenge of the political and social revolution which ran through the whole century and gave logic and direction to its history. But it was also powerfully affected by such blind forces as the increase of population and the progress of the Industrial Revolution and the increase of wealth, and not by these only but by other factors less easy to trace, by fashion, by the flux and reflux of opinions which might seem to be tangential to the main argument of history, by the kind of emotional appeal which affects particular people at a particular moment, by snobbery—one of the most elusive but not the least powerful of the factors that influence human affairs—and probably by other things not identified. Historical analysis may find it necessary to treat these forces separately, but it must be remembered that they are all, conscious or blind, the power of fashion or the deposit of wealth, working on the same people at the same time in the same community. Like the different currents in a fast-moving river, they rush forward together in the same bed, through a period like the reign of Queen Victoria, past the observer of a later date and into the future to make and remake that in its turn.

The Business Interests of the Gentry in the Parliament of 1841-47

By Professor W. O. AYDELOTTE

[Originally produced as an answer to a question by the Author]

It has never been settled how far the landed gentry in the mid-nineteenth century were or were not involved in the world of business, despite the obvious importance of this question for the political history of the period. It is well known that some land-owners did have active business careers or incidental business interests, but what matters is how many or how large a proportion did and what is the general tendency of the evidence. I have some information on the gentry who sat in the Parliament of 1841-47 which may shed light on this subject. Though these were not perhaps a representative sample of the gentry, they were at least a politically important section of them, and hence an appropriate group to examine in considering the political rôle of that class.

It would be helpful if this question could be studied in the light of a detailed examination of estate papers, such as Professor David Spring has made for some of the families of the nobility. Unfortunately I do not have this kind of information. The large numbers of the group with which I am dealing make so detailed a survey out of the question. I do, however, have a good deal of information of another kind: the business activities and business connexions of these men as reported in Dod's *Parliamentary Companion*, biographies, handbooks of various sorts, minutes of the meetings of railway directors, company prospectuses, and a great variety of other sources. This information amounts altogether to a good deal of material, ample enough so that most points established by it can be confirmed several times. The picture it presents is, at least in its general outlines, reasonably clear.

The extent of the business interests of the gentry cannot be established simply by ascertaining the figures and reciting them: there are some difficult problems of interpretation. Neither the term 'gentry' nor the term 'business' has a precise meaning, and the results will depend on the significance assigned to these two words, on how inclusive we make them. I doubt that any firm definition of either can be devised which, on the one hand, will be acknowledged by all as conforming to accepted usage and, on the other hand, will be sufficiently detailed and precise to cover all cases. However, it is still possible to follow some rough rules on a common-sense basis.

In regard to businessmen, the principal danger is that of making this category too inclusive and too uncritical. To describe as businessmen all individuals with business connexions of any kind, no matter how minor or incidental, will, I believe, produce an exaggerated picture of the extent of the representation of commercial interests in Parliament. It seems more useful to count as businessmen only individuals engaged in undertakings that would presumably demand a substantial amount of their time: merchants, manufacturers, brewers and distillers, partners in private banks, and merchant bankers. I have not included among the businessmen, unless they were exceptionally active in commercial affairs, East India and West India proprietors or directors of joint-stock banks, of insurance companies or of railways. I have also excluded silent partners, as well as men who owned business properties but did not manage them or who drew income from business enterprises in which they did not take an active part. In other words, I have sought to make a rough distinction between a major and a minor business involvement. My contention is that the number of businessmen among the gentry was, though significant, not large while the proportion of those involved incidentally in business was, on the other hand, very considerable.

It is still harder to work out a rule of thumb for identifying the landed gentry. What general guide should one follow?

Should the sons be included, or only the heads of families? Do the baronets belong in the gentry? (Sir Lewis Namier has told me that he would include them.) What about men more distantly related in the gentry, or for that matter to the baronetage and peerage, grandsons and great-grandsons, for example, or those connected only by marriage?

An abstract discussion of these questions seems unlikely to lead to fruitful results. The solution of them depends in part on the nuances of contemporary usage, which are difficult to recapture after the lapse of a century and which, for all we know, may not even have been consistent at the time. To avoid an unprofitable argument I have simply taken an empirical approach and given, in the tables, separate figures for various groups. As a starting-point I have used the second edition of Burke's *Landed Gentry*, the one most nearly contemporary to this Parliament. This is not wholly satisfactory, for Burke does not adequately explain his basis of selection, and I have every reason to believe, after much use of the work, that it was compiled with something less than meticulous care. Yet an attempt to produce a more refined criterion would lead to ambiguities and would probably be useless since the gentry cannot in any case be defined precisely.

In the tables, the figures for the 'gentry' include only men listed in Burke's second edition. Of the 815 men who sat in this Parliament throughout its length I found 234 in Burke, of whom 166 appeared as heads of families, 35 as eldest sons of fathers still living, and 33 as younger sons of fathers living or dead. I found 129 men related to the baronetage: 81 baronets, 22 eldest sons, and 26 younger sons. Figures for the gentry and baronetage, broken down into heads of families and sons, appear in the tables above the horizontal line; they have been thrown together in the figures immediately below the horizontal line.

To provide a basis for comparison I have added to the tables three other groups: (1) the 180 close relatives of peers (8 Irish peers and 172 sons of peers, including sons of Irish and Scottish ones); (2) 115 men more distantly related by descent to the peerage, baronetage and gentry, or related only by marriage; (3) 157 men who so far as I have yet discovered were not related to the peerage, baronetage or gentry at all. These three groups, together with the gentry and baronetage, make up the whole of the membership of Parliament.

The advantage of presenting separate figures for these several groups is that this procedure makes no assumptions as to which ones belong together. By keeping them distinct, it permits the differences between them to appear. The disadvantage is that such small figures are undesirable for statistical purposes, since they are likely to produce freak errors. The larger the figures, the more confidence we can have in the conclusions we derive from them. It would therefore be helpful to coalesce some of these categories, to make them fewer and larger, if this can be shown to be justified. Figures for the gentry and the baronetage were close enough in most cases to make it seem legitimate to put them together, and I have done this in Tables I-V. Table VI, which summarizes part of the information in Tables I-V, shows comparative figures for the gentry according to the narrowest and according to the broadest definition. The percentages are very close. In other words, while there are many different ways of combining this information, it does not in practice seem to matter much which alternative we choose. The general results are much the same, and the heavy involvement of the landed class in business stands out clearly enough no matter how the figures are arranged.

1. Of the 166 heads of families in the landed gentry I find about one-sixth who can be described as businessmen. This is a total of 26 men, or 16 per cent., the first figure in Table I. The group included 10 partners in private banks, 8 merchants, 6 manufacturers, a merchant banker, and an eminent railway chairman.

The railway man was William Ormsby Gore, and the merchant banker William Brown. The 6 manufacturers included 3 in textiles, Peter Ainsworth, William Feilden and Edward Strutt, 2 ironmasters, Joseph Bailey and Richard Blakemore, and the copper-smelter John Henry Vivian, a brother of the first Lord Vivian. The merchants were: William Astell, Daniel Callaghan, Thomas Gisborne, James Matheson, James Oswald, George Palmer, Thomas Sheppard and Robert Wallace. The private bankers were: William Baillie, Reginald James Blewitt, William Joseph Denison, William Evans, John Scandrett

Harford, Kedgwin Hoskins, John Pemberton Plumptre, William Morris Read, Edward Royd Rice and Charles Gray Round.

There might be some question about one or two of these. Thomas Gisborne is better known as a landowner; yet his mercantile interests are confirmed by several sources. It is not clear how closely Edward Strutt was connected with the family business; yet he put himself down in Dod as a cotton manufacturer, and he seems to have been identified in the public mind, notably at the time when he received his peerage in 1856, with the manufacturing interest. On the whole the list seems to me fairly reliable.

None of the eldest sons of the gentry were businessmen. Six of the 33 younger sons were, 18 per cent., a proportion close to that for the heads of families. Three of these men were private bankers, Raikes Currie, William Tyringham Praed and Richard Spooner; and three were merchants, David Barclay, Henry Broadley and Aaron Chapman.

The figures for the baronets were very close to these: 12 per cent. of the heads of families and 27 per cent. of the younger sons were businessmen. Only one heir to a baronetcy was a businessman, James Power, a distiller in Dublin. His father was also a distiller in Dublin and received his baronetcy only in 1841.

It must be admitted that on close inspection some of these baronets do not look like very authentic members of the landed class. Of the 10 baronets I have classed as businessmen, 7 were first baronets, of whom 1 obtained his title in 1837, 2 in 1838, and the remaining 4 only in 1841. These first baronets were: Sir William Clay, who had been a merchant and shipowner in partnership with his father; Sir John Easthope, who had been a stock-broker; Sir Josiah John Guest, the ironmaster; Sir George Larpent, a partner in the mercantile house of Cockerell & Co.; Sir John McTaggart, a merchant in London; Sir David Roche, a merchant in Limerick; and Sir Matthew Wood, the hop merchant and former Lord Mayor of London. Two more were only second baronets: Sir John Rae Reid, a partner in Reid, Irving & Co., whose father had also been a merchant; and Sir George Thomas Staunton, the Oriental scholar, who had been active in the East India Company and whose father had business interests in the West Indies. Only 1 of the 10 seems to have had any antiquity of descent, Sir Alexander Cray Grant, the West India planter, who was an 8th baronet, and whose title had been created in 1688.

The sons of baronets in business, also, seem to derive from families recently established and not necessarily connected with the land. James Power, an eldest son, was, as mentioned, the son of a distiller in Dublin who had received his title only in 1841. Of the 7 younger sons who were businessmen, 4 were sons of first baronets: William Beckett, a banker at Leeds; his brother Edmund Beckett Denison, the chairman of the Great Northern Railway; Henry William Hobhouse, a banker at Bath; and Charles Russell, the chairman of the Great Western Railway. Thomas Baring, the leading partner in Baring Brothers, was the younger son of a second baronet. Humphrey St John Mildmay, the fifth son of a third baronet, married into the Baring family and was a partner in the firm from 1823 to 1847. Patrick Maxwell Stewart, a merchant interested in the West Indies, was the son of a fifth baronet whose title dated from 1667, and was brother-in-law of the Duke of Somerset. Of these, perhaps only Mildmay, Stewart and Russell came from families which belonged in any meaningful sense to the landed class.

Clearly the baronetage was a mixed group. Baronetcies were apparently conferred not only on landed families but also on mercantile families which had little connexion with the land. It might, then, seem mistaken to count the baronets with the gentry. Perhaps they should rather be divided into two sections, a landed and a mercantile one. Yet, if the baronets were a mixed group, the gentry were also. It is necessary to distinguish between the contemporary *mystique* or folk-lore about the gentry and what seem to be the facts. Sir James Lawrence in his *On the Nobility of the British Gentry*, the fourth edition of which appeared in 1840, has a good deal to say about the prescriptive recognition and prestige of the gentry, which baronets or even peers did not necessarily share. The descendants of yeomen, he asserts, can never be gentlemen, though they may make very respectable lords: gentlemen must belong to families whose ancestors have always borne arms. Such a view bears little relation, if we may judge from Burke, to what was accepted as a working guide in practice. The extravagances of Lawrence must be balanced against the methods apparently used by Burke in compiling his reference work, and I incline to give the preference to Burke. In his volumes there appear a substantial number of families of commercial background and obviously recent descent. Indeed, the number of these may actually be larger than it seems on the surface, since genealogies might be exaggerated or distorted, and coats of arms were notoriously falsified. The prefaces to the later editions of Burke are full of apologies for the genealogical absurdities of the earlier editions. The prefaces to the fifth edition (1871) and to the ninth edition (1898) disclaim responsibility for the heraldic bearings cited in the text.

I conclude that the evidence does not warrant the arbitrary exclusion of the baronets, or any section of them, from the landed class. Both the gentry and the baronetage were rapidly recruiting new members from the commercial and professional classes and, in comparing two orders of society, it seems incorrect to exclude recent arrivals in one case while including them in the other. The extensive degree of coincidence in the figures for the baronetage and the gentry is perhaps an additional reason for thinking of them together. What does appear to be true is that in both the baronetage and the gentry the businessmen were usually, though by no means always, either younger sons or recent arrivals.

2. The business connexions of the landed class were, however, far more extensive than the figures in Table I reveal. Many of the gentry, and many also related to the baronetage and peerage, who were clearly not businessmen had, nevertheless, important connexions with the business world. The 166 heads of families in the gentry included 29 railway directors, 21 insurance directors, 9 directors of joint-stock banks, 2 East India proprietors, 3 West India proprietors, 4 interested in coal-mining, 3 in other types of mining in England, 4 involved in docks, 3 in canals, and so forth. Adding together the businessmen and those with minor business interests of this kind produces a total of 70, or 42 per cent., who were connected with business in one way or another. This information is set forth, for the gentry and the other groups, in Table II.

Perhaps the figures in Table II are the crucial ones for your purpose, since you are interested not merely in the gentry who were businessmen but also in the business associations of those who were principally oriented towards the land. I cannot say how far these connexions involved a subsidiary income from a non-agricultural source. Yet it seems not improbable that they frequently did. A director of a railway, for example, would be likely to have shares in it. Even if he did not, the mere fact that he was a director constituted a significant connexion with the business world.

The figures in Table II are rather high. Yet they are probably an underestimate, and do not tell the whole story. I have excluded a good deal of information that I found, when it did not seem reliably confirmed. Doubtless there was further information that I failed to get and possibly there were other business connexions of this kind, no evidence for which now survives. Also, these figures include only formal business associations, and not investments. Though the field for investment was restricted in these days before the extensive use of joint-stock financing, it was still possible to put money into railways, insurance companies, Government securities, mortgages and urban real estate. If I had the story on all this, the picture might be still more impressive. I did at one time go through the trouble of compiling the information in the two lists of railway investors published in the 1840s. However, I was informed by those who knew more about railway history than I did that these lists were unreliable, and I finally decided not to use them.

3. You did not ask about lawyers, but you might be interested in the fact that, of the 166 heads of families in the gentry, 28 were barristers. (I am not including in the figures the tiny group of solicitors in this parliament.) Only two of these barristers were also businessmen. Thus the 26 businessmen and the 28 barristers, cancelling out the 2 overlapping cases, make a total of 52, or 31 per cent., of the gentry who were either businessmen or lawyers. That nearly one-third of the group was active in either business or the law seems to me a substantial finding. You will see from Table III how the other groups compare. Very few of the relatives of peers were lawyers—none of them were businessmen, of course—while a large proportion of those unrelated to the landed class were either businessmen or professional men.

The figures for barristers may be a little high. I have tried to exclude men who were called to the bar but never practised. However, this fact was not always easy to establish, and I may have counted as barristers a few who did not have active careers in the law.

4. Table IV includes not only businessmen and barristers but those with minor business interests as well. The proportions now become very high: over half for the heads of families in both the gentry and the baronetage, while figures for the other groups also increase. Certainly Table IV makes it clear enough that the proportion of the landed class which had some connexion with business or law was very substantial.

One figure in Table IV may raise a question. Of those wholly unrelated to the landed class, I found that 76 per cent. had some connexion with business or the law. This leaves 24 per cent., or 38 men, who are, so to speak, unaccounted for. If these men belonged neither to the landed group nor to the business and professional group, you may wonder what was their means of livelihood. Most of these left-overs can, however, be explained by a more detailed analysis than it seems necessary to present here. In brief, a few of them were solicitors, quite a number were the sons of successful businessmen or professional men, and most of the rest were landowners who resembled the gentry in external characteristics though they did not happen to belong to the families included by Burke in his survey.

5. The connexion of members of the landed class with business can be shown in still another way. A substantial proportion of each group, in most cases just under or just over one-third were descended from or had married into families which had, or had had significant business interests. The information I have been able to find on this point is summarized in Table V. The connexion was not always close: in some cases the father or grandfather was a businessman; in other cases a distinguished family, even one with a high rank in the peerage, proved to have been established by a merchant or secured by marriage to a mercantile fortune several centuries before. The figures for the relatives of peers in Table V may be a little high, since I have taken account of certain great landed magnates who were actively concerned with exploiting their mineral resources or their urban real estate holdings, men like Earl Fitzwilliam, the

Marquess of Downshire, the Duke of Portland or the Duke of Bedford, all of whom had sons in this Parliament. Such individuals were not businessmen in the usual sense; yet their involvement in business enterprise seemed important enough so that, after some hesitation, I decided that it should be reflected in the statistics.

6. I mentioned earlier that the story came out much the same whether the gentry was defined narrowly or broadly. Table VI summarizes the information in Tables I-V for the gentry according to the narrowest and also according to the broadest definition. (To get the information on one page in a form where its purport could be easily grasped I have made the table add vertically, instead of horizontally like Tables I-V.) The first column, the 'Gentry by narrow definition', includes only the 234 men listed in Burke's *Landed Gentry* either as heads of families or sons of heads of families. The second column, the 'Gentry by broad definition', includes not only the 234 men listed in Burke but also the 129 men related to the baronetage, i.e. baronets and sons of baronets, and the 115 men more distantly related to the peerage, baronetage or gentry. The larger group is 478, just over double the smaller one.

The percentage figures in the two columns are extremely similar. The men in Burke resemble the men left out of Burke very closely, at least in the characteristics considered here, as soon as the figures are large enough to show some stability. This suggests that the broader definition of the gentry may be the more useful one, and that we should think of it as including not only the men listed by Burke but also the baronetage and those whose relationship to the landed class was more remote. At any rate, the general purport of the data is unmistakable. Further, the fact of the correspondence of the figures, regardless of whether a narrow or a broad definition is adopted, leads me to have increased confidence in their reliability.

TABLE I

| | Businessmen | | Not businessmen | | Totals |
	No.	%	No.	%	
Gentry:					
Heads of families . .	26	16	140	84	166
Eldest sons . . .	—	—	35	100	35
Younger sons . .	6	18	27	82	33
Baronets:					
Heads of families . .	10	12	71	88	81
Eldest sons . . .	1	5	21	95	22
Younger sons . .	7	27	19	73	26
Gentry and Baronets together:					
Heads of families . .	36	15	211	85	247
Eldest sons . . .	1	2	56	98	57
Younger sons . .	13	22	46	78	59
Irish peers and sons of peers	—	—	180	100	180
More distantly related to peerage, baronetage or gentry . . .	16	14	99	86	115
Wholly unrelated to peerage, baronetage or gentry .	73	47	84	53	157
Entire Parliament . .	139	17	676	83	815

TABLE II

| | Businessmen, or had minor connexions with business | | Not connected with business in any way | | Totals |
	No.	%	No.	%	
Gentry:					
Heads of families . .	70	42	96	58	166
Eldest sons . . .	5	14	30	86	35
Younger sons . .	9	27	24	73	33
Baronets:					
Heads of families . .	36	44	45	56	81
Eldest sons . . .	6	27	16	73	22
Younger sons . .	10	38	16	62	26
Gentry and Baronets together:					
Heads of families . .	106	43	141	57	247
Eldest sons . . .	11	19	46	81	57
Younger sons . .	19	32	40	68	59
Irish peers and sons of peers	49	27	131	73	180
More distantly related to peerage, baronetage or gentry . . .	38	33	77	67	115
Wholly unrelated to peerage, baronetage or gentry .	102	65	55	35	157
Entire Parliament . .	325	40	490	60	815

TABLE III

	Businessmen or barristers		Neither businessmen nor barristers		
	No.	%	No.	%	Totals
Gentry:					
Heads of families . .	52	31	114	69	166
Eldest sons . . .	4	11	31	89	35
Younger sons . .	12	36	21	64	33
Baronets:					
Heads of families . .	18	22	63	78	81
Eldest sons . . .	7	32	15	68	22
Younger sons . .	14	54	12	46	26
Gentry and Baronets together:					
Heads of families . .	70	28	177	72	247
Eldest sons . . .	11	19	46	81	57
Younger sons . .	26	44	33	56	59
Irish peers and sons of peers	14	8	166	92	180
More distantly related to peerage, baronetage or gentry . . .	38	33	77	67	115
Wholly unrelated to peerage, baronetage or gentry .	100	64	57	36	157
Entire Parliament . .	259	32	556	68	815

TABLE IV

	Businessmen, men with minor business connexions, and barristers		No connexion with business and not barristers		
	No.	%	No.	%	Totals
Gentry:					
Heads of families . .	86	52	80	48	166
Eldest sons . . .	7	20	28	80	35
Younger sons . .	13	39	20	61	33
Baronets:					
Heads of families . .	41	51	40	49	81
Eldest sons . . .	9	41	13	59	22
Younger sons . .	16	62	10	38	26
Gentry and Baronets together:					
Heads of families . .	127	51	120	49	247
Eldest sons . .	16	28	41	72	57
Younger sons . .	29	49	30	51	59
Irish peers and sons of peers	55	31	125	69	180
More distantly related to peerage, baronetage or gentry . . .	54	47	61	53	115
Wholly unrelated to peerage, baronetage or gentry .	119	76	38	24	157
Entire Parliament . .	400	49	415	51	815

TABLE V

	Father or other relative in business		No known relative in business		Totals
	No.	%	No.	%	
Gentry:					
Heads of families · ·	47	28	119	72	166
Eldest sons · · ·	10	29	25	71	35
Younger sons · ·	14	42	19	58	33
Baronets:					
Heads of families · ·	30	37	51	63	81
Eldest sons · · ·	9	41	13	59	22
Younger sons · ·	12	46	14	54	26
Gentry and Baronets together:					
Heads of families · ·	77	31	170	69	247
Eldest sons · · ·	19	33	38	67	57
Younger sons · ·	26	44	33	56	59
Irish peers and sons of peers	67	37	113	63	180
More distantly related to peerage, baronetage or gentry · · ·	41	36	74	64	115
Wholly unrelated to peerage, baronetage or gentry ·	74	47	83	53	157
Entire Parliament · ·	304	37	511	63	815

TABLE VI

	Gentry by narrow definition (234 men)		Gentry by broad definition (478 men)	
	No.	%	No.	%
Table I:				
Businessmen	32	14	66	14
Not businessmen	202	86	412	86
Table II:				
Businessmen, or had minor connexions with business . .	84	36	174	36
Not connected with business in any way	150	64	304	64
Table III:				
Businessmen or barristers . .	68	29	145	30
Neither businessmen nor barristers .	166	71	333	70
Table IV:				
Businessmen, men with minor business connexions, and barristers .	106	45	226	47
No connexion with business, and not barristers	128	55	252	53
Table V:				
Father or other relative in business .	71	30	163	34
No known relative in business .	163	70	315	66

Index